FAIR DAY

By the same author:

IRISH COUNTRY CURES

THE OLD GODS: THE FACTS ABOUT IRISH FAIRIES

MEDICAL DUBLIN *(with Liam C. Martin)*

FAIR DAY

The Story of
Irish Fairs and Markets

PATRICK LOGAN

Illustrated by
Liam C. Martin

Appletree Press

to
the memory of my father
John Logan
who
bought and sold at many fairs and markets

First published and printed by
The Appletree Press Ltd
7 James Street South
Belfast BT2 8DL
1986

Copyright © the estate of Patrick Logan, 1986
Illustrations copyright © Liam C. Martin, 1986

9 8 7 6 5 4 3 2 1

British Library Cataloguing in Publication Data
Logan, Patrick
Fair day: the story of Irish fairs and markets.
1. Ireland—Fairs—History
I. Title
394'.6'09415   GT4647.5

ISBN 0-86281-146-5

Contents

Editorial Note

Patrick Logan's sudden death, while this book was in production, deprived him of the opportunity of reading or amending his original text. He would have done both with his usual enthusiasm and good humour, despite the postscript which concluded his last letter to this office: 'Pray for the poor hard-working scribe. As one of them wrote in the margin of an Irish medieval manuscript, *Is fuar an lá agus mo laimbh tinn* – The day is cold and I have a sore hand.'

Foreword

Fifty years ago the local fair was a most important event in every part of Ireland outside Dublin. Almost everybody was affected by it in one way or another. The parish priest might wish to buy or sell a cow, the children got a holiday from school and the tinker had a supply of tinware to sell. People who had sold cattle had money which was used to pay outstanding bills, and when the buying and selling was completed everybody had a holiday. Those whose business it was to travel on Irish roads often complained about the fairs, which often created a major difficulty for the driver of a motor car because neither the people nor the cattle gathered on the streets took any notice of the car no matter how loudly he might sound the horn. The least the driver was likely to suffer was to have his car spattered with cow dung, but the car might collide with some of the cattle and that could lead to serious trouble. Experienced drivers took care to avoid fairs.

Then suddenly the fairs were no longer there. Cattle marts were established, usually on the outskirts of towns with space for lorries to load or unload cattle. For a few years some of the fairs managed to continue – Strokestown for example – but now one of the few old style fairs is held at Maam, County Galway. A few of the famous horse fairs are still held, such as Cahermee and Boherboy in County Cork, Tallow in County Waterford, Spancil Hill in County Clare, and Ballinasloe in County Galway. A few have continued as pleasure fairs – the Ould Lammas fair in Ballycastle, and the Puck fair in Killorglin are still famous – and in 1980 the fair of Ballyboggan in County Meath was revived as a sort of agricultural show.

This change took place without anybody realising what a difference it would make. Clearly marts are much more efficient than fairs could ever be, so they will continue, and this book is written not with regret for the fairs (nobody who ever made his living at fairs would ever do that) but to leave a record, however incomplete, of what they were and what they meant to different people.

It only remains to thank some of the people who helped in so many different ways. I am particularly grateful to Liam C. Martin for providing the excellent illustrations. My friend Father Con O'Donovan

7

told me all about Bartlemy Fair and the other fair lore from County Cork. Then there is Cyril Chapman who told me about his life selling at fairs in every part of Ireland. As usual my friends in the place names section of the Ordnance Survey were courteous and helpful, and my dear old patient Peter Casey told me about the horse fair in Drogheda. Johnny Maher told me about the travelling people, and very politely corrected some of my mistakes. Then there was Michael J. Molloy who told me about his local fairs, and he also was kind enough to read and correct my script. Many of my nephews and nieces helped me in different ways. These were John and Michael Logan and their sisters Mary, Ann and Edel, as well as Fergus Mulligan. I felt that they all had a family interest in Irish fairs, though removed by a generation from them.

I am also very grateful to the Northern Ireland Tourist Board, to Damien Mitchell, Dr Joe Kelleher, Mrs Hugh Ramsey, Dr J. Logan and to my sister-in-law Dr Ita Logan for their help.

Ireland's most successful cattle dealer, Seamus Purcell, spoke about his training as a buyer at Irish fairs: 'It was a great way of life. I wish my sons could get the same. It would be better than sending them to Oxford or Cambridge. I remember buying sheep at a fair one day when I was about sixteen years of age. A farmer had sixty lambs to sell and I agreed to buy thirty of the best of them. I got in to mark the thirty best lambs and when I had done it I said to the farmer, "Here I'll buy the other thirty", thinking I might get them for a couple of shillings less. He said no and I ended up paying five shillings more than for the ones I had marked. So that was an education.'

1

The Beginning

IN MODERN Irish the word for the local fair where livestock were sold is *aonach*. This is an old word and in the ninth century, spelt *oenach*, it was the word used for a provincial or tribal assembly which was held at Lughnasa (1 August). Some of these assemblies were very famous. Aenach Tailten, the assembly of the men of Meath, was held at Teltown along the County Meath Blackwater. For the men of Connacht the assembly place was Rath Croghan in County Roscommon and the Ulster assembly met at Emain Macha, a short distance from the city of Armagh. Oenach Carmain was the assembly of the men of Leinster. This is the only *oenach* of which a contemporary description is extant, but in this case the site of the assembly is not certain. There is some evidence that the Munster assembly place was Cashel and this is likely, but little is known about it. These provincial assemblies met every fourth year and were presided over by the provincial king, whose duty it was to summon people to attend.

As well as the provincial assemblies, there were local assemblies where the men of the *tuath* (tribe) met. The word is found in a number of Irish place names. A good example is Nenagh (Aonach Urmumhain) which probably marks the assembly place of the men of Ormond, and it may be that in some of the other places a local *oenach* was held.

The *oenach* was not a fair in the modern sense. It was essentially a legislative and judicial assembly, and D. A. Binchy has written:

> From several statements in the [ancient Irish] Laws it is clear that the king of every tribe was bound to convene an *oenach* at regular intervals. The site where it was held was normally an ancient burial ground: indeed the tradition reflected in many poems and sagas suggesting that the *oenach* originated in the funeral games held for kings and heroes may have a kernal of truth. Doubtless many of the modern fairs throughout Ireland are, or were, formerly held on the site of an old tribal oenach. At such gatherings, besides the exchange of goods, and the holding of games, horse racing and various athletic competitions, the 'public business' of the *tuath* (tribe) including

9

important lawsuits between different kindreds, and the issue of special ordinances were enacted.

Among the ancient Irish there were some other types of assembly. One, held on the hill of Uisneach in County Westmeath, was called a *dail* and was held at Bealtine (1 May). A third natural feast day, Samhain (1 November), was the time when another assembly, Feis Tara, was held: it may have been a harvest festival. During later centuries these three – 1 May, 1 August, and 1 November – became fair days in many places.

In order to run a market or a fair efficiently, it is necessary that there be a medium of exchange, a coinage of fixed and recognised value. In Ireland the earliest coinage was not minted until late in the tenth century by Sitric, ruler of the Norse kingdom of Dublin. These coins were imitations of the contemporary coins issued in England by King Aethelred and King Cnut. It has been pointed out that the quality of these Hiberno-Norse coins declined steadily after the year 1020, and some of the later coins were so thin that they could be struck on one side only.

Although there are references in early Irish writings to payment of such sums as ounces of silver, or even of gold, such references are rare. There was, however, a system of 'cattle money' in which the largest unit was a *cumhal*, originally the value of a bondmaid. This was equal to three cows. The cow was defined in the Irish laws as a *bo-tri-laeg*, and this has been translated as 'a three-calf-cow'. It was worth one third more than a cow in calf. Dr Binchy has told me that the words *bo-tri-lǫeg*, may also mean a recently calved cow with its calf. One such cow was equal to two *sets*. Smaller units were a *samaisc* (a three-year-old heifer, which was half the value of a cow, or one *set*) and a *dairt* (a yearling heifer, which was one-sixth the value of a cow). The smallest unit mentioned is a fleece of wool.

In ancient Ireland cattle were valued for their milk yield. This was sound econony, because a good cow will provide three times as much food in the form of milk as it would if fattened for beef. Some of the later law tracts provide details of the standard and size of the cow. A calf increased in value as its girth increased from four to six feet, and a two-year-old bullock was seven feet in girth. As no means of weighing such an animal was available, this was an efficient and simple method. The girth of the standard cow was twenty *dorns* (fists) – about ten feet – which was clearly a very large cow. Among the Irish of the twelfth century, cattle served many purposes and would nearly correspond to what today is called capital. In modern Irish, the word *airneis* means property: originally it meant cattle. Rents were often paid in cattle, and doweries which were made up of many kinds of property were mainly cattle.

This cattle money was further divided. The value of an animal was measured in three parts. One part was the value of its body – the meat and the skin. Another part was its expectation – how many calves and how much milk it was likely to produce in the future. Thirdly, the value of its present production of milk and of the present season's calf was considered.

It is likely that in ancient Ireland it was difficult to fatten cattle except in districts where the land was very good. Later jurists commenting on the ancient law texts wrote that the cow should give enough milk to fill a vessel twelve inches high and twelve inches in diameter – in other words, about 4-4½ gallons daily. If, when fed on good grass, it failed to give the required amount, its value was judged that much less.

It is of interest to find this method of deciding the value of a cow still being used during the early nineteenth century in County Cork. In the *Statistical Survey of County Cork,* Townsend wrote: 'When a milking cow is sold she is engaged to give not less than a fixed amount of milk. If she does not there is an adjustment of the price.' The amount was twelve to sixteen quarts a day. Townsend added that few cows gave less than twelve quarts and many small cows gave more than sixteen quarts daily.

This system of 'cattle money' did not die out when a money economy was introduced, but continued in use for centuries. An extant medical manuscript in the Irish language, written in 1482 (probably in County Clare) had a note written in it a few years later which has been translated:

> A prayer for Earl Gerald who bought this book (Justiciar of Ireland) for a score of kine. Two and twenty quaternions are what this book contains. The rent of Ormond, six score kine just come in to the earl, on the day when this reckoning up was written. Thomas O'Mulchonry it was that for the earl lifted such rent. The year in which I am is the year of grace 1500.

The market house, Callan, Co. Kilkenny

2
The Normans

TOWARDS the end of the twelfth century the Normans invaded Ireland, and within a generation or two they had occupied most of the good land of Meath, Leinster and Munster. Their economy was based on the rents paid by those who worked the land and produced goods which could be sold at fairs and markets. In most cases a patent to hold a fair or market was granted by the king, though sometimes a powerful lord might grant such a right to the burgesses of one of his towns.

In order to run markets it is necessary that all those coming to buy or sell in such places should be able to do so safely and efficiently. There should be strict rules about the quality and the quantity of the goods brought for sale. It is also necessary that there be a coinage, recognised and accepted as a medium of exchange by both the sellers and the buyers. The problem of having standard and honest weights and measures appears to have been insoluble. Complaints about this never ceased, and even though heavy fines were imposed on those convicted of using false weights the complaints did not stop. It was most important that order be maintained at the fair, and in one case at least (New Ross) a number of men were recruited and paid to act as a police force during the time of the fair.

Most important of all, a special court, called in the legal language a Court of Piepowder *(curia pedis pulverisati),* was set up and remained in session during the time of the fair. The person who presided over this court might be the chief magistrate of the town or someone appointed by him, and any disputes which arose during the fair about prices, the quality of the goods or goods which were mislaid or stolen, were tried before the Court of Piepowder. This was the end of the dispute, as there was no court of appeal against its decision. This regulation shows a high degree of common sense, because if an appeal was allowed the case might drag on indefinitely, and clearly it was in the interest of everybody concerned that the case be concluded quickly and with justice to all parties.

During the time of the fair, and for some days before and after it, there was a rule that no summons might be served on anyone for debt. It was laid down in a thirteenth-century manuscript, *The Customs of Dublin*, that no summons should be issued in the city during the time of the fair, and a similar rule, in almost exactly the same words, is found in *The Customs of Waterford*. This custom continued and is mentioned during the seventeenth century and even as late as the eighteenth century in New Ross. The object of the rule appears to have been to enable a seller to come to the fair and sell his goods in order to discharge his debt without fear of arrest.

Not long after his return to England in 1172, Henry II granted the lordship of Ireland to his younger son John. John came to Ireland for the first time in 1185 and it is likely that his first Irish coins were minted then. Between 1190 and the end of the century coins were minted at Dublin, Waterford, Limerick, Kilkenny and Carrickfergus. These were silver halfpennies and farthings and bore the inscription 'John Lord of Ireland'. At about the same time coins were minted at Downpatrick and at Carrickfergus by one of the new Norman conquerers, John de Courcy. These coins issued by de Courcy were also half pence and farthings and bore his name and also the word 'Patricius'. When John became king of England, he had a new coinage minted in 1204. The coins were of silver, pennies, halfpennies and farthings, and the weight and fineness of the silver was 22½ grains, the same as the English standard. Many of these coins were exported, but large numbers of them must have been issued from the mints at Dublin, Limerick and Waterford, because they are not very rare.

Also in the year 1204 John made an order declaring: 'We wish that a fair be established at Donnybrook lasting for eight days at the feast of the Finding of the Holy Cross' (3 May). This was the beginning of the famous – or infamous – Donnybrook Fair which in later centuries became a great popular carnival for the people of Dublin. There were many complaints about the brawling and drunkenness of the crowds which gathered at the fair during the eighteenth and nineteenth centuries, and in 1855 it was finally abolished by the city authorities.

There was a second fair established in Dublin by King John. This was to be held at the bridge of Blessed John the Baptist, which may have been near the hospital of St John the Baptist at the New Gate.

In 1204 John also gave a charter to the city of Waterford granting the right to hold an eight-day fair starting on the feast of St Peter's Chains (1 August). In this case the dates of the fair may not have been suitable, because the St James's Fair in Bristol began on 25 July and it would not be possible for a merchant to attend both fairs.

At the same time John also granted a fair to the citizens of Limerick. According to its charter the fair was to begin on the feast of St Martin (11 November) and was to continue for eight days, but this may have been found to be too late in the year. A new charter from Edward I given on 4 February 1292 had a clause which read: 'Also we grant to the citizens of Limerick that they have a fair once in the year in Limerick, lasting for fifteen days, namely on the vigil, day, and morrow of St James the Apostle [25 July] and on the twelve following days.'

This fair continued for centuries, and in the late 1600s Dinley wrote in his diary about his visit to Limerick: 'There are two fairs a year viz. that of St John the Baptist, and St James. The latter which is after the manner of St Bartholomew fair in London continues for a fortnight'.

On 6 March 1226 Henry III granted to William Baron 'that he have until the King's majority a fair at the manor of Nas [Naas] lasting eight days from the vigil of the feast of SS Simon and Jude' [28 October].

At the end of the thirteenth century there are references to a great annual fair at New Ross. This town may have been founded by William the Marshal, and at the time the references were written it was part of the Irish estates of the Earl of Norfolk (1279-94). During the fair a temporary exchequer court was opened to receive payment of debts due to the earl, and it is recorded that a *teptum* with chess board lines on it was bought for 2s. This was to be used to help with the accounting – a thirteenth-century calculator. It must be remembered that the system of Roman numerals in use at the time made simple arithmetic a very complicated business. The records also say that a special force of watchmen was recruited to keep order during the time of the fair. Their wages amounted to 10s.

The first charter of Drogheda on the Meath side of the Boyne was granted by Walter de Lacy in 5 July 1194. However a charter from Henry III says: 'We grant also for us and our successors that the aforesaid burgesses and their successors may have one fair in the year in the aforesaid town, lasting for eight days namely on the vigil and day of the Assumption [15 August] and the six following days'. The charter goes on to say that the burgesses may have a weekly market on Wednesday in the town. Later, on 7 December 1318, a charter of Edward II added the right to hold a second weekly market on Saturday. On the Louth side of the Boyne a town had also been founded, and charters were granted to it by John and by Henry III. The charter of Henry III issued on 12 December 1252 granted a fair on the vigil, day and morrow of St Luke the Evangelist (18 October) and on the twelve following days unless the fair would be harmful to the neighbouring fairs. Dundalk was granted a charter for a fair from King Richard II (1375-99). The fair was to continue for fifteen days from the feast of SS Philip and James (1 May).

In Kinsale a charter of Elizabeth I cited one of Edward III which had declared in the year 1333:

> And we have granted to the Sovereign, Burgesses and Commons [of Kinsale] that they may hold one market on Wednesday and another on Saturday, and hold fairs in the town whensoever they will within the franchise once every year viz. at the feast of St Bartholomew the Apostle [24 August] and for the three following days, and that the Sovereign be clerk and governor of the market and a Court of Piepowder by reason of the market and fairs aforesaid.

In Kilkenny a fair was established early in the thirteenth century, probably by William the Marshal or by one of his sons. In 1383 the citizens claimed to have a fair which began at the ninth hour on the vigil of Pentecost and continued for fifteen days. They also said that four men of the town were elected to act as barons of the fair. Their duties were to see that order was kept, to supervise the weights and measures used, and to preside at the Court of Piepowder. The town of Callan was founded by William the Marshal, and a document dated 10 June 1407 said that the fair in the town began at the ninth hour on the vigil of St Michael the Archangel (28 September) and continued during the following three days.

All these fairs – and there must have been many others, of which no records survive – greatly stimulated trade during the thirteenth century.

The records of the fairs and markets held in Dublin are more extensive than those for any other Irish city. The fair had been established in 1204 on the feast of the Finding of the Holy Cross (3 May) and was transferred in 1252 to the vigil of the translation of St Thomas (6 July). The fair lasted for fifteen days and it was ordered that the first two days were to be the property of the archbishop of Dublin.

Markets

At all fairs and markets tolls were paid by the seller and sometimes also by the buyer. Normally these were paid to the civic authorities in the towns and were a valuable source of income for the town. In some cases the fair might be owned by the local lord or by the bishop of the diocese and the tolls were paid to them. In return for the tolls, it was the duty of the owner to organise the fair and to provide such things as weights and measures.

The amount paid on each article is found in the Dublin records. On a tun of wine being taken into or out of the market 2*d*. was paid, and the same was also paid on a sack of wool. One penny was paid on an ox, a cow, a batch of six pigs or six sheep. In the case of a horse or a mare, 1*d*. was paid by both the seller and the buyer. A saddle was taxed at ½*d*. and the seller of a *crannach* of salt was also charged this amount. Both the saddle and the salt may have been imported. A *crannach* was a skin-lined wicker basket and was used as a measure for such things as grain, salt, peas, beans, coal and apples. It was said to be equal to a Bristol barrel and held the amount of grain which would be derived from seven score sheaves of corn. The word is Irish, and the *crannach* may have been a measure used by the native Irish or in the Hiberno-Norse towns.

A fisherman who regularly brought fish to the market paid ½*d*. every Saturday. If a boat came to the quay with fish for sale, the owner was free to sell it aboard the boat, but if the fish was taken ashore and sold on a stall the seller had to pay ½*d*. per day for each stall. A horse load of eels paid ½*d*. and a load of eels carried by a man paid ¼*d*. A merchant stranger – one who was not a citizen of Dublin – paid 1*d*. if he brought a carcass of beef to the market and ¼*d*. was paid for the carcass of a pig or goat.

In addition to these tolls, there were many other taxes which for one reason or another had to be paid by the sellers or buyers. Among these were *murage,* a special tax to pay for the building of the town walls, and *pontage,* which was used to pay for the building of a bridge. Another was *pavage*, which was used to repair the streets of the town.

Weights and Measures

Many efforts were made to ensure that the weights and measures used at all fairs and markets in Ireland were uniform and honest. In 1244 an order was sent to the Justiciar, Maurice Fitzgerald, ordering him to see that this was done. Again in 1268-9 the Justiciar, Robert de Ufford, and his council made an order that all weights and measures used in Ireland were to be the same as those in use in London. The complaints continued, however, and in 1277 the king, Edward I, sent his clerk, Elias of Wynton, to Ireland. He was ordered 'to hold pleas of market, assizes of bread and wine, and also to inspect bushels, gallons, ells and weights and to correct transgressors'. Finally in 1307 a set of standard measures, scales, beam and weights were delivered into the Exchequer of Dublin to be used as standards for Ireland.

This was not the end of the complaints or the solution to the problem. All through the centuries people continued to complain and apparently with good reason – it appears that on at least one occasion Henry de Kissok paid a fine of 40*d*. for using bad weights.

It is very likely that in every case an official called the 'clerk of the market' or the 'baron of the fair' was appointed. In some cases, such as Ardee and Kinsale, the mayor or sovereign of the town so acted – personally or by deputy – and he might appoint people like the constables and petty constables to assist him. In Callan and in Kilkenny two men were elected to preside over the Court of Piepowder which was so important.

Naturally the people of the town were anxious that fairs and markets be conducted properly, as they were a great source of profit. Efforts were made to ensure that the bread, beer, wine and other foodstuffs brought for sale were of good quality, and there are references to such things as the stocks and the pillory being in constant use. Great care was taken about what was called the 'assize of bread'. In the *Laws and Usages of Dublin*, drawn up in the thirteenth century, it was laid down that a baker must have his name stamped on his bread. Unstamped bread was forfeited and given to the poor. The fines to be imposed on offenders were also set down – 15*d*. for a first offence, 2*s*.6*d*. for a second offence, and for a third offence the baker had to stand in the pillory and swear to leave the city for a year and a day.

Next to Dublin, the city of Kilkenny has preserved the most extensive records of how it was administered during the Middle Ages. Its oldest manuscript, the *Liber Primus Kilkenniensis*, begins with an entry referring to the year 1231. One of the first entries in the book deals with the regulation of the fish market. It says that fishermen and those who brought fish for sale in Kilkenny had to take it all to the place ordered for the sale of fish and the sellers had to remain there all the day. If any of the fish remained unsold it might be kept overnight, taken back to the fish market early next morning, and sold there. If against this order the sellers sold any fish in their houses, all the fish was forfeited to the community. This regulation was made on the Monday after Ash Wednesday in the year 1333, by Thomas Oweyn, Superior, and the commons of the town of Kilkenny

Further, it was ordered that 'six lawful men must gather all the measures in the town, namely bushels, half bushels and quarter bushels, all gallons, bottles and quarts, both those from taverns and from other places. Also scales and weights, namely pounds, half pounds, *tronas*. . . by which bread is weighed and they are also to see the name [of the baker] distinctly written on each loaf. In the same way they are to collect (and examine) the measures used by the millers'.

The 'six lawful men' were directed to question each of the bakers about the price of corn, wheat, oats and barley, and the price at which he sold his bread. If his loaves were less than the standard quartern loaf, he would be fined or sentenced to the pillory, according to the judgement of the court. However, in cases where the baker was sentenced to the pillory, the seneschal or the bailiff had to see that it was used 'without danger to the body of man or of woman'. The court would then have to enquire about the assay and the selling of wine. The members had to ask the names of those who sold wine and for how much they sold a pint *(sextarius)* and they had to decide if any wine in the town was 'corrupt and not healthy for man's body'.

In every town there were strict rules against those who forestalled the market. The Kilkenny regulations mentioned those who bought goods before the hour laid down in the statute and those who went outside the town to meet and buy goods on the way to the market. Their guilt was all the greater if, having bought outside the town, they then brought the goods to the market and sold them, at profit. The regulations also tried to stop those who took goods which should be sold at the market and brought them to some other place. There are similar regulations found in the Dublin records and during later centuries in the records of Youghal, Waterford and Kinsale. It is not difficult to see why this should be so. The town was dependent on its own neighbourhood for supplies of corn, wool, hides and other essentials and it would be possible to buy up these before the market opened and so raise the market price. The idea of cornering the grain market is not new.

Fair Symbols

The fair was always held in a definite place and continued for a fixed number of days. This fact was publicly shown by some sign which people could recognise. In Limerick, Dinley recorded in his *Journal* that during the time of the fair a white glove was hung out at the prison and while the glove remained there no arrest for debt might be made in the city.

The use of a glove as a fair symbol is mentioned in the records of the town of New Ross on 6 July 1726. On that day it was decided by the corporation 'that for the future the glove be sett up two days before each faire day, and it to continue up for two days after and no more'.

A few years earlier, on 8 August 1710 the corporation of New Ross had declared: 'that there will be annually a faire on the eleventh day of August, being St Laurence's Day, the first four years free of all customs, and standings, of which all persons may take notice, and the same is to continue three days, viz. the faire eve, the faire day and the day after and noe longer, and to be free from arrests five days before the said faire day and three days after'.

Again this is an English custom and there are references to the use of a glove as a fair symbol in a number of places, including Southampton, Exeter, Liverpool and Preston.

Animals were sometimes used as fair symbols, and MacNeil believes that some of these have survived in Ireland. One of these is the Puck Fair in Killorglin, County Kerry which is held from 10-12 August. During the afternoon of the first day a white buck goat, decorated with garlands, is led in procession from the bridge to the town square. There the animal is hoisted on to a high platform where it is fed with cabbages and remains as King of the Fair until the third day. During the afternoon of the third day the goat is taken down and carried on the shoulders of four men through the town, calling on the different shop-keepers who contribute to its 'expenses'. It is then sold by auction.

MacNeil discusses all the evidence available about this custom. She suggests that the goat was a fair symbol at a fair which was established there by the Normans early in the thirteenth century. In the Irish annals it is recorded that the Fitzgeralds built a castle there in the year 1215, and the district remained under the control of the earls of Desmond until the last quarter of the sixteenth century.

The custom of having an animal as a fair symbol has also been recorded in Greencastle, County Down. A fair known as 'the Ram Fair' was held at Lammas in Greencastle and during the time of the fair a ram was enthroned high on the walls of the ruined castle.

In Mullinavat, in the Walsh Mountains of south Kilkenny, there was a fair called the Puck Fair. In this case all the buck goats were decorated, and the best one chosen, put into a cart and set up in the field where the fair was held. At Cappawhite, in County Tipperary, a white horse was paraded through the fair and then put on top of a fort there as long as the fair continued. Recently I have heard of a custom of decorating the rams at the fair of Dungarvan. It may be of significance that Greencastle, Mullinavat, Cappawhite and Dungarvan were all in areas which came early under the influence of the Normans.

In the *Calendar of Judiciary Rolls* for around the year 1300 there are some references to fairs which had been established by the Normans.

Here is one such reference:

A certain William Douce complained to a court in Kildare that one of his serving men with a packhorse load of merchandise going to the fair of Kilkenny came to the town of Naas and deposited the packs. . . . Christiana la Salelhackere, while the serving man went for the key. . . took a box of William's containing small things. The Marshall was commanded to attack [arrest] her and she being demanded how she wished to aquitt herself says she is not guilty. But she admitts that the said box as well as a pair of linen webs, a pair of shoes and a pair of hose came to her hands by gift (of the serving man) in pledge for 2s. which he promised her that he should lie with her and [she] gave the box in pledge for twelve gallons of ale as she was entitled to do, and she has the small things ready if anyone will demand them: and that this is so she puts herself on the country. The Jury found Christiana guilty and so let William have the goods. The Jury also found that the goods were not worth more than 20d. Christiana is a *mulier communis*. She has abjured the country. The man who got the box knew she had stolen it but they pardoned him.

Some other references to fairs can be found in the *Calendar of Judiciary Rolls*. At a court in Cork in 1300 the mayor, bailiffs and commonality of Cork summoned twenty-four men for trading at Shandon. Formerly they had been ordered to stop trading at Shandon in the prejudice of the city of Cork but they had persisted in holding markets there. All but two of the defendants were found guilty and committed to jail. Later they were each fined 20s.

In 1298 Maurice, formerly serving man of Thomas Maunsel, was charged that 'he took in the market of Cloncurry eighty afers [horses] under avowry of said Thomas then sherriff, and falsely feigned that they were required for carriage and afterwards took for sending back each afer 6d. or at least 4d. to its owner'. Cloncurry in County Kildare was a Norman town and it must have been a market of some size if there were eighty horses there. In any case the jury found Maurice not guilty.

It would appear from all this that by the year 1300 the Normans had establised fairs and markets in every part of the country where they had gained control. During the thirteenth century some of the towns had grown rapidly and were tending to become small independent republics. It is of interest to learn that in 1285 representatives of some of the larger towns – Dublin, Cork, Limerick, Waterford, Drogheda (Louth) and Drogheda (Meath) – met and drew up a compact for mutual benefit. They also decided that representatives of these towns should meet each year in Kilkenny on the day after Trinity Sunday to consider matters of common interest.

3

The Fourteenth and Fifteenth Centuries

UNTIL the end of the thirteenth century the Anglo-Norman colony in Ireland continued to prosper, and some of the larger towns were developing an urban way of life with a degree of local autonomy. Gradually the two races began to blend. Unfortunately for Ireland, the English kings became involved in wars both in Britain and Europe and, as a consequence, Ireland and its problems were of little interest to the London government.

Then early in the fourteenth century a disaster occurred. In 1315 Edward Bruce invaded Ireland and for three years he ravaged the country. The famine and pestilence which followed the years of war were made much worse by a number of bad seasons and crop failures and conditions in every part of the country were so bad that in 1318 the Four Masters wrote:

> Edward Bruce the destroyer of [the people of] Ireland in general both English and Irish, was slain by the English through dint of battle and bravery at Dundalk. . . and no achievement had been performed in Ireland for a long time before from whence greater benefit had accrued to the country than from this: for during the three and a half years that Edward was in it a universal famine prevailed to such a degree that men were wont to devour one another.

The country had scarcely recovered before an even greater disaster struck. An epidemic of bubonic plague spread across Europe from east to west between the years 1346 and 1351. This was caused by a micro-organism called *Pasteurella Pestis,* which is carried by the rat flea which lives as an octoparasite on the black rat, *Rattus Rattus.* The epidemic reached Ireland early in August 1348 and the district between Dublin and Drogheda was first affected.

All the evidence would suggest that the epidemic was more severe in the towns. The native annals do not mention the plague in the year

1348, and in 1349 the Four Masters say, 'a great plague in Moylurg, and in all Ireland in this year. Matthew, son of Cathal O'Rourke died of it. The earl's grandson died of the plague.'

The disease begins as an epizootic among the rats of the community and when these have been killed off the flea will tend to carry the infection to man. The common flea may also transmit the disease, and in very acute cases it may be spread directly from man to man. Few of the native Irish aristocracy died during this epidemic; if they had the annals would have said so. This would indicate that the epidemic was more severe in the towns than among the Gaelic Irish, who did not live in towns. In the cluster of cabins and cottages around the home of an Irish lord or around a large monastery there would not be enough rats to keep the infection going, so it was likely to die out quickly.

On 30 March 1399 Richard II made an order to the provost, bailiffs and commons of Kinsale. By it he granted them permission to treat with the Irish enemies. As the prosperity of the town depended on its trade, it is very likely that this order was only recognising the fact that Kinsale merchants had been doing this for a long time.

During the fifteenth century the Statute Rolls of Henry VI refer to the town of Carrickmagriffin (Carrick-on-Suir). In the document it is described as 'a market town burned by rebels.' The parliament ordered that the town be rewalled 'for people from Waterford, Fethard and Clonmel.' The provost and commons were to have power to hold a fair there twice in the year, on the vigil, day and morrow of St Barnabas (10 June), and also on the feast and morrow of Michaelmas (29 September). There were to be no tolls or customs charged at these fairs, but instead people were expected to pray for the king and for the Lord Lieutenant, the Duke of York. The ordinary tolls and customs were to be paid at all other times.

The practice of establishing fairs and markets continued. The parliament ordered that:

> Richard, Duke of York [Lord Lieutenant 1447-60] and his heirs forever, lords of the Manor of Ratoath in the liberty of Meath, that they, in the town of Ratoath, parcel of the same manor, may have their market in the said town to be held on Monday from week to week, and also that the said Duke and his heirs may have a fair to be held in the said town twice in the year, one on the vigil, day and morrow of St John the Baptist and the other on the feast of the Innocents at Christmas and on the two following days.

The duke was also given the right to hold a market on Saturday at

Carlingford within the liberty of Ulster, and a fair there on the vigil of Holy Trinity until the following Saturday. The Duke and his heirs were to 'have and receive such customs of all things brought for sale to the said markets and fairs as the authorities in Dublin have'. It was also decided that citizens of Dublin, Drogheda and other towns were to be free to trade in Ratoath and in Carlingford. At this time the Duke appears to have been trying to reassert some claims to Irish lands, and these grants were part of the claims. However, he later returned to England and was killed in battle, and little more is heard of the grants.

In 1449 it was claimed in the parliament that Luke Cusack had been granted a Monday market at Killeen by Edward III in the forty-sixth year of his reign. For this reason the parliament granted the same right to Cusack's heir, Christopher Plunket, even though the market had not been held. It was also ordered that tolls and customs the same as those collected by Richard Marwood, Baron of Skreen, at his market in Skreen be collected at Killeen. For this grant Plunket was ordered to pay a fine of 13s.4d. and also to pay 20s. into the hanaper.

One reference to a market in Navan may be of interest. It is recorded in the Statute Rolls that in full time of the market there a man was led in procession and publicly excommunicated, with a bishop present to carry out the ritual.

In 1450 Esmond Mulso was granted permission to build a town called Mulscourt in Fercullen, County Kildare. In the grant he was given the right to appoint the portreeve, burgesses and so on of the new town and to hold a Tuesday market there and fairs on the feast of SS Philip and James (1 May) and on the three following days, and at Michaelmas and on the three following days. He was to establish a Court of Piepowder, before the barons of the fair and to take tolls and customs. The grant went on to say that the lordship of Fercullen was situated on the frontiers of the marches and the town was to protect County Dublin and County Kildare. Fercullen is almost exactly the present parish of Powerscourt but the name Mulscourt does not appear to have survived and it may never have been established.

In 1458 the commons decided that:

> Whereas the Earls of Kildare, lords of the town of Kildare, and all other lords of the same town have heretofore from time whereof memory runs not, held a market in the said town of Kildare, on the Saturday from week to week. And foreasmuch as there is a market held in the Naas in the county of Kildare on Monday, the which market of Kildare if it were held on the Saturday would be injurious

to the market of Naas held on the Monday, and the said market of Naas, held on the Monday would be injurious to the said market of Kildare, held on the Saturday.

The parliament agreed to change the Kildare market to Thursday. At the same time the Earl of Kildare was given the right to hold a fair in the town on St Brigid's Day (1 February) and the two following days. The parliament also ordered that he might take customs at the rate prevailing at fairs in Dublin, and that:

> all manner of men and persons of whatever condition they be, shall have free coming staying and going at the said market and fair and that a court be held there for causes commenced in the said market and fair, saving to every man his action who will sue in the said town of Kildare. And that Holy Church and all other persons who ought to be free of custom in the said town of Kildare be free. And this for a single fee of 20s. to be paid into the hanaper.

It is likely that during the fifteenth century many of the small towns outside the Pale and on the marches had declined, and some had disappeared completely – Rathwire and Kilbixy, for example. In the year 1429 the Irish parliament declared:

> Likewise, in as much as diverse Irish enemies of Our Lord the King, levy, raise, and hold among them different fairs and markets, and Sundry merchants, liege Englishmen go and repair to the said fairs and markets, and some send their merchandise to the said enemies by their people called laxmen, and there sell and buy diverse merchandises, and things vendible, whereout the said enemies take great customs and benefits, to their great profit, and the depression of all the boroughs and trading towns of this land, and of the liege subjects of the said land. It is agreed and established that henceforth, no manner of merchant, nor any other liege person shall go or resort in time of peace or of war to any manner of fair, market or other place among the said enemies with merchandise or things vendible, or send the same to them, unless it be to redeem some prisoner from them who may be the King's liege man. If any liege man do the contrary of this ordinance let him be held and adjudged as a felon of Our Lord the King.

This must be one of the earliest references to the establishment of markets in the territories of the native Irish lords. It may have resulted from the decline of the Meath towns where the Irish had come and traded for centuries.

Later the parliament decided:

That whereas diverse Irish merchants, lately supplied with stock of good by concourse of English merchants, in Irish country have lately found great means of destroying and injuring the markets of Athboy, Kells, Fore, Mullingar, the Oldcastle, and other ancient English market towns, by means, namely that they have commenced markets in Orailly's Country and in Offerroll's Country at Cavan, Granard, Longford and other places, which if they are long continued will bring great riches to the King's enemies, and great poverty to the King's subjects.

Whereupon it is ordained by authority of the said parliament that no English merchant, shall take any good or merchandise to any of the said markets of Cavan, Granard, Longford, or to any Irish country out of English country or carry any goods from the said markets, or make any concourse, or resort to them, on pain of forfeiture of the said goods and merchandise, and their bodies to the King's will.

These documents speak for themselves. For years merchants established in the Anglo-Irish towns had traded successfully with the native Irish – they could not have survived without this trade. The Irish needed many things; salt and wine were very important, as were luxury goods, and they were willing to pay well for them. However, when some of the towns declined at the end of the fourteenth century it was natural that the more enterprising and energetic of the merchants should look for fresh markets. The easiest places were Cavan, Longford and Granard, but there were probably others. In order to trade successfully in these places, the merchants needed the protection of the local lord, for which they were prepared to pay. Naturally those merchants who judged it wiser to stay at home and wait for the buyers and sellers to come to the towns objected to this, and complained loudly to the Dublin officials; hence the action by the parliament.

Money

From 1307 until 1460 few coins were minted in Ireland, and the shortage was made up, to come extent, by forgeries. This was a cause of continuous complaints by the Irish parliament, and the condition of the coins found in the hoards of the time shows that these complaints were justified. Some of the coins were clipped, some were forgeries, and some had been imported from Scotland or England. Coins from many parts of Europe were also in circulation in Ireland during this time. In 1447 the Irish parliament meeting in Trim made an order that

from May, clipped money must not be circulated, 'nor the money of O'Reilly, or any other unlawful money, provided that a coiner be ready at the same day to make the coin'.

In 1456 the complaints had become louder still. It was stated that:

> The country is greatly impoverished by the great withdrawing, taking and carrying of the said land into England, of silver plate, broken silver, bullion, and wedges of silver, made of the great clipping of the coin, of our Sovereign Lord the King, by his Irish enemies, and English rebels, within the said land, by which the said coin is diminished and greatly impaired, and the Irish silver called Reilly's increase from one day to another, to the great injury and impoverishment of his said people, of this his said land, and annihilation of his said coin.

The parliament then ordered, 'For every ounce of broken silver, bullion, and wedges of silver, taken by any person or persons out of the said land, the person shall pay to the King twelve pence for every ounce taken out.' Lords and messengers going to England were excepted from this rule.

In different parts of the country locally made coins were being widely used, as substitutes for the official coinage. Such forgeries had probably been made and used for centuries but little was done about the problem until Edward IV (1461-83) became king.

One of these counterfeit issues was knows as O'Reilly's money. In an article written in the *Journal of the Royal Society of Antiquaries of Ireland* it is stated:

> We have been informed by Dr O'Donovan that according to the pedigree of Count O'Reilly, compiled by the Chevalier Thomas O'Gorman, the money called *Croise Caoile* (Slender Cross) was said to have been coined by O'Reilly (Lord of Briefne) at Crossakeel, a village in the county of Cavan. At parliaments held at Trim and Naas in 1447 and 1457 the money called O'Reilly's Money was forbidden to be circulated.

In the parochial survey issued by Shaw Mason during the early years of the nineteenth century one of the writers said that at Kesh, near Ballymote in County Sligo, a Calais groat of Edward IV had been found and he went on to say that the local people refer to such coins as *Airgead na Croise Caoile* (Money of the Slender Cross). Many of the coins minted by the Dublin government from the thirteenth century onwards have what might be called 'a slender cross ' on the reverse side and it is likely that this is the reason for the name. In any case, Crossakeel is in County Meath, and a considerable distance from the territory of O'Reilly. The money has been shown by Dolley and Sealy to be clever counterfeits of groats which had been clipped. They were made of a core of base metal covered with silver.

It appears likely that this money was used at the fairs of Cavan, Granard and Longford and used in this limited area it would serve its purpose admirably. Since the local lord had complete control of the fairs, and markets in his territory, he would have been responsible for any money used there, hence the name O'Reilly's money.

Similarly the coiners were at work in the south of Ireland. The parliament found that there were diverse coiners in the city of Cork as well as in Youghal, Kinsale and Kilmallock, and said that their names were 'John Fannyn, John Crone, Patrick Martell, William Synnott, Morytagh O'Hannigan, Nicholas Rury and diverse others, which coiners from one day to another make and strike false coins, without any Authority of Our Sovereign Lord the King'. Fannyn claimed to have been granted letters patent for coining money, but no such patent letters were in the official records, and these were forgeries. The parliament went on to declare that the circulation of these counterfeit coins had destroyed the trade of Cork and the other towns, 'so that no bulk of merchandise came to them by sea or land'.

In this case it was ordered that Fannyn and the others should appear in person before the Lord Deputy in parliament, and when they did not do so, they were found to be 'traytors attainted'. Orders were then sent to the Earl of Desmond, to the mayors of Cork and of Youghal, and to the Sovereigns of Kinsale and Kilmallock. They were directed to 'take the bodies of the said coiners' and execute the law upon them as 'traitors attainted.' It was also decided that all the money minted in Cork and in other places in Munster, except Waterford, be condemned.

It is very likely that the coiners had been acting with the authority of the Earl of Desmond and certainly no coiners could work in Cork, Youghal, Kinsale or Kilmallock without the approval of the local authorities in these places. In any case, the money issued by them was used to enable people to buy and sell and so help the trade of these towns rather than injure it, as the Irish parliament said.

It is probable that the mayor of Cork was wise in undervaluing the groats from the royal mint. He had to pay for them, while it was much cheaper to employ a local tinker to make the coins, and there is no doubt that the technical skill to do this was available in fifteenth-century Munster. It is likely that coins issued in Wexford at this time, and those struck in the Munster towns, were also for local circulation – like

O'Reilly's money.

All this is evidence of the efforts of the people concerned to buy and sell efficiently. Since the government of the time did not provide an adequate supply of money, different substitutes had to be found and it was in the interests of everybody that these should be acceptable to buyers and sellers.

4

Bishops' Fairs

IN THE present century it would seem strange to us if a bishop were granted a patent to hold fairs and markets in some of the towns and manors of his diocese. This was, however, a common practice in Norman England and early in the thirteenth century similar patents were granted to some of the new Norman bishops in Ireland. It will be realised that in Norman England a bishop was not only the spiritual ruler of his diocese, he was also a powerful temporal lord with all the powers and duties which went with such a position.

There are references to Bishops' fairs at Winchester and at York. Naturally, the Irish dioceses which were controlled by the Normans were administered as they were in England, and so it is no surprise to read that on 26 July 1193 John Count of Mortmain and Lord of Ireland granted to his 'Most dear father in God, John (Comyn) Archbishop of Dublin [1181-1212] the right to hold a fair once a year at Swords for eight days, commencing on the vigil of St Columcille' (8 June). As the old Irish monastery of Swords was associated with St Columcille, his feast was celebrated there and it is also likely that the town was part of the temporalities of the archbishop of Dublin: the mediaeval archbishops had a house there.

Not long afterwards, on 10 July 1211, John granted to the city a fair lasting for fifteen days beginning on 2 May within the boundaries of the city of Dublin. The grant stated that the first two days of the fair were to be the property of the archbishop.

The next such grant is dated 30 September 1234, when Henry III granted to Luke, archbishop of Dublin, and to his successors a weekly market on Saturday at his manor at Slagunnilde (now Powerscourt) and a yearly fair at his manor of Ballymore (Eustace) beginning on the vigil of the Assumption (14 August), and continuing for eight days.

The duties and responsibilities of the archbishop were set out in a document written late in the fourteenth century, and were similar to those of a temporal lord.

As was general at fairs, no summons might be served during the two days of the Dublin fair which were the property of the archbishop. Complaints about matters arising during these two days had to be made to the archbishop within twenty-four hours. If the complaint was made later than this, the plaintiff had to pay 20s. If he was unable to pay, he might be kept in jail for forty days, unless pardoned by the mayor and commonality.

There is some evidence that the archbishop of Cashel had similar rights in his own town of Cashel. On 12 July 1230 the archbishop, Mairtin O'Brien, granted to the provost and twelve burgesses of the town of Cashel certain rights and privileges in the town, but reserving to himself the control of the market there. In the *Calendar of Patent Rolls of Ireland* a charter cites one of Edward IV. In it the archbishop claims to have assize of wine, bread and beer in the town of Cashel and also of the standards there – ells, weights, bushels, gallons, yards and other measures and weights. The charter also declares that the king's clerk of the market and keeper of the measures should not interfere in that office within the lordships, manors and crosses of the archbishop except once a year when they might see and examine the standards of the archbishop.

In 1666 a lease was made to James Langford:

> . . . of all and singular the tolls and customs of the two fairs belonging to the said Lord Archbishop and his successors, and yearly kept within the liberties and franchises of the city of Cashel aforesaid in the suburbs of Connafee Street in the east side of the city one of which two fairs kept yearly on the fifteenth and sixteenth days of March [the two days before St Patrick's Day] and the other fair is kept on the Friday and Saturday before the Sunday of the dedication of the church of St Patrick aforesaid and in Irish called *Domhnach Crom Dhu*, falling always in the month of July.

The yearly rent was £4 sterling.

These fairs are now held on 26 March and 7 August in Lady's Well Street. The late Archbishop Lawrence, at the instance of Dr Cotton, remitted the tolls – since his time they have been toll free. *Domhnach Crom Dhu* means Cromdu's fair or pattern. There is a common saying, 'Things were not so dear (or so cheap) since the days of the Cromdu'.

In the diocese of Ossory the bishop, Geoffrey de Turville, was given a royal grant of a fair in the Irishtown – Kilkenny – in 1245, with a weekly market on Wednesday. This fair continued and was held on 22 October, when it was known as St Canice Fair. The Irishtown was that part of the present city which lies on the left bank of the little river

Bregagh which runs under Parliament Street into the River Nore. It includes the mediaeval cathedral of St Canice on its hill, as well as the deanery and the other buildings around it and also some streets on the lower ground.

In the *Calendar of Patent Rolls I* a writ can be found which prohibits the provost and commonality of Kilkenny from interfering with the customs of the market of the Irishtown of Kilkenny which were parcel of the possessions and temporalities of the see and had been expended on the reparation of the walls of the city.

Irishtown continued as an independent corporation and returned two members to the Irish Parliament until the Act of Union in 1800. The place appears to have been a sort of Vatican city, but it will be remembered that the archbishop of Dublin had a similar area, called the Archbishop's Liberties, outside the jurisdiction of the mayor of Dublin.

During the seventeenth century the religious differences which arose out of the Reformation became fixed, and the Anglican bishops who had acquired the temporalities of the Irish sees now continued to possess the rights to hold fairs and markets. Before the Reformation the archbishop of Armagh, an Englishman, lived at Termonfechin in County Louth and seldom visited Armagh, which was administered by an Irish dean.

When the Plantation of Ulster began early in the seventeenth century the archbishop, Christopher Hamilton, was granted a patent for a Tuesday market in Armagh, 'where a market has been held time out of mind', as well as two fairs, one on St Patrick's Day (17 March) and the other on Lammas Day (1 August). He was also given two fairs at Carnteele (County Tyrone), one on 15 August and the following day, and the other on 8 September (Nativity of the Blessed Virgin Mary) and on the following day. These were popular feasts in Ireland and were each referred to as 'Lady Day in harvest'. Later, in 1634, another fair on 29 June was established in Armagh.

The *Patent Rolls* also contain grants to the archbishop of markets on Monday at Termonfechin in County Louth and at Nobber in County Meath, as well as a Wednesday market at Inniskeen, County Monaghan. It would appear likely that these three markets were part of the temporalities of the mediaeval archbishops, because the archbishop had property in all three places and the patents were issued to make sure that his rights were maintained.

At these fairs and markets the archbishop was given the right to have 'pillory tumbrell and thewr'. He was also told to appoint coroners, clerks of the market and masters of assay, as well as establishing Courts of Piepowder and collecting the usual tolls. Not long afterwards he was given a Friday market at Tinan, County Armagh, with two fairs there, one on 15 June and the other on 13 April.

In the *Patent Rolls of James I* Thomas Jones, archbishop of Dublin (1605-19), got a patent to revive a market formerly held in Ballymore (Eustace) and a fair on the feast of the Assumption and on the two following days. This patent was dated 18 April 1609.

The Anglican archbishop of Tuam was granted a Friday market at Kilmaine in County Mayo and a fair there on St Luke's Day. By the year 1800 this fair was being held on 28 October, due to the calendar change.

John Todd, who was bishop of Down, Conor and Dromore, was granted a patent 'to hold a Saturday market in the place near the Cathedral of Dromore where the great cross now stands' and also two fairs to be held in the same place on the feast of SS Philip and James and the two following days and on the feast of St Michael and the two following days. He was to appoint a coroner, an escheator, and a clerk of the market. As lord of the manor of Down he was to grant leases to English, Welsh and Scots of sixty years possession at not less than £8 a year for each holding.

Another of the new men, George Montgomery, was bishop of Derry, Raphoe and Clogher, and when he was translated to Meath he retained Clogher. He was given a patent for two fairs, probably the two 'Old fairs' which were held there on 6 May and 26 July.

One of these, the fair held on 26 July, appears to have been a very special occasion known as the Gooseberry Fair and the Spoilin Fair. This word refers to the tents and bothies put up at the time of the fair to cook meat for the crowds. These tents were to be seen at many country fairs and sold food and drink of different kinds. The name Gooseberry Fair was used for a number of fairs, since they occurred at the time the gooseberries were ripe and were on sale there.

In the diocese of Killaloe the bishop, John, was granted a patent for a Wednesday market and a fair on 10 October and on the day following in Killaloe town. Early in the nineteeth century this fair was being held on 21 October due to the change in the calendar in 1753.

Also in County Clare the bishop of the tiny diocese of Kilfenora was granted a Thursday market and two fairs, one on the Wednesday, Thursday and Friday before Whit Sunday and the other at Michaelmas and the two following days. The Michaelmas fair continued into the nineteenth century, held on 10 October due to the calendar change.

The field in which the fair of Kilfenora used to be held is on the opposite side of the road from the partly roofed pre-Reformation cathedral of Kilfenora. In the middle of the field is a circular stone structure about twelve feet in diameter and with battlements on top. It is approached by three steps at one side and resembles a very large pulpit. I was told that this was a 'paying stand' where people paid for the cattle which they had bought at the fair. There is also a story concerning a man who lost his money on the paying stand and found it still there in a hole in the wall on the next fair day. I heard the same story about the wall round the fair green in Kilkenny.

There was also a Bishop's fair in Elphin. The bishop there, Edward, was given two fairs on the feasts of St George (23 April) and of St Andrew (30 November). To this, Lewis adds, 'a market has been established by the bishop on Wednesday for which a market house will be erected'.

The butter market, Cork

5
The Sixteenth Century

THE sixteenth century was a time of change in Ireland. The Reformation was followed by the Counter Reformation, and the power of the Earls of Kildare and of Desmond was finally broken. Early in the following century the power of the native Irish lords in Ulster was destroyed after nine years of war, and at the death of Queen Elizabeth in 1603 the conquest of Ireland appeared to have been completed.

During this century, charters for fairs were granted to some Irish towns. These included such famous fairs as Trim, Mullingar and Athenry. On 8 July 1584 a patent was addressed to the provost, burgesses and commonality of Mullingar, County Westmeath, and to Walter Hoppe, constable of the castle or gaol there, and his heirs. Power was given to them to hold two fairs in the town, one on 1 November and the three following days, and one on St John's Day (24 June) and on the three following days. In this case, if Sunday fell on any of the fair days it was ordered that the fair should begin on the following Monday and tolls were to be levied 'as in other towns'. The patent went on to order that these tolls and all other customs levied there were to be expended on the fortification of the town by the provost and the constable.

On 9 January 1562 a lease was given to the portreeve and burgesses of Trim. This granted them the tolls of the market of Trim, as well as the ground or soil of the market and all shops or stalls there, 'parcel of Her Majestey's Ancient Inheritance'. This lease was granted for twenty-one years at an annual rent of £4. The lease was renewed on 22 July 1578 in much the same terms as those mentioned in the lease of 1562, but in addition it mentioned all customs of cattle and all other merchandise coming to or going from the market.

There are some more details in a charter granted to the town of Athenry in 1575. This ordered that a common clerk was to be appointed, as in Trim. He was to have assize of bread and ale in the town and he was also given the authority to examine the measures and weights used in the town 'and other things belonging to the clerk of the market'. This charter also referred to 'the Queen's Clerk having only the power to view and correct the town standard'. The charter also declared that a fair was to be held in Athenry from the Eve of St John's day to the feast of St Thomas the Martyr. Two of the burgesses were to be elected barons of the fair and were to hold court for the settlement of disputes arising there. The provost was ordered to proclaim the price at which all victuals were to be sold. The town was to have a pillory and a ducking stool. The provost, in directing their use, was to obtain the counsel of four burgesses in difficult cases.

In the year 1553 a charter was given by Queen Mary to Thomastown, in County Kilkenny. This granted the right to hold a Monday market with the same liberties, privileges, tolls, customs, profits, and commodities as in Kilkenny. It also granted a fair within the town, or in its franchise, on May Eve and during the fifteen following days – just as in Kilkenny and in other Irish towns holding fairs.

On 10 November 1552 Edward VI instructed the Lord Deputy to grant to the Baron of Delvin the markets and customs of Fower (Fore) and Templeton.

Carrickfergus, with its strong castle and easy approach from the sea, had been an English outpost since the early years of the thirteenth century. In 1569 it was visited by Sir Henry Sydney, the Lord Deputy, and in a memoir written some years later he said that when he was there a fat cow could be bought for 6s.8d. and twenty-four eggs for 1d. He went on to say that at Carrickfergus there was a good market twice a week where:

> Not only all kinds of things of that country breed were to be sold, but out of the English Pale, the Isle of Man and Scotland came much merchandise, victuals and other comodities, and out of France in one summer three barks of forty tuns apiece discharged their loading of excellent good Gascoigne wine, the which they sold for nineteen cow skins the hogshead [fifty gallons].

Athenry acted as an outpost for the Galway merchants, and it is likely that Enniscorthy acted in the same relationship to the town of Wexford. It was favourably placed for trading with the native Irish who had regained control of north Wexford. Sydney referred to Enniscorthy in his memoir. He wrote that in 1569 Sir Edmund Butler:

> Utterly spoyled a great fair held at Enniscorthy, a house and town of the Queen's in the county of Wexford. I am sure that fair is far the greatest of any in Ireland and held yearly and usually at a day certain. The horrible rapes, the shameful murders with the total

rapine of all the goods that could be carried away were too loathsome to be written or read. There were assembled (beside a multitude of country people) the most of the merchants of the good town of Wexford, either in their own persons, their wives, or their servants, who were ravished, killed or spoiled, all looking for no such unheard of harm there, whither placably they came by water.

The town of Callan had also suffered when it was attacked by Sir Piers Butler, and a certain Fulke Comerford, 'a wealthy man of plate', was especially ill-treated there. At about the same time a concordat of the lord deputy and council declared that the town of Callan had 'had of long and ancient time two market days weekly on Wednesday and Saturday'. It then went on to grant the sovereign, portreeve, burgesses, corporation and commons that they 'might keep two weekly market days within the town as they anciently had done'. It also exonerated them from Irish cess and custom, and granted them a licence to erect a tan house. The concordat went on to say that the butchers and fishers of the town should have free liberty to 'provide abroad in such place as to them should seem meet, such store of victuals and other necessaries as should suffice for victualling and provisioning the town'.

In County Kerry there were at least two important fair towns during the sixteenth century. One of these was Tralee, a town owned by the Earl of Desmond. The fair was held at the time when the earl came there to collect his rents, and the duties paid by merchants who attended the fair added to his income.

The Earl of Desmond had castles both in Kilmallock and Rathkeale. Kilmallock had been for long an important trading town until it was sacked and burned during the rebellion of James Fitzmaurice Fitzgerald, and it is recorded in the inquisition of the lands held by the earl that he levied a tax 'on every cart and beast that were brought to the markets at Kilmallock and Rathkeale'.

At this time there are references to what were called 'grey merchants'. These were men who travelled from the larger Anglo-Irish towns to sell and buy in the areas where the native Irish were still in control. Some of these men came from England, or even from Europe, to trade in the most inaccessible parts of the country. In order to do this in safety and with success it was necessary to have a safe conduct from the local lord, and when the merchant moved on into a neighbouring lordship a further safe conduct became necessary. It is clear that the profits of such trading must have been very large to make such difficult and dangerous journeys worthwhile.

People asked that the activity of these men be stopped, and a law was passed stating 'that no merchant, neither his servant, shall go out of the citys and towns, wherein they dwell, to the extent to buy or sell any manner of wares: and that they which dwell in Dublin and Drogheda shall bargain wares with them which dwell in the Borrough towns in the country'.

Similarly the merchants of Dundalk had been paying black rent to O'Neill at least since 1430. No doubt the merchants who traded at the market in Cavan also paid O'Reilly, whose castle of Tully Mongan overlooked the town. By the 1560s the towns of Trim, Ardee, Navan, Athboy, Kells and Mullingar, which had once thrived on trade with the Irish, were 'sore decayed and in manner desolate'.

In the south of Ireland too, merchants who wished to trade had to obtain the good will of the local lord. MacCarthy Mor, Earl of Clancar, was paid by an English merchant, John Corbine, when in 1568 MacCarthy assured him that 'any man may pass' in his name.

Towards the end of the century there are references to the appointment of an official called the 'clerk of the market'. There had been many such appointments during earlier centuries, but now an effort was made to ensure that the official did his work honestly and efficiently. On 14 February 1586 the queen granted to Richard Kimuelmershe of Dublin:

> the office of general clerk of the market throughout the realm, as well within the liberties, as without, with all fees belonging to the office. To hold during good behaviour. He shall yearly certify to the exchequer. The patent recites that diverse disorders are daily comitted in buying and selling by false weights and measures and other deceitful means for want of such an officer.

Kimuelmershe appears to have experienced some difficulties in carrying out his duties because on 23 January 1589 Elizabeth wrote to the lord deputy about the matter. She told him to accept the surrender of the office of clerk of the markets and fairs from Kimuelmershe and to regrant the office to him, 'with authority to reform diverse inconveniences and abuses, which in consequence of the insufficiency of his former patent he was fain to leave unreformed'. On 22 April 1596 the patent was renewed, but a few days later a certain Philip Williams was appointed to the office.

Two years later there was another change. On 5 May 1598 a grant was made to Walter Williams of the office of clerk of the market throughout Ireland. He was to hold it 'during his good behaviour' with power to search for, and commit to jail, tradesmen using false weights and measures, forestallers and regraters. His salary was £10. The document also stated that the office had been surrendered by Philip Williams.

Unfortunately there is no evidence to show how these men carried out their duties. We do know however that during the following centuries the complaints continued.

It is clear from all this that fairs and markets continued to be held in many parts of Ireland. At that time the produce of the country consisted largely of flax, linen yarn and linen cloth, wool, wool yarn and woollen cloth, and hides, butter, tallow, salt beef and fish. There was even a beginning to the export of live cattle. These are the products which the grey merchants were seeking when they attended fairs and markets, and in return they supplied wine, iron, salt and manufactured goods.

All this suggests that trading in Ireland during the sixteenth century was like trading on the west coast of Africa until the early part of the present century. In each case primary products of the country were exchanged for more sophisticated goods which were not produced locally. It was also necessary that the local lord be paid for his protection; without this it was not possible to trade. Naturally the established merchants in the Anglo-Irish towns objected to the fairs which were held among the native Irish. For centuries they had prospered by trading with the Gaelic Irish who came there, but they could not manage when their markets were being forestalled by their more energetic and enterprising – and often more courageous – rivals. It is remarkable how far a man will go in search of a good bargain. This trading was to expand greatly during the next century and eventually spread to every part of the country. It was then that the modern system of holding fairs and markets began.

The market house, Newtownards, Co. Down

6

The Seventeenth Century

SOME of the records of the administration of Waterford, Youghal, Cork and Kinsale are available for the seventeenth century. Reading through them it becomes clear that the problems associated with the running of fairs and markets during earlier centuries continued, with the addition of further problems following the religious change of the sixteenth century.

In 1626 Charles I granted a new charter to Waterford city. This mentioned weekly markets on Wednesday and Saturday and a fair at midsummer. It also stated that 'no person, not being free shall retail in the city except at fair or market, under the penalty of forfeiting the goods or the price to the city.'

There appears to have been continuous trouble about the buying and selling of corn in the city markets. During the seventeenth century the people of the town, as well as the baker and brewers, were dependent on the surrounding country for supplies of grain. In Ireland the weather is not always suitable for ripening or harvesting it, and when conditions were unfavourable prices inevitably rose. At such time there were great complaints about those who forestalled the market by buying up all the corn before it opened — presumably to sell at higher prices. In Youghal in 1612 it was ordered that 'If any of the inhabitants after 1 December next, bring any corn into the said town or liberties on any other day than the official market days, Wednesday and Saturday, or bring it to any place other than the market place, (the fish shambles and the flesh shambles excepted) he shall forfeit the corn with a fine of 5s.' The corn was kept and sold on the next market day.

In Youghal in 1612 market tolls were collected by the town bailiffs who were paid 2s. in the pound for their work. In Waterford the market tolls were farmed to people who paid a fixed sum to the city for the right. There appears to have been some trouble about the way the collectors did their work, because on 28 August 1669 it was ordered that 'John Carroll and his wife employed by Joseph Cooper, in taking up the toll and custom be forthwith turned out of the said employment

43

by said Cooper and not received in again for future'.

In the following year the city authorities agreed that Mrs Joseph Barr and Mr William Launder were to be collectors of tolls for the year, excepting the tolls of the midsummer fair. Barr and Launder paid £35 for this, and in addition they were obliged to keep the market-place clean. At the same meeting it was ordered that the toll gatherers for the previous year, Joseph Barr and Joseph Cooper, 'do clear forthwith last year's arrears'. It is not now possible to decide who were the culprits, but Barr and Launder gave satisfaction and the following year they were continued as toll farmers. In this case they paid £40 to the city and were allowed to collect the tolls at the midsummer fair. It may have been as a result of the peculation that on 28 August 1696 the city council decided that 'the present sherriffs bee allowed fifty shillings out of the revenue for their expenses and charge at midsummer fair'. In Cork the tolls and customs of the market were also farmed. On 12 June 1610 the city council decided that 'the customs and profits of the next fair on St Matthew's Day shall be granted and farmed to him who shall pay most'.

In Youghal in 1634 a proclamation was issued about passing good farthings and against counterfeiting the coin of the realm. This was a serious effort to stop counterfeiting as the punishment for offenders was to have their ears cut off. The town council of Youghal then made an order that farthing tokens might not be used to pay any sum greater than 2*d*. Later in the century the traders in most Irish towns issued tokens which they were prepared to exchange on demand for coin of the realm. During the year 1653-59 hundreds of different types of tokens were issued and of these sixteen different types from Waterford, seventeen from Youghal, and ten from Cork are extant.

Stories and rumours of a 'popish plot' were widely circulated and believed during the reign of Charles II, and in 1677, as a precaution against such a plot, the town council of Youghal made an order which forbade papists from coming inside the walls of the town. As a further precaution it was ordered that markets be held outside the walls. During the following year the rumours continued, and a proclamation was issued by the Duke of Ormond and the Irish Council. This ordered that markets and fairs should be held outside the walls of Drogheda, Wexford, Cork, Limerick, Waterford, Youghal and Galway. When the city authorities in Waterford learned of this, they decided that 'the Garrison have liberty to make use of the old market house near the Key Gate for a guardhouse till the market be brought within the gates again'.

On 30 June 1684 the city council in Waterford had to consider a petition from a certain William Orpin. The council decided that 'upon reading the peticion of William Orpin it was concluded by vote of the mayor and Councill that the peticioner shalbe discharged of his imprisonment, acording his peticion, he being arrested in the time of the fair, and the mayor and Sherriffs shalbee idempnified'.

This appears to have been a case in which Orpin invoked the old law, which stated that no arrest might be made during the time of the fair. It may have been that Orpin was threatening to sue the Mayor and Sherriffs for unlawful arrest so they were very quick to have him released.

In contrast to the relatively steady life of the towns, there were many changes in the ownership of land in parts of the country during the seventeenth century. Many new patents were granted during the reign of James I (1603-25). Generally the patent set out the extent of each man's lands and granted the owner the right to hold fairs and markets at fixed times and place on these lands. As a result, the system of fairs and markets was extended to almost every part of the country.

Ulster

The greatest change in the ownership of land was in Ulster, where nearly all the native Irish landowners lost their lands. At that time only Carrickfergus, Armagh, Downpatrick and perhaps Cavan could have been considered towns, and Carlingford Lough was one of the few ways which led easily into the interior of the province.

In 1611 Arthur Bagnall was granted a Thursday market at Newry, with two annual fairs there, one on Low Monday and the two following days, and the other on St Luke's day (18 October) and the two following days. Bagnall was also granted similar privileges at the old town of Carlingford. These included a Saturday market, with a fair at Michaelmas and on the following day.

Shortly after the end of the Nine Years war two Scotsmen, James Hamilton and Hugh Montgomery, had managed to get possession of the O'Neill lands of Clandeboy (North Down and South Antrim) and were busy settling the Lowland Scots there. Hamilton was given patents for fairs and markets at Castlereagh, Bangor, Holywood and Greyabbey on 5 October 1605. Early in the following year he got some more licences for fairs and markets at Antrim and Ballycanure, as well as at Castletown in the Little Ards.

By now the Flight of the Earls had taken place and the way was clear for the Plantation of Ulster. By January 1609 it had been decided that twenty-five incorporated towns should be established, and the Lord Deputy, Sir Arthur Chichester, travelled with a number of commissioners through the counties in the same year and found that all the land there was at the disposal of the king. The towns were to be established at three forts, Mountjoy, Mount Norris and Charlemont, which had been built during the war. There were also three episcopal towns, Armagh, Clogher and Raphoe. Derry had already been incorporated. Then there were Dungannon, Enniskillen, Cavan, Belturbet, Dungiven, Limavady, Ballyshannnon, Donegal, and Killybegs.

The new arrivals faced a difficult and dangerous task in establishing themselves on their lands. Despite this, however, most of the planters prospered, as they were often able, energetic and, like true conquerors, greedy for land and power. They founded families which were to hold that land and power for centuries. Names like Chichester, Brooke, Cole, Caulfield and Hamilton appeared in Irish history for the first time as they set about establishing a new order in the country.

In most of the new plantation towns the system was much the same, and Enniskillen was typical. After the plantation it was decided that it should be the county town, and the man who was given responsiblity for it was an Englishman, William Cole. In 1609 he became governor of the castle of Enniskillen and in 1611 he was granted lands in County Fermanagh as a servitor of the plantation.

The grant declared that he was to 'bring, or cause to be brought, to the site twenty persons, being English or Scotch and chiefly artificiers and mecanics, to make, erect and construct a town in a convenient place to be decided by Cole, to be burgesses of the town of Enniskillen'. He was to mark out and set apart sites for a church and cemetery, for a market house, for a jail or prison for the county, and for a public school with a court and garden adjoining. He was to 'build or cause to be built in a decent or uniform manner' twenty burgages or houses of stone or framed timber according to the form of building usual in England. Cole and his heirs were empowered to hold a Thursday market and fair on Lammas Day and they were also appointed clerks of the market and were to keep the toll book. No persons, except the freemen of the town, were allowed to sell by retail within three miles of it without licence.

Cavan was a different type of town. Its first charter was granted on 15 November 1610. This declared that the corporation should have a weekly market and two fairs in the year, one on 14 September and on the day following and the other on 1 November and on the day following, with all the usual trappings – a Court of Piepowder, a market jury, constables, appraisers and petty constables. The charter was issued on the direct instructions of Sir Arthur Chichester. A surprising thing about this was that the first sovereign was Walter Brady and the two portreeves were Owen Mor Brogan and Farrel Mac Eregules. The area of the borough was to be the area within one mile of Walter Brady's house. Even more surprising was the fact that only two of the twelve burgesses were of the New English or Scots.

During the Confederate Wars, Masari, a Roman emissary to the Confederation, wrote in July 1646 about:

> the great fair held in a field near Cavan. It is attended by crowds and great quantities of merchandise are brought thither by the people of the surrounding districts. I was amazed at the abundant supply especially of animals, and of all kinds of eatibles, which were sold at an absurdly low price. A fat ox cost three crowns, a fine wether three guilii [6*d*.] a kid or a pair of fat chickens six *baiocci* and so on, for the supplies were as plentiful as money was scarce in the country.

The oaths to be taken by the holders of office are of interest. The sovereign was to take the oath of a justice of the peace, the oath of allegiance and an oath to fulfil his duties. The foreman of the market jury swore to:

> discharge the duty of said office without favour or affection and do justice to the poor as well as to the sick and to the rich as well as to the poor, to the best of your skill and knowledge: that you will examine, the victuals of every kind, the weights and measures of said Corporation, and prevent all manner of forestalling as often as you receive information, or suspect any frauds are committed.

Belturbet, which was intended to be the urban centre of the barony of Loughtee in County Cavan, was different. One of the undertakers was Sir Stephen Butler, who held 2,000 acres near the town as well as 3,000 acres in County Fermanagh. He was given a Saturday market in Belturbet with two fairs, one on the Wednesday before Ash Wednesday and the other on St Bartholomew's Day, (24 August). The Town was officially established on 18 July 1610, when Butler was given the town lands, and the other undertakers in the neighbourhood were told to procure settlers for the town. They were also told to build a church there. A charter was granted in March 1613 to the provost, free burgesses and commonality of Belturbet, and Butler was made 'chief officer'.

By the next year the inhabitants were building boats there in order to make use of the waterways of the Erne, and in 1618 Pynnar found 'houses built of cage work, all inhabited with British tenants, and most of them tradesmen each of these having a house and garden plott, with four acres of land, and commons for certain numbers of cows and garrans'. The commissioners for the plantation were very pleased and referred to 'that well begun corporation which is fitt to be cherished', adding that there was 'great store of Protestants in and about the town'. They recommended that a church be built there, and in 1623 a parish minister was living in the town – although no church had been built. William Bedel (whose father was bishop of Kilmore), writing before the year 1641, described Belturbet as 'the only considerable town in the whole county' but one which 'was built as one of our ordinary market towns here in England, having only but one church in it'.

Clearly Cavan and Belturbet were different types of town. Cavan had acquired and retained many of the characteristics of a mediaeval Anglo-Irish town, with its Franciscan friary and the friars still living quietly in the town. Belturbet was a Protestant town from the beginning, and a plantation town in the true sense.

At the other plantation towns, such as Dungannon – where Sir Arthur Chichester was established – and Donegal – where Basil Brooke was in charge – the same system was followed. Fairs and markets were established, a town laid out in streets, and English or Scottish colonists were settled. It is a little surprising to find small grants of land, with rights to hold fairs and markets, given to some of the native Irish. In Fermanagh Brian Maguire was given a Wednesday market and a fair in Inseylougherne, and James MacGrath of Termon Magrath got a Saturday market and a two day fair on 16 July at Cowlinser.

In County Down Sir Arthur MacGenise was granted a Tuesday market and two annual fairs at Rathfriland. There were at least two grants in County Tyrone. Catherine Ny Neale got a Monday market at Kinard and a fair on the vigil and feast of St Barnabas (10 June), and Henry O'Neil got two fairs at Edencarrickduff, one at midsummer and the other at Michaelmas.

Munster

The destruction of the power of the Earl of Desmond and his death meant that by 1585 a large part of the good land of Munster was forfeited to the English crown. Preparations were made to plant large areas of Cork, Kerry, Limerick and Waterford with English undertakers who were to settle English tenants on their newly acquired lands. During the Nine Years War the native Irish rose against the colonists and destroyed the settlement. At the end of the war the work of planting the forfeited lands was resumed and, with the grants the new owners were given, the right to hold fairs and markets. In the first plantation the largest grant, 42,000 acres of arable land, went to Sir Walter Raleigh at a rent of £66 a year.

In County Clare Donough O'Brien, the loyalist Earl of Thomond, got new patents for his lands as well as a number of fairs and markets. These included two fairs at Clarecastle. Later he was given fairs at Ennis and at Sixmilebridge. In Clare some other patents were granted to followers of the Earl.

In contrast to County Clare, most of the fairs in County Kerry were given to the New English. These included Thomas Roper, who had one at Castleisland and another at Castlemaine. Richard Harding had two fairs at Ballinskelligs and Giles Herbert one at Cowrins. Still another was Valentine Browne, who was granted a fair at Killarney.

Among the Old English in Kerry, Thomas Fitzmorris, Baron of Lixnaw, got fairs at Listowel and Ardfert and a market at Liselton.

In County Limerick a number of New English came into possession of the Desmond lands. Sir John Dowdall had a Thursday market 'at the high cross of Rathkeale and in the street thereto adjoining within the Seigniority of Knockfillingsley' and two fairs, also in Rathkeale. Next Sir Francis Berkley was granted fairs and markets at Askeaton: Rathkeale and Askeaton had been important places under the control of the Earl of Desmond.

In County Tipperary the most important landowners were the Butlers, headed by the Earls of Ormond, of whose loyalty there was no doubt. One member of this family, Thomas, Baron of Cahir, got a Thursday market and an annual fair in his town. Oliver Grace had fairs at Tyone, near Nenagh, on 22 July and 29 August and William Dran got a Thursday market and fairs on the eve, day and morrow of St George (23 April) at Solighod, and also on the eve, day and morrow of St Andrew (30 November) at Tipperary town. At least two of the native Irish landowners obtained patents for fairs. One was Mortagh O'Brien, son and heir of O'Brien of Ara', who got a fair at Palaice.

In County Waterford, Richard Boyle, the most successful of all the New English, bought Sir Walter Raleigh's lands. He took over Lismore castle and held a fair in the town. Later he was granted fairs at some other places on his Waterford lands. John Poer, grandson and heir of Lord Poer, had a fair at Kilmackthomas, while another of the Old English, Sir John Fitzgarrett, had two fairs – one at Drumcanny and the other at the Rocke near Whitchurch.

In County Cork some new towns were founded and patents for a large number of fairs were granted. Bandon was founded by Richard Boyle in 1608. Then Henry Beecher at Castlemahon was granted a Saturday market and two fairs 'in the town, lately built on the south side of the River Bandon near the Bridge'. Beecher appears to have been the provost of Bandon and later he was given the power to appoint a clerk of the market and to licence butchers, brewers, bakers, merchants and so on. Boyle was also granted a Saturday market and two fairs in Ballydehob in 1614 as well as two fairs at Clonakilty. Another of the New English, Thomas Petley, had a market and fair at Carrigaline. Sir Richard Aldworth had a market and two fairs at Kilmacroghan (*alias* Newmarket), and Elizabeth Lady Jephson, wife of Sir John Jephson, was granted a patent for fairs and a market at Mallow.

Among the Old English of County Cork, John Lord Courcy got a patent for two fairs at Ballinspittle. Another, Sir Dominick Sarsfield, had a fair at Carriglemleary, a village near Midleton. Perhaps the most notable of the Old English, however, was David Lord Barry (Ballymore). He was granted fairs in Castlelyons, Timoleague, and Carrigtowhill.

Leinster and Connacht

In Leinster the Anglo-Irish landowners generally remained, although some of the New English were granted land and fairs. Leix and Offaly had been planted during the sixteenth century and this was continued while new plantations were begun in north Wexford in 1610 and in County Longford in 1615.

In County Meath fairs which may have lapsed were re-established in Kells, Old Castle, Navan, Kilcock and Ballyboggan. In County Dublin, fairs were established at Rathfarnham, St Margarets and at Newcastle Lyons. In County Louth fairs were established 'at the old chapel on the Lorgan' and also in Louth, where a house for tanning hides was to be established. In County Kildare fairs were established at the Abbey at Comnail, Monasterevin, and Kilcullen, Ballysax, Kildroght (Celbridge) and Scollockstown. Most of these were monastic sites.

In Westmeath and Longford some of the New English were able to displace the original holders. For example, church lands at Kilkenny West were granted, with a fair, to Sir Theobald Dillon, but some years later this was granted to two of the New English, John King and Adam

Loftus. Fairs were established also at Multyfarnham, Abbeysruel, Finea and Fore. In County Longford, Richard Nugent was granted a fair at Longford town and Sir Francis Shaw got two fairs at Granard. Later Francis Auinger was granted two fairs at Longford and a patent for the two fairs which had previously been given to Shaw.

In County Wicklow fairs were established or re-established at Newcastle, Carnewe and Baltinglass.

In County Carlow they were established at Knockmullen and at Orchard, and Viscount Butler obtained a patent for fairs at Tullow. This man was also granted fairs and markets in Inistioge in County Kilkenny. Fairs were also established at Graigue Duiske, the site of the famous abbey. In Offaly, fairs were established at Kilcormack, Clonona, Birr, Banagher, Shinrone and Geashill. In Leix they were established at Stradbally, Clonegaune, Ballybrittas and Timahoe.

The most notable change was in north County Wexford, where an Ulster-like plantation was started in 1610. Part of this was the establishment of a town called Newburg (Gorey), with fairs and markets. Patents were granted to members of the New English with names like Wallop, Marwood, Parsons, Wingfield and Loftus.

According to Hardiman, the earliest patent for a fair in Galway city was granted on 14 June 1613. This was to be held at Fair Hill or at the Abbey of St Dominick near Galway on 24 August and the two following days, and was known as the Cladagh Fair.

In contrast to the displacement of the native landowners and people which followed the plantation of Ulster, and the establishment of fairs and markets, there was no such disturbance in Connacht. Some of the New English got grants of land, but generally this made little difference to the tenants who must have been relieved that the war was finished and there was no more cattle driving. Most of the grants were given to the Old English.

Ever since the Norman invasion of Connacht early in the thirteenth century, the newcomers had to a great extent replaced the native landowners, especially in Galway and Mayo, even though by the year 1600 there was little to distinguish them from the native Irish.

The most powerful of the Old English was Richard Bourke, Earl of Clanrickard, whose lands extended from the Galway-Mayo border to Portumna at the top of Lough Derg on the River Shannon. At this time Clanrickard was changing from Irish chieftain to English earl, and he was quick to see the advantages of having fairs and markets at convenient places on his lands. His first patent was for two weekly markets on Wednesday and Saturday and a fair on 1 August at Shrure in County Mayo. This was a most important ford on the road running north from Galway, and is now the village of Shrule. There are still the ruins of a strong castle there. This might be regarded as Clanrickard's northern border. By the same patent two more weekly markets and a fair on 25 July were to be held at Collure in County Galway, also markets at Oughelbegg with a fair on 25 March. The patent also granted the right to collect tolls and establish a Court of Piepowder, at a rent of £1 yearly for each place.

The next patent, granted in 1605, was for a Monday market at Ardrahan, a Tuesday market at Clare (Galway) and a fair in the earl's own town, Loughrea, on 1 May. On 14 July 1609 he was given a Tuesday market at Portumna with a fair on St Matthew's Day. At the same time the earl got a Tuesday market at Tyaquin, a Thursday market at Fertimore and a Saturday market at Tynagh, with the usual courts and the right to collect tolls. Rent was 6s.8d. for each market.

It would appear that Clanrickard was given the right to establish some further fairs and markets, because when Edmund Skerrett of Cahermorrish, County Galway, was granted a market there – as well as a fair on St Laurence's Day (10 August) and the two following days – he was to hold it from the Earl of Clanrickard. Others were Ulick Bourke Fitzjohn of Castlehackett, who had a fair on St Matthew's Day (21 September) and the two following days, and Oliver Martin who had a Saturday market at Kinvarra. Both these men were also to hold their grants from the earl.

Some other Old English obtained patents for fairs in County Galway. Richard Birmingham got a market and an annual fair on the 29 June and the following day at Dunmore, an old Norman town which had been held by the Birminghams since the Normans invaded Connacht in the thirteenth century. It still retains something of the look of a mediaeval town. Moyler Boy Birmingham was granted a patent for a market at Conogher with a fair on 14-15 September.

Richard Blake of Galway, merchant, had a Thursday market with a fair on 28-29 October at Ballintubber in County Mayo. The most powerful of the Mayo Bourkes was Sir Theobald Bourke, who got patents for fairs at Bellahene, Bellanamore, Bellanacarrcu and Cloghmacadam. Another was Thomas Bourke, who held fairs at Ballyloughmask, Newtown and Ardnery. Josiah Browne of the Neile was granted a licence for a fair there on 25 July with a Saturday market.

Also in County Mayo Thomas Nolans of Ballinrobe had a three day fair starting on Whit Monday and a market on Thursday at Ballinrobe, 'where a market had been formerly held but was discontinued for many years'. John Moore of Bries was given a Monday market and a fair on 1 August.

In Connacht many of the native Irish landowners were given fairs and markets. These included Colla O'Kelly, who got fairs at Knockcrockery and Ballinamore Bridge. Two of the O'Connor lords, Hugh O'Connor, Don of Ballintubber and Charles O'Connor Roe of Bellanafadde also received grants. Others were Brian MacDermott of Carrick MacDermott and his neighbour Donogh O'Berne. In Roscommon William Molloy got a fair at Croghan, while in Sligo at least two of the native Irish, Brian MacDonough and Rory MacSwine, were granted fairs.

Perhaps the first of the New English to be given a fair in Connacht was Sir James Fullerton: he had a Saturday market and fairs at midsummer and Michaelmas in Sligo town. Shortly afterwards, in June 1604, he got a Monday market on May Day, and another on 24 August at Ballymote. The next were John Bingley and John King, who were granted markets and fairs on 20 May and 20 September 'at the town or Abbey of Boyle'. They already had markets and a fair at Cong, County Mayo. Later King was also given fairs and markets at Tulsk. These three grants were part of the grant of some of the property of the suppressed abbeys of Cong and Boyle. Other members of the New English were Edward and William Crofton. Edward Crofton was given a fair at Ballymurry in County Roscommon and one at Ballisodare, County Sligo, and William had one at Templehouse, County Sligo. Another founder was Sir Charles Coote, who was granted two fairs in Fuerty, County Roscommon.

The city stocks, Dublin

7

The Modern Fair

The Day

A QUICK and incomplete examination of the *Patent Rolls of James I* revealed patents for 386 fairs — approximately two-thirds of the total number granted during that king's reign (1603-25). Between the year 1625 and the time when most fairs ceased to be held, the numbers increased steadily until most towns had about twelve fairs during the year. It had also come about that during the twentieth century the fair was held on a fixed day in each month, for example on the first Tuesday in each month, rather than on a fixed date.

Of the fairs mentioned, one fair was held during January and one during February. Then followed ten fairs in March, eleven in April and thirty-one in May. In June there were forty-three fairs, in July thirty-seven and in August ninety-seven. In September there were fifty-five, in October thirty-nine, in November twenty-seven and only two during the month of December.

In addition, there were thirty-two fairs held on days related to the day on which Easter fell. One of these was held on a day related to Ash Wednesday and five were held during the week following Easter. Seven were held during the week of the Ascension, fourteen during Whit week, two during the week after Trinity Sunday and three on the Feast of Corpus Christi.

During March three fairs were held on St Patrick's Day. One of these was in Armagh, where the fair was granted to the archbishop, and another was in Downpatrick, where it was granted to Thomas Cromwell. The third was in Kilpatrick, County Cork, and it was granted to Bernard Grenville. Three fairs were held on the Feast of the Annunciation (25 March). Five fairs were held on the Feast of St George (23 April), and five on the Feast of St Mark (25 April). To these must be added the five fairs held during the week after Easter, as they almost always fell during April.

During May fifteen fairs were held on May Eve or May Day (SS Philip and James) and six were held on 3 May, the Finding of the Holy Cross. Three were held on the fifteenth. June had two popular times for fairs. One was the eleventh, the Feast of St Barnabas, and the other was on the twenty-third, twenty-fourth and twenty-fifth – the time of the summer solstice, St John's Day, and Bonfire Night. During these three days nineteen fairs were held. In addition there were five fairs held on 29 June, the Feast of SS Peter and Paul.

In July the fairs were spread more evenly. Four were held on the second, the Feast of the Visitation, and five were held on the twentieth, St Margaret's Day. Five were held on the twenty-second, the Feast of St Mary Magdalene, nine on St James's Day, the twenty-fifth, and seven on St Anne's Day, the twenty-sixth. Thirty-seven fairs were held on 1 August, called Lammas Day (Lughnasa) or the Feast of St Peter's Chains. Eleven were held on St Lawrence's Day, the tenth, and fourteen were held on the fifteenth, the Feast of the Assumption. The Feast of St Bartholomew, the twenty-fourth, had nineteen fairs and on the twenty-eighth, St Augustine's Day, there were four.

In September there were seven fairs on the eighth, the Nativity of Our Lady, and nine on the fourteenth, the Exaltation of the Holy Cross. On St Matthew's Day, the twenty-first, there were seventeen, and at Michaelmas, the twenty-ninth, there were also seventeen. In October there were three on St Francis's Day, the fourth, and on St Luke's Day, the eighteenth, eighteen fairs were held. Twelve were held on the twenty-eighth, the Feast of SS Simon and Jude. In November twelve were held on the first, All Saints Day (Samhain) and three on the eleventh, St Martin's Day. On the twenty-fifth, St Catherine's Day, there were six, and three on the thirtieth, St Andrew's Day.

The Place

Most often the fair was held in the centre of the town, spreading out during the bigger fairs in spring and autumn into the adjoining streets. In many cases when a field had been designated as the fair green it remained unused, and there were often good reasons for this reluctance to use it. In some cases traders in the town wished to have the fair on the street – it increased their sales – and in some cases they tried to move neighbouring fairs into the town. For example, traders in Kingscourt, County Cavan, tried to have the fair of Muff moved to the little town. They failed. However, the traders did succeed in moving the horse fair of Cahermee to the neighbouring town of Buttevant. In some cases there was a more compelling reason for not using the fair green. Anyone who has ever attended fairs will remember the condition to which the fair green had been reduced by the evening of the fair.

Usually it had been trampled into a mixture of soft mud and manure – a miserable place on a wet day – and, very reasonably, people preferred to show their cattle on the streets which had been paved. 'You'd go to your knees on that fair green' was an expresson often used about such a place, as people remembered the misery of the damp, cold and dirt.

Not all fair greens were muddy, though – as could be expected – all were dirty by the end of the day. Some were very well maintained, such as Kilkenny and Mullingar, and were well ordered. In some towns the central square was made especially large to accommodate the fair. This was done generally by the landlord, who could be said to own the town. As a result, some towns have now got fine squares. Listowel and Mitchelstown are examples, but the village of Crossmaglen is the winner: it claims to have the largest central square in Europe. In many of the northern towns the town centre was called 'the diamond'. In some other cases the streets were made unusually wide to accommodate the fairs. Such were Ballymahon, Moate, Strokestown and Gort. Since the fairs are no longer held, these areas have been put to other uses. In the village of Tyrrell's Pass the area is now laid out as a park and carefully maintained, and the trees planted along the wide streets in Strokestown have added much to the town. In Carrick-on-Suir the fair green has been converted into a sportsfield. When it was proposed that houses should be built on the area when it was no longer needed for a fair green the local people objected successfully.

At present one might not realise that a river could be a major obstacle if one wished to move cattle across it. It might mark the boundary of a county, a parish or a diocese or in some cases the boundary of the property of a landlord. Until the nineteenth century, bridges were few and sometimes difficult to negotiate, and in some cases tolls were paid by those crossing the bridge. When there was no bridge, the ford might be deep and dangerous after heavy rain. Sometimes it was necessary to drive the cattle through the narrow streets of an old town, in order to approach the bridge.

As a result of these difficulties, towns might be established on opposite sides of the river, and in some cases fairs were granted to these towns.

These difficulties are well illustrated in the case of Galway. The old walled city was built on a firm piece of rising ground on the left hand bank (east) of the River Corrib and there was only one bridge. The river was a difficult one, making it necessary to use the bridge to move cattle from one side to the other, with the added difficulty of getting through the narrow streets. This problem was solved by having fairs on both the west and east sides of the town. The fair on the west side was to be held near the site of the pre-Reformation Dominican friary, but on a map dated 1818 the site is marked Fair Hill, some distance from the original site at the Cladagh. On the east side of the city fairs were held on the Square Plot outside the East Gate. This is now called Eyre Square and was used as the fair green as long as fairs were held in Galway.

There is another Galway fair mentioned in the Almanack for 1844. This is referred to as Galway Town, and was held on 4 September. I have heard of no tradition attached to this fair, and I wonder if perhaps it was a survival of a mediaeval fair.

Something similar is found in the records of the fairs in New Ross, County Wexford. There the town is separated from Rosbercon, its western suburb, by the River Barrow, and the two sides are connected by a bridge. The river is wide and tidal and the bridge has been destroyed on a number of occasions. In 1844 New Ross had thirteen fairs during the year and Rosbercon had six. It is of interest to see that five of the six fairs in Rosbercon were held on the same day as five of the New Ross fairs, no doubt to the benefit of both places. It was much easier to have the buyers cross the river than to take the cattle across.

It would seem likely that similar difficulties arose in getting cattle across the Shannon at Limerick and through the streets of the old city. The fact that part of the city was built on an island in the river meant that two bridges had to be crossed. In the year 1844 fairs were held in the city on 4 July and 4 August, and in the same year a fair was held at Thomond Gate, on the Clare side of the river, on the twenty-second day of each month. At the same time fairs were held at Singland a short distance from the old city on the Limerick side on 9 April and 11 December.

Fairs were also held at Carrick-on-Suir and Carrickbeg, on opposite sides of the River Suir. In 1844 Carrick-on-Suir had twelve fairs and Carrickbeg across the bridge in County Waterford had nine during the year. The dates of the fairs are of interest. In January there were fairs in both places on the twenty-sixth, and in February Carrickbeg fair was on the twenty-sixth and in Carrick-on-Suir on the twenty-ninth. In March Carrickbeg was on the twenty-fifth and Carrick-on-Suir on the twenty-eighth, and in April Carrickbeg was on the twenty-eighth and Carrick-on-Suir on the twenty-fifth. Then in September Carrick-on-Suir was on the twenty-sixth and Carrickbeg was on the following day.

In contrast to this there are Strabane and Lifford on opposite sides of the River Foyle. In Strabane, on the Tyrone side, there were eleven fairs during the year, but there were no fairs in Lifford during the first half of the nineteenth century. In Drogheda, divided by the River Boyne, the fairs were all held on the Louth side of the river.

In the majority of cases where a river presented an obstacle to the movement of cattle, as at Carlow on the River Barrow, at Killaloe on the Shannon and at Ballina on the Moy, fairs were held separately on both sides of the river. In each of these cases it is clear that the fair days were arranged so that there was a suitable interval between them.

Some people took exception to the way fairs were managed. Dutton, in 1806, wrote:

> Fairs held in towns are a great nuisance, and towns are surely most inconvenient places to both buyer and seller, for the cattle are packed so close together that it is not easy to form a judgement of their quality, and great difficulties are experienced to keep each person's cattle separate. Great abuses are permitted by unnecessary blows, especially at Ballinasloe after they are sold: severe blows on the legs are viewed with perfect indifference by the graziers.

He then continued:

> Great losses are sustained by having fairs in harvest: almost every person for many miles around Ennis and Killaloe deserted their reaping, which almost universally began the day before, to idle away their time at these fairs which were held on the third of September: I saw very great quantities of oats lying on the ledge, and as the following day was very wet and cold, and Sunday followed, they must have sustained very considerable losses: besides the money spent on whiskey, and consequent debility of both body and mind, must have been a serious addition.

Dutton also wrote about the Dublin cattle market which in the early years of the nineteenth century was held in Smithfield:

> Smithfield market is much too confined, and by no means adequate to the business transacted there, and which is likely to increase. I beg leave to suggest the necessity of opening it up to Brunswick Street at one end and down towards the river Liffey as far as a stable lane in West Arran Street at the other end: this could be easily accomplished as the houses are of small value. On many market days there is scarcely room to pass, and hay carts are frequently obliged to stand in the ajacent streets, liable to the depredations of pilferers of every description. The state of this market is always very filthy and as a day intervenes between each market there is no excuse for it: those who want hay or straw are frequently obliged in wet

weather to ride through it. . . .

The present mode of keeping cattle at random, close to the houses is a very great nuisance: were they ranged with their heads towards the sheep leaving a broad passage between them they could be more easily and safely handled and viewed, and a much less space of ground would answer: at present they are only kept in order by the sticks of the penny-boys: and I am sorry to say the abuses cattle and sheep sustain from these ruffians do little credit to the humanity of the sales masters, who are the only persons that can redress this grievence, simply by refusing to deliver any beast to one possesed of a stick.

Archer also wrote about the Dublin cattle market at about the same time as Dutton. He said that the market was held on Tuesday and Thursday and cattle, sheep and pigs were sold there. The principal buyers were the Dublin dairymen and the Dublin butchers.

Cattle fairs began very early in the morning in most places, often in the cold darkness of a winter morning. This may have developed because men wished to be on the fair green early in order to secure a good position. In some cases the practice so developed that at length the buying and selling was almost all completed on the previous day. This was so in the fairs held in Caherciveen in County Kerry and on the first occasion when my father arrived there, on the preceding evening, he discovered that the fair was over.

This holding of the fair on the preceding day in Athlone was a matter of grave concern to the Reverend Annesley Stream. In 1815 he wrote:

Though the numbers sold in these fairs are difficult to be acertained, the collectors of the tolls and customs say there are about 500 horses shewn for sale in the fairs of January and September, besides other cattle: and in the fairs held in the months of March and May besides horses (not in such numbers as in the other fairs of the year) there are from 3,000 to 4,000 sheep and about 2,000 cows and bullocks.

There are no other fairs in this parish and in a religious point of view it is well there are not: for painful is the sensation that must be excited in the breast of every sincere professor of Christianity to hear of, and how much more grievious to those who are periodically, as these fairs return, witness to the assemblage of graziers, horse-jockeys, sellers and buyers of cattle etc. etc. from twelve or one o'clock on the Sundays which precede these fairs (some of which are held on Mondays) in the public street as earnest in selling and buying and with as much unconcern, as if they were ignorant that a Sabbath existed: and as reguardless of its sanctity, as if the respect due to it made no part of the decalogue which the God of Heaven delivered to man and ordered him to obey by keeping that day holy, and to such excess has the depravity of this profane practice grown that even the public worship is superseded by it, as the parishoners cannot make their way to the church through the numbers of cattle etc. etc. which obstruct the street. It might be reasonably concluded that some temporal advantage must arise from this practice: yet no one can be benefited by it – no interest, public or private be served: nor could either of these be a motive originally to promote or still to cause such profanation to be continued: for the slightest refection would show that no temporal benefit can be promoted either collectively or individually by such unsabbatical pursuits, and unchristian contempt for God's laws: for were the business of these fairs confined to the three days, on which, by the charter they are appointed to be held, it would not only render them more beneficial to the town (as there are many whose conscientious reguard for the Sabbath will not suffer them by their attendance to profane a day dedicated to more sacred uses than that of public fairs (though they thereby forego the opportunity of selling the articles they have to dispose of) but even the tolls and customs would be increased by the additional numbers who would thus be induced to Athlone on the days appointed by the law. It appears then that it would not only be a public as well as individual advantage, but an act of Christian charity if a public notice were given from legal authority, some time before these fairs, setting forth a caution that they will not be suffered to be held on Sundays, as heretofore, under the penalty the law may inflict which by 7th of William III Chap. 17.Sec.i. is 'a forfeiture of every kind of goods, wares, chattels shewed forth or exposed for sale on Sundays'. This would at once deter sellers from risking their property under such circumstances and the law of the land would thus effectivly remove a shameful abuse, which the law of God has so long failed to prevent. If the Corporation is also empowered to hold that species of court, denominated Pie powdre or *curia pedis pulverizati,* and a most useful sort of court this is, as it is calculated for administering Justice for all injuries done during the fair but extends no farther, and is thus framed to promote and protect the trade of the place where the fair is held 'by deciding disputes as speedily as dust can fall from the feet, or before the litigating parties could have time to wipe the dust off their feet.'

Seamus Fenton, author of *It All Happened,* described the fair of Sneem, County Kerry. He recalled that in 1885, at the age of eleven years, he set off with some other lads of his age to drive a batch of Kerry cattle to the June fair of Sneem. Before they set out at dawn, they were warned not to sell – the adults would come later to do that – and they were also warned to take special care of the *bradaighe* (the wanderer) of the herd. He added that the women of the house were very fond of the *bradaighe*.

One of the drivers was Tomás Óg, who was old fashioned and had been to Sneem before. He explained to the others that Sneem was a fine city full of wealthy shops – after Cork, Dublin and Boston it had few equals. The priest there was a canon and they had a doctor who could cure all diseases. Another of the party was a lad called Padraig Ó Grada. He later became professor of Irish at Indiana University, was ordained a priest by Cardinal Gibbons and died parish priest of Dallas, Texas. Trade must have been good that day because Fenton says that the cattle were sold easily and the *Luach Impidhe* (Luck Penny) paid.

When the selling was finished, the boys were all gathered by the women – their relatives – and taken to a big room in a grocer's shop where there was a long table of boards laid on trestles. There was white bread, butter brought from home, cold roast pork, *crubeens* and strong tea poured from a huge tin tea pot made by one of the Coffeys. The adult men drank porter and the old men drank whiskey, which used to cost 4*d.* for a half pint.

Next there were dancing competitions on the square. A number of large wooden doors were laid side by side to make a dancing floor, and it must have been a great occasion because it was the last time Morty O'Moriarty adjudicated at the dancing competitions. Morty was from Glenbeigh. He was a very famous teacher of dancing and used to judge very honestly at parish championships, as well as at fairs and patterns – no easy task.

Fenton mentioned the ballad singers. One sang a ballad in Irish called *Fáilte is Fíche* written by Tomás Ruadh. There was also Paddy Nangle from Killarney, who sang ballads which he had himself written. There was some difficulty with another of the ballad singers. He sang a song in praise of William O'Brien as 'a greater man than glorious Dan'. It was, of course, heretical in south Kerry to say that anyone was a greater man than Daniel O'Connell. Happily the ballad singer was equal to the occasion. He blamed the Mallow printer who had changed the ballad to glorify his fellow townsman.

As Fenton recalls it, the fair had everything associated with Irish fairs – tinkers, useful to help in the selling or buying of a horse or an ass, and simpletons like Seanín, Colonel Prince Patrick O'Sullivan and others. With the money made on the cattle, shop bills were paid and accounts settled with the blacksmith and the tailor. To this he adds the story of the tailor who was so skilful that he did not use a tape measure:

once he called to a customer in a boat some distance from the shore, 'Stand up,' then, 'Turn sideways' – and with that he was able to go ahead and make the suit. Fenton also writes about the courting and matchmaking that went on at fairs and the explanation offered by the girl's mother when one of the neighbours said, 'I am sure that you thought it hard to lose Mary.' 'Aye, it was hard. We were afraid it would fail again, but we got the match fixed in the end.' He ended the references to Sneem fair with the visit to the fair of a local lad, William Melville, who had gone to England, joined the police force, and risen to high rank in Scotland Yard. On the day of the fair a telegram for him had come to the RIC barracks in Sneem and a constable was sent to find him. Melville answered with the necessary instructions to Scotland Yard and the people of Sneem looked on with admiration.

There is another description of what was called the Old Fair of Magheramore by P. J. MacGill. This was established on 13 November 1620 by a patent given to John Murray, Earl of Annandale, to hold markets on Friday at Magheramore in the Manor of Ballyweel and 'a fair at Magheramore on 1 November and two days after' – but not on Sundays. This patent was regranted in 1629. Later the fair was brought forward to the first week in October.

For about 200 years it was a great social occasion in south-west Donegal. Magheramore was a sandy area west of Sandfield on the north shore of Loughrosmore Bay. Thousands came to it from as far away as Letterkenny, Ballyshannon and County Tyrone, 'and friendships started at the storied fair of Carney in Sligo were renewed on the Plain of Magheramore.' Every house had its quota of visitors for the fair, paying return visits from the Aonach at Largy, the Port of Inver, or even from Ballina.

The fair lasted for a number of days. First the livestock and other goods were bought and sold and then the festivities started. They had sports, horse racing and faction fighting and then the matchmaking, courting and eloping went on day after day. There must have been a great sensation when Miss Montgomery, the daughter of the local rector, ran away with young O'Boyle of Maghera. Such doings must have been in the air then, because MacGill quotes:

A withered old maid of three score and ten
Goes to Magheramore with her eyes on the men.

I visited the site of the fair on a July day during a holiday in west Donegal some years ago. It was a dry and sandy level area and I saw what were said to have been the fire sites in sheltered hollows where food was cooked and sold at the fair. According to the traditions, tradesmen all brought their wares to sell at the fair. Weavers sold frieze, drugget and linen. Coopers sold churns, noggins and firkins. There were also blanket makers, nailers, iron workers and tinsmiths. There were hawkers, quack doctors and showmen gathered there from as far away as Malin Head and Galway. There were, of course, musicians, singers and dancers, and also sellers of poitín. It was remembered that on one occasion the dancing competition was won by the son of the local landord, 'young Nesbitt of Woodhill and the daughter of a tinker'. Much of the faction fighting at Magheramore was between two famous gallowglass families, the O'Boyles and the Gallaghers, and sometimes the women joined in the fighting using a *doirling* stone in a strong woollen stocking. During the wars against the French at the end of the eighteenth and during the early years of the nineteenth century prices were high and trade brisk. In those years people at the fair of Magheramore used to say, 'God damn ar Napoleon, nach breá an Fear é' ('God damn Napoleon, isn't he a fine man')?

The original fair declined when the war ended in 1815, and finally died with the famine. Later it was transferred to the neighbouring town of Ardara, and the fair held there on 1 October was known as the Fair of Magheramore. MacGill had of course a long memory of fairs in Ardara and he was able to compile a splendid description of the original fair from the local traditions. In Ardara horses were sold at the hill head, cattle on 'cow hill', sheep were ranged and tied at the side of the street and homespun and hand woven tweeds were laid out on tables and benches along the main street. Donegal tweed was famous before the 1914 war and as well as local people, some buyers came from Dublin, Belfast or even London. As might be expected, there were cockles, dulse and fish, with fruit, wool, hardware, secondhand clothes, delph, creels and baskets.

When the buying and selling was finished the activity got started on the diamond. The quack doctor got to work selling medicines which would cure all diseases. The blind fiddler from Glenfin was there, as well as the three card trick men and the thimble-rigger. MacGill describes the skill of the man who sold gold watches and half-crowns which he wrapped up in a paper bag. A gold watch and a fistful of half-crowns would seem good value for a pound until the buyer opened the paper bag. However, trade was good and the seller also appeared at the fair of Glenties, still selling the large gold watch from his waistcoat pocket. A fair was usually a great place when the world was young.

Here is another description of a nineteenth-century fair. This time the writer is Thackeray, the year 1842, and the place Castledermot:

> The long street of the place was thronged with oxen, sheep and horses and with those who wished to see to sell or to buy. The squires were all together in a cluster at the police house: the owners of the horses rode up and down showing the best paces of their brutes: among them you might see Paddy in his ragged frieze coat seated on his donkey's bare rump and proposing him for sale. I think I saw a score of this humble though useful breed that were brought for sale to the fair. 'I can sell him,' says one fellow with a pompous air 'wid his tackle or widout.' He was looking as grave over the negotiation as if it had been for a thousand pounds.
>
> Besides donkeys of course there was plenty of poultry and there were pigs without number, shrieking and struggling and pushing hither and thither among the crowd rebellious to the straw rope. It was a fine thing to see one huge grunter and the manner in which he was landed into a cart. The cart was let down on an easy inclined plane to tempt him. Two men ascending urged him by the fore legs, other two entreated him by the tail. At length, when more than half of his body had been coaxed upon the cart, it was suddenly whisked up causing the animal thereby to fall forward: a parting shove sent him altogether into the cart: the two gentlemen inside jumped out and the monster is left to ride home.

In this description Thackeray reminded me of some things which I had forgotten; one was the custom of driving a pig with a straw rope tied to one of its hind legs. The other was the ceremony of loading a big fat pig into a cart. This was often a difficult job, remembering that then the animal might weigh over 400 pounds, quite unlike the present-day pig. Thackeray was then approaching a part of Ireland famous for the size of its pigs.

The Puck Fair of Kilorglin, County Kerry, still continues, though now it is a tourist attraction and pleasure fair rather than a gathering of people for buying and selling. I was at Puck in the year 1938 and, as I recall it, the fair was like any other fair at the time. Since then I have read a description of it by Richard Hayward, who had been there some years before. At first he looked out at the fair from a hotel window and, as he said:

> It all seemed much the same, the streets of the small town below, jammed with people and beasts, shoulder to shoulder. Now a man jostling a cow to make his way into a pub, now a cow jostling a man to reach a bunch of grass growing from some old masonry: the tall wooden scaffold-like construction rising in front of my window,

flagged and be-ribboned for the reception of His Majesty King Puck when the great moment arrived: the concourse of showmen and their stalls, crowding the small square to bursting point: the movement of frightened herds with their loud cries and bellows: the streets and pavements in many places ankle deep in cow dung, the rather savage feeling of sound and colour and raw humanity. It was all very primitive and lively and pagan-seeming, and it was all intensely exciting. It was in short Puck Fair on the day of the Gathering.

Then he decided to venture out into the streets and continued:

As I walked about the sounding streets of this usually quiet little market place for I had left my perch at the window for a space and was making my way down the long street to the foot of the town where a stone bridge carries the highway over the wide-flowing Laune the single outlet through which the Lakes of Killarney dispense with the surplus of their sweet waters. For wherever I went was colour and movement and animation, and no poet worth his salt could fail to be infected with the immense energy of it all. Horses and cattle, hounds and sporting dogs, pigs and sheep, little foals crying for their mothers, cocks crowing, dealers shouting and laughing and making large gestures, sightseers getting in everybody's way, and the attendant train of show people, with their flashy attire and alien-sounding language, and then over the bridge, along the road to right and left were the caravans of the gypsies and the distinct and smaller portable habitations of the tinkers. A great riot of nomadic colour this, with swarms of children playing under the caravans or about the openings of the lower tilts, and the buxom brightly shawled women busy taking silver in exchange for news of dark-avised strangers whom they saw in the upturned palms of laughing country boys and girls.

Hayward was not familiar with the sights and sounds of an Irish fair. As I try to recall that visit to Puck Fair in 1938, I am surprised at the things which I scarcely noticed at the time, the street so filled with cattle that it seemed impossible to find a way through. The buying and the selling of the cattle was the real business of the fair, and all the other activities depended on it. If prices were good and there was a good number of buyers available, then it was a 'good fair', but of course that was not always the case, and times and fairs were often 'bad'. Then cattle were sold at poor prices, or worse still brought home unsold to be taken anxiously to the next available fair.

This was the part of the fair which the outsider never saw or understood. He saw the stands selling delph or secondhand clothes or sweets, and watched the three card trick man busy, and stood looking into the crowded public houses, but these were only the incidentals. He might never realise that in most cases all the dramatics of bargain making, slapping hands, dividing pounds and the buyer going off in disgust was just ritual and that in the end the deal was finished and the play came to its inevitable end.

Then when the cattle were sold, the outsider watched the singing and dancing and all the talk and laughter of the fair evening in the dirty and often wet streets. By this time I was usually some miles away driving cattle from the fair and often tired, wet and cold. The glamour was mostly in the eye of the outsider, or in the minds of those to whom a fair day was a holiday. To the people who made a living at it, a fair was certainly no holiday.

Punishments

In many towns there were such unpleasant things as jails and other methods of punishing offenders. There are some references to different forms of punishment found in the records available from the seventeenth, eighteenth and nineteenth centuries and it is possible to form a picture of what might be thought of as the justice of the market place. In the year 1662 the city authorities in Waterford agreed that a whipping post and a pillory should be provided.

Such things might be considered usual at the time and there are some references to them. In the Youghal records of the year 1653 there is a reference to a 'cage and ducking stool' and in 1664 the reference is to a 'pillory and cage for boys'. These unpleasant instruments were probably available and used in most towns at the time, because in the patents for fairs and markets granted by James I, one of the rights granted was the use of 'pillory tumbrell and thew'. The pillory was a most unpleasant instrument. When sentenced to it, the prisoner stood with his head bent forward and resting on a plank while another plank rested on the back of his neck. There is a sketch of the pillory used in Dublin, taken from the Dublin city records, and it appears from this that the hands of the prisoner were also secured in holes in the infernal machine. The printed sketch shows that it was built in the shape of a large box and had room to punish four prisoners at the same time, one facing outward on each side of the box. The 'thew' was a pillory which was used to punish women and was, one hopes, less unpleasant. In fairness to those who used the pillory and to those who ordered it to be used, it may be added that one of the regulations said that it was their responsibility to make sure that it was used 'without bodily peril either of man or of woman'.

Punishment by placing the prisoner in the stocks was much less severe than the pillory. In this case the prisoner was seated on a wooden bench with his legs placed in holes in a wooden frame in front of him. The ducking stool was also used to punish women. It was in the form of a chair in which the prisoner was seated and tied firmly. The chair was built on the end of a long wooden beam by which the stool could be raised or lowered. When required for use, the apparatus was moved on wheels to the edge of a stream or pool and the prisoner was strapped into the chair, which was then dipped under the water. The 'cage for boys' may have been found necessary because the boys could have managed to get out of the stocks. The 'tumbrell' was a cart in which the prisoners were moved through the streets of the town. The whipping post continued in use in Kilkenny until 1770, when an official called the 'whip-beggar' was paid £3 a year for his services.

These punishments were partly a form of public humiliation, and prisoners held in the stocks or the pillory were often reviled and insulted by the crowd. Complaints were made to the city authorities in Dublin on many occasions about the pillory. It was in the Cornmarket beside the water conduit and the citizens asked that it be removed because 'large store of filth is cast into the water'. The *Liber Primus Kilkenniensis* gives some details of the way these things were used to punish forestallers and dishonest traders, and it seems likely that they were also used to punish those who sold bad bread, meat or beer.

The records of the town of New Ross contain a number of references to such things. On 16 August 1669 the sum of £2.7s.6d. was paid to the man who made a ducking stool for the town, and this included the cost of the material used. Later, on 7 April 1710, the town council ordered that a pillory, a whipping post and a ducking stool should be made and erected in the said town. A year later, on 18 April 1711, the town council ordered that 'forthwith a ducking stool be made and the day after it is fixed Frances Rooke be ducked'.

Ducking appears to have been the standard method of discouraging a scold, and the article has a picture of a ducking stool which is preserved in England. There is also mention of something called a 'scold's bridle', which was in the Kilkenny Museum. About 1815 there is mention of a pair of stocks kept at the market house in Maghera, County Derry, 'which is seldom unoccupied on fair or market days'.

8

Cattle at Fairs

CATTLE have always been the most important part of Irish agriculture and made up the greater part of the stock offered for sale at Irish fairs. By the eighteenth century they had become a most important source of money rent – until then they had been the source of wealth – and landowners, Old Irish, Old English, and those known as the New English, saw this clearly. During the early years of the seventeenth century the export of live cattle, as well as butter and beef, to England increased and some of the landowners imported English cattle which were considered better than the native stock. These new breeds of cattle were referred to by Dr Gerald Boate, a Dutch physician living in Dublin, in the year 1652. He referred to:

> the goodly beasts. . . that are brought thither out of England. . . so that before this last bloody rebellion, the whole land where the English did dwell or had anything to do was filled with as goodly beasts, both cows and sheep, as any in England, Holland or other the best countries in Europe.

The Confederate wars (1641-52) saw the destruction of a great part of the cattle of Ireland by the different marauding armies. With peace, recovery was rapid and the export of cattle and cattle products again began to develop. The practice of introducing English breeds of cattle was also resumed. In 1672 Sir William Petty estimated that a milking cow of English breed fed on two acres of pasture and half an acre of hay would produce 384 gallons of milk during one season. Unfortunately he does not give any figure for the amount of milk given by a cow of the native breed – perhaps he looked at the native cattle and decided that they were poor and useless. If this is so, many others during the following centuries made the same mistake in dismissing the native cow as worthless.

In a few years the export trade had so increased that the English producers objected. They complained that the imports from Ireland were ruining them and were able to frighten or persuade Charles II into passing the Cattle Acts in 1665. These placed an embargo on the import of Irish cattle and cattle products into England. Naturally, the Irish landowners, led by the Duke of Ormond, objected to the embargo, but the English influence was stronger and the acts remained and were made permanent in 1680. When the Irish continued to object, Charles II, in an effort to placate them, allowed the free export of all Irish products to countries other than England. This concession had a dramatic effect on Irish exports, and trade with European countries and with the plantations, which had been illegal, now expanded rapidly. In the year 1685, 75,000 barrels of salt beef, 135,000 hundred-weights of butter, 95,000 raw hides and tanned hides were exported. During the same year English traders loaded 25,000 barrels of beef and 43,000 hides at Irish ports. It seems clear that the Cattle Acts which forced Irish exporters to seek out new markets were in fact of great benefit to nearly everyone concerned with the cattle trade in Ireland.

Native Irish Cattle

It must be remembered that among the native Irish, cattle were kept almost exclusively for their milk. This is mentioned many times during the seventeenth century. Sir William Petty wrote in 1672:

> The diet of these people is milk, sweet and sour, thick and thin, which is also their drink in summer time. . . . Their food is bread in cakes whereof a penny serves a week for each, potatoes from August till May. . . eggs, and butter made very rancid, by keeping in bogs. . . . The common sort of people of Ireland do feed generally upon milk, butter, curds and whey. Most of their drink is buttermilk and they. . . but seldom eat flesh.

In 1690 Stevens said much the same when he wrote that the Irish were 'the greatest lovers of milk I ever saw which they eat and drink above twenty several sorts of ways and what is strangest for the most part love it best when sourest'.

It is only when we come to the eighteenth and early nineteenth centuries that the native Irish cattle are described in detail. These descriptions were generally written by men who were keen 'improvers' and to them 'improvement' was the replacing of the native cattle by a large handsome English breed which matured early and fattened easily. Unfortunately many of these cattle were poor milkers, and in addition they damaged the soft pasture by their size more than the smaller, lighter Irish cattle.

This difference of opinion between the advocates of the new foreign breeds and those who favoured the use of the native breeds continued all through the eighteenth and nineteenth centuries. Sir William Wilde, who was a good witness, described what he called 'the Old Irish cow'. It might be of any colour but most usually was black or red. It was a medium sized animal, but in general the better the land the bigger the cattle. Generally the cow was short legged and with a big belly and it certainly did not fatten easily. It was in fact what it was bred to be, a good milking cow.

The *Statistical Survey of County Derry* describes two types of native Irish cow. One was 'light in the bone, small in size, extremely active, crooked in the ham, with a good eye and a sharp nose, and nice thin neck, a crooked horn frequently turned upward. The strain is generally black, reddish or brindled, with some white'. Clearly this is a description of what we now call the Kerry. The other was 'a coarse-boned ill-shaped breed. . . . these have swollen bellies, heavy head, a dewlap very pendant and a bull-like aspect'.

In Munster the Irish cows were able to hold their own against the improved breeds. Smith wrote in 1746 about County Waterford: 'A large quantity of butter is made here, though but little cheese, the former being most profitable.' More than sixty years later Wakefield wrote the following also about Waterford:

Notwithstanding the great number of cows in the dairies of this county the breed is as bad as any in the island which may be ascribed chiefly to two causes. The first is that the old native breed produce the greatest quantities of milk: and the second that the breeding counties in the West of Ireland where the best stock is established are at a considerable distance.

In some of the Leinster counties the foreign breeds had been established before the year 1800, but in the better dairying areas the Irish cow remained predominant. This was especially so in south Kildare, Carlow, Wexford and Kilkenny, and the butter produced in County Carlow was generally considered the best in the country. In making the butter the same methods were used in County Carlow as in the Golden Vale, but with a much greater degree of cleaniness and care, and in addition the average yield per cow was one and a half hundred-weight of butter during the milking season.

The writer of the *Statistical Survey of County Kildare*, T. J. Rawson, gave a long description of Irish cattle. He concluded:

On a comparative view of the particular merits of the different breeds of English cattle, it will appear that though each may have its local advantages, they should not, except on the clearest conviction, be the object for pursuit of the Irish breeder: crossing from the most perfect long-horned (originally our native breed) may improve but a change of breed might greatly endanger the wealth of Ireland.

After a long discussion of Irish conditions he summed up:

It is most evident that the neat stock already in our possession are the best adapted to soil, climate and Irish treatment and better answer the wants of the country: nothing is necessary, I will be bold to say, but a selection of the best males, of the shapes I have endeavoured to describe. I am sensible that no remark of mine will retard the exertions of gentlemen who may wish to speculate in the improvement of cattle. I have gone into great length on this subject from an anxious desire to induce my countrymen to hold fast that which is good.

The most notable of the Irish breeds is the Kerry, an ancient and very distinct breed which was first clearly identified in south Kerry and south-west Cork. Cattle of the same type were probably found in other parts of Ireland, and such a breed was described in County Derry in 1800. At present pure-bred Kerries are black, but many of the cows in Kerry with all the other characteristics of the breed are red or brown, and some have white back markings. It is a small dual-purpose breed and a mature cow is not likely to weigh more than 900 pounds. In appearance it has a smooth shiny coat, is lithe, active and quick moving, with a bright sharp eye, small head, thin neck and a well-shaped udder placed well forward. The tail is quite characteristic. It springs like an arch from the root and is long and thin. The horns are usually white with black points, and grow out and upwards with the points facing backwards. Some Kerries, if left in an open field, will seek out any little hillock which may be available and stand on it for hours. I remember one which regularly took up its position on a small heap of sand.

Towards the end of the eighteenth century people became interested in this breed. Arthur Young described the Kerry cow in 1780 as being 'much the best for milking in quantity of good milk', and not long afterwards, in 1800, we learn that in County Dublin the native breed had been replaced by English and Dutch breeds and 'a few from Kerry which the dairymen consider less productive in milk but more advantageous for the butcher'. This is the first reference I know to the Kerries as a beef breed, and while they are strictly dual-purpose cattle this is a surprise. In any case the reference shows that at the end of the eighteenth century Kerry cattle were being taken to County Dublin farms.

Wakefield was asked to find some of the true breed of Kerries about 1808 but was unable to find any. He reported that the Kerry stock 'are a distinct breed but they are not to be procured of the true blood because the Long-horned are now so much dispersed throughout the country that the breeds have become intermixed'. As the century went on we get some other references. Low wrote in 1845: 'The cultivation of the pure dairy breed of the Kerry mountains ought not to be neglected by individuals or public institutions.'

There were some other native Irish breeds, all of which appear to have died out. These included the Donegal Red and the Irish Dun, and I used to hear old men speak of a breed which they called the 'Yellow Polly'. These were said to have been specially good milkers. Finally there was a very special ancient Irish breed. These were white with red ears and were comparable to the ancient herd of wild cattle still preserved at Chillingham in County Durham. They survived in Ireland until the early nineteenth century.

Foreign Breeds of Cattle

As the export trade in salt beef, hides and leather developed, it was realised that the native breeds of cattle were not very suitable for this trade. Some of the English stock grew larger and fattened more easily and more quickly. Therefore it became the practice during the eighteenth century to import English cattle, and this continued all through the century. Lord Masserene imported some cattle in 1735 from the English midlands:

> They were of the Longhorned kind, and though not exactly of the same appearance and shape as the New Leicester breed they were very fine beasts and grew to a very large size. . . . An idea of the value set upon them. . . may be formed from the price at which old bulls were sold. . . five pounds were usually given for them. . . . At the same period the value of an ox is known to have been two pounds to two pounds five shillings.

After the year 1750 food prices rose in England, and in 1758 the British parliament passed an act which allowed the import of salt beef and butter from Ireland. As the price of food did not fall, and as industry continued to expand, it became clear that if England was to get cheap food she could only get it from Ireland. Then when the American War of Independence made it still more necessary to get cheap food, the

Cattle Acts were finally repealed. This boom in trade continued all through the years of war against the French, until prices fell again after the Battle of Waterloo in 1815.

About the year 1750 some other Irish landowners, including the Earl of Farnham and the Earl of Altamont:

> imported some excellent longhorned stock from Staffordshire, being the same breed which the celebrated Bakewell afterwards took so much pains to bring to perfection in England. Mr Waller of Allanstown in the county of Meath introduced cattle of the same kind nearly at the same period and the shape and qualities of this longhorned species are now so completely transfused into the native Irish cattle as to render their appearance almost the same as that of the pure blood.

Wakefield added in 1812 that this work had been continued 'by many noblemen and gentlemen of late years'.

Some more details about the Longhorns were provided by Dr James McParlan. He said that the breed of cattle in the barony of Murrisk in County Mayo had been as much improved 'as the moory mountainy pasture admitts of by the importation of English breeds by the Marquis of Sligo and his father'. Later he wrote: 'Forty years ago the English bull called Johnny Ghant was introduced by Mr Lindsey of Turin. About that time Mr Annesley Gore of Ballina and subsequently the Earl of Altamont introduced good English breeds which greatly refreshed and improved the blood not only of this barony but of the county in neat cattle'.

The most dramatic description of the Longhorns was written by William Wilde in 1858, and it is clear that as he wrote he was remembering the cattle which he had seen as a young lad in County Roscommon:

> They were generally a red or brindled colour, had large bones: grew to great size, particularly as bullocks. They were covered with a plentiful supply of hair which protected them from the inclemency of the weather. This together with the peculiarity of their constitutions rendered them an exceedingly hardy race of cattle never requiring winter fodder except when the ground was covered with snow. They were not much used as milkers but were the principal cattle sent to the Dublin market or exported to England thirty years ago. Their hides were of great value being, when tanned, at least half an inch thick. This breed principally abounded in the plains of Roscommon and might be termed the Connaught ox. . . . They grew

to a great size but they took four or five years to come to perfection.

This description recalls another breed, the Texas Longhorns, now most often seen in cowboy films. These, like the Irish Longhorns, were descended from the English breed, and at the end of the nineteenth century were driven in great herds to the nearest markets. In Ireland this happened on a smaller scale when the Connacht Longhorns were driven in thousands to the October fair of Ballinasloe. By the year 1812 they had become the standard cattle in Meath, Tipperary and Limerick as well as Clare and every part of the Connacht plain, and in some other areas they had been crossed with the native cattle. They were mainly a beef breed and as such better than the old Irish cattle. Certainly in the west of Ireland they tended to grow bigger than their English ancestors, a tendency which has also been observed in the Texas Longhorns.

The success of this breed can also be noticed at the shows held by the Irish Farming Society. In 1816, commenting on this success, the *Irish Farmers' Journal* wrote: 'The Longhorned cattle continue in high estimation and are considered to be best adapted to improve the general stock of Ireland as they are supposed to unite to a greater degree than any other breed hardiness, early maturity and fitness for the dairy.'

In 1817 it was decided by the Irish Farming Society to have all the different breeds compete against each other in open classes for the Society's premiums and prizes, and in this case the Longhorns won twenty-five of the thirty awards. Commenting on these results, the *Irish Farmers' Journal* wrote:

> It must appear that the Longhorned cattle are those to be most encouraged especially under the influence of another most striking fact that the total number of horned cattle above stated amounting to nearly 7,000 sold on the fair green of Ballinasloe scarcely one appeared on this or any former year except of the longhorned description – a kind too of excellent form and description according to the best English breeders who have visited the fair.

By this time the breed which was going to replace the Longhorns had arrived in Ireland and was spreading, slowly at first. This new breed, the Shorthorn, had been developed in the country east of the Pennines in the north-east of England and was known as the Durham, or the Teeswater. A similar breed, the Holderness, was also used as the foundation stock. These cattle were 'mainly Dutch descent but with a discernible admixture of Scandinavian blood' and were a dual-purpose breed from which many strains have been bred, such as its close relation the Northern Dairy Shorthorn.

The earliest reference to this breed in Ireland may be in the year 1801 when 'at Carrickglass in the county of Longford this gentleman (Sir George Newcomen) has the Shorthorn breed, highly improved on the Teeswater'.

In 1802 Dubourdieu wrote: 'A few years ago Sir Henry Vane Tempest brought a bull and some cows from Durham to Glenarm: they were of the shorthorned breed from Collings: they were large and well shaped of a fine deep red colour mixed with white, but reckoned too heavy for general use'.

At first they spread slowly, and in 1816 the *Irish Farmers' Journal* wrote:

> The Teeswater cattle of a large handsome frame, good handlers and many of them valuable for the pail: they are preferred to all other breeds in the North Eastern districts of England from whence they have been imported into this country, but from their appearance at this show it is very much doubted whether they will bear the harsh westerly winds and the moisture of our climate as their pile is in general short and thin.

Any breed of cattle which could survive the harsh easterly and north-easterly winds east of the Pennines would not find an Irish winter harsh.

Finally, in 1829 there was a dispersal sale of a famous Shorthorn herd owned by Christopher Mason at Chilton, County Durham, and seven Irish buyers bought four bulls and thirteen females for 1,183 guineas. The highest price of the sale, 270 guineas, was paid by a Mr La Touche for a three-year-old bull which Mason said was the best bull he had ever bred. By 1842 they outnumbered the Longhorns at the Cork Show, and in the following year at Belfast there were 139 Shorthorns and 166 of all other breeds. This position was maintained at the Limerick Show in 1844.

The Hereford breed has been in Ireland for 200 years and has contributed significantly to the quality of Irish cattle. This excellent beef breed originated in Hereford, where they were famous as draught oxen, of which they still show signs. They are deep red in colour with white head, crest and underneath, and these colour markings are predominant in the calves regardless of the breed with which the Hereford bull is crossed. This shows that the calves are half-bred Herefords and therefore excellent beef stores.

They appear to have been well established by 1800, when they were described thus in County Kildare:

In size come next to the Holderness: they are famed for some excellent qualities, but for that they are indebted to the great attention paid to their preparation for the London market by Mr Wescar of the Vale of Aylebury in Bedfordshire, the most careful feeder, and possessing the best tract of land in England. They handle kindly, feed well when at an advanced age, are good in draft but indifferent milkers as the Herefordshire dairies are filled with a mixed Shropshire longhorned. They are deep in the breast, very fine in the chin and shoulders, but flat in the sides and long in the couples, very wide in the hips and thin in the thighs, they are rather leggy and loose from whence their deficiency in early maturity as they are never put to fatten until six years old.

The Hereford has been changed greatly since that was written and now the body is more uniform, shorter in the leg, and the animals mature at an earlier age. There was a class of Herefords at the show in 1812 but there were few entries and no awards were made. However, in 1815 Herefords won the two premiums given to Leinster entries and in 1819 a four-year-old Hereford bullock weighed 1,750 lb. and had a carcass weight of 1,120 lb. It was, however, later in the century that the breed established its position as an economical beef breed on the heavy wet land of the Irish midland counties.

Ayrshire in the south-west of Scotland had given its name to a famous breed of dairy cattle. It is said that this breed is descended from the indigenous cattle of the district and these were improved by crossing with the Teeswater and the Holstein. The earliest reference to this breed in Ireland may be in 1819 when at a sale of a herd at Ballymascanlan, County Louth, a number of Ayrshire cows made over £30 a head and the average price of the thirty-eight cows sold there was £21. Since many of the Scots who settled in the north of Ireland in the seventeenth century came from the south-west, it is likely that some of them brought their cattle with them. At that time the Ayrshire breed had not been fixed and we do not hear of them as a distinct breed until the nineteenth century. They became popular in the first half of the century and there was a class for them at the Farming Society's Show in 1824. There were also classes for Ayrshires at the Cork Show in 1842, and in Belfast in 1843 there were 73 Aryshires entered compared with 139 Shorthorns and 20 Devons.

Another breed which contributed significantly to the story of cattle in Ireland was the Devon Red. There is a reference to some red cattle which were landed at Dingle from Cornwall in 1587. These were probably the forebears of the Devon Reds, a small hardy breed derived from the indigenous cattle of the south-west of England. They were triple-purpose animals, strong and smart in draught, giving good milk and able to thrive on the high rough pastures of Dartmoor and Exmoor. During the eighteenth century they were taken to west Cork by improving landlords such as Lord Bantry and Lord Doneraile, and did well in a district not unlike the west of England. Unfortunately an epizootic of pleuropneumonia which had spread across Europe between 1835 and 1840 reached Ireland in 1839 and infected the cattle in many parts of the country. This disease, called *an scamach* in Irish, severely affected the newer foreign breeds, and especially the Red Devon, which appears to have fared badly.

Two more breeds which must be mentioned are the Aberdeen Angus and the Poll Galloway, both of which were successful in the west of Ireland. The Galloway, which became known as 'the Galway maol' was a larger rough-coated version of the Aberdeen Angus and did well in west Mayo and west Galway. The Aberdeen Angus did well in County Sligo, and I have seen hundreds of them grazing in north Roscommon. Another Scottish breed, the West Highland, had become the native cattle of the Antrim Glens by the year 1802, probably brought there by the MacDonnells some hundreds of years before. By 1842 they must have been in Ireland in some numbers because there was a class for them at the Cork Show in that year. They were probably used as park cattle, and, along with ivy clad ruins and other fashionable follies gave a romantic touch to a rich man's estate.

There are a number of references to some Dutch cattle. In 1802 Dubourdieu wrote that Mr MacNeil of Larne kept a number of Dutch cows for their milk. These cattle were black, with some white. It is possible that they had been brought across the short sea passage from south-west Scotland, where Holstein cattle had been used to improve the Ayrshire breed. There were some other references to Dutch cattle which were introduced to supply milk to the Dublin market. These were forerunners of the Friesians, which are now the predominant strain in all the dairying districts in Ireland.

During recent years French breeds of cattle have been brought to Ireland, notably the Charollais and the Limousin. Strangely, these were not the first of such breeds, because Wakefield mentioned a French breed of pale cattle called Normans, which were found in County Wicklow early in the nineteenth century.

The economics of the eighteenth and early nineteenth centuries were the reason for the difference of opinion about Irish cattle. The new breeds flourished in the grazing areas of the west and parts of the midlands and supplied the salt beef and hides which were so important for the Irish economy. On the other hand, the native cattle were much the better milkers, and were small and hardy. Much Irish land is wet and soft for part of the year and cattle will do great damage to the pasture by poaching it when the ground is soft. In such conditions one might hear the expression 'every baste has five mouths'. When the small farmers of County Cavan refused to accept the new breeds they knew that such big heavy cattle would do great damage to their land. In this matter their common sense prevailed.

The search for improved breeds continues, and it is proper that it should; but no matter what changes may occur, the most efficient use of Irish grass is to feed milking cows. It should therefore be remembered that the genetic strains carried by Irish native cattle are of great value for the future and care should be taken to preserve them.

The front of the market yard, Ardee, Co. Louth

9

Horse Fairs

IT IS a pleasant experience to look down on the world from the back of a good horse, and the horse and rider together have always been a great status symbol. This has been the case in every society since the horse became domesticated, and the word chivalry, with all that it implies, expresses this superiority. In Ireland, as elsewhere, the horse has always been such a symbol, and during the eleventh century a poet, having written a poem for his lord, expressed thanks for his fee – a horse. Many people in Ireland will have learned that under the Penal Laws no Catholic might own a horse worth more than £5 – surely the most effective way of humiliating an Irish aristocrat. Indeed, the expression 'horse-Catholic' – meaning a Catholic with social pretensions – was in current use until about fifty years ago. At present, a visit to the Dublin Horse Show will show clearly that the horse is still the greatest status symbol.

Nowadays the horse trade is limited to the breeding and sale of thoroughbreds, hunters, showjumpers and children's ponies. In some parts of Ireland farmers still keep brood mares, and their half-bred foals are reared to become high quality hunters and showjumpers. Children's ponies are still bred and sold at good prices – the Connemara pony show and sale still flourishes – and in the horse-breeding districts some thoroughbreds are bred, reared and even trained by farmers.

Despite this, the great trade in horses has come to an end, largely because the internal combustion engine has now superseded the horse. At present it is difficult to realise that thousands and thousands of horses were needed to pull carts, brewers' drays, bread vans, mowing machines and ploughs, as well as traps and side cars. Then there were the armies. They needed a limitless number of horses as mounts for the cavalry regiments and to pull guns and wagons, as well as pack animals for use in places like the north-west frontier of India. In my childhood I saw a cavalry unit of the British Army as it moved from Enniskillen to Longford. The well-groomed horses and the smart uniforms made a splendid sight. During more recent years the glamour was kept up by a unit of the Irish Army called the Blue Hussars, and even more by the famous Army Jumping Team.

Today it is still possible to see what a real horse fair was like, because a number of them are still held in the old way and in the old places. Nowadays the sight of a working horse is rare, and the great Guinness horses with their hard-hatted, well-fed drivers – living proof that Guinness was good for you – are no longer seen and will soon be forgotten. Similarly, the smart ponies of the Court Laundry, or of Bewley's, are not now seen trotting along the Dublin streets. Even the horse brasses which once decorated the harness must now be sought in antique shops.

The selling and buying of horses was a very serious business indeed. People used to say that a horse was worth four times the price of its worst foot, and this sums up very briefly much of the practical pathology of the horse. The feet of the animal have gone through many changes during the course of evolution which has produced the modern horse. For example, the hooves were evolved for moving across open grassy plains and would not stand up to the wear of travelling on hard stony roads unless protected by iron shoes. As a consequence of the evolutionary changes, defects and deformities sometimes occur in the feet – rudimentary toes, for example – which may cause the horse to go lame. These can only be diagnosed by an expert, and in the horse trade it is always essential that the buyer beware.

Dealing in horses has often been compared to dealing in secondhand motor cars. During an election campaign in the United States, a Democratic Party poster showed an unflattering picture of the Republican candidate Richard Nixon. Under the picture were the words: 'Would you buy a secondhand car from this man?' Some years earlier the question would have been: 'Would you buy a horse from this man?' There were so many things that could go wrong with a horse and so much skill was used to disguise these faults that even the greatest experts in such matters were sometimes deceived. Most men who have spent their lives dealing with horses will tell you of some occasions when they had been tricked into buying a bad one. The story will probably end with, 'I was able to get him away all right'. This is shorthand for 'I patched up the old nag and paid a lackey to take him to a distant fair and sell him to another dupe'. Only a man who knew nothing about the trade would think such horse dealing dishonest, and such an idea would never occur to anyone connected with the horse trade.

Most horses were probably bought at the local fair. This was a mixed fair where cattle, sheep, pigs and horses were sold, but if a man had an outstandingly good horse he would be wise to take it to one of the great horse fairs where there were certain to be large numbers of buyers. The horse fair always began rather late in the day, usually about eleven o'clock when most of the other buying and selling was finished. This was a very sensible arrangement, because a man might, for example, have cattle to sell and wish to buy a horse, and in this way he was able to do both his buying and his selling. Also, it was essential that a buyer examine a horse carefully before buying and this could only be done in the clear daylight. It was also important that cattle be moved away and the noise and shouting associated with the selling of them be finished. At horse fairs there were usually a number of fences over which the horse might be tried before the customer would make a bid. This trial over the jumps could only be done in quiet conditions because an inexperienced horse is easily excited by noise.

There was still another reason why the horses should be sold apart from the rest of the fair. Normally there were fewer people at the horse fair – only those who were doing business of some sort were there – because it could be quite dangerous. One might notice that people never passed behind a horse, and always spoke to the animal before striking it or leading it. Few children were to be seen at horse fairs, though they were always dodging in and out among the cattle and sheep.

In Drogheda there was a horse fair every month where a County Louth farmer could buy a good plough horse or cart horse. It was held in St George's Square, and horses to pull bread vans, milk floats and brewers' drays were on show at every fair. By far the most important horse fair in Drogheda was held in May and lasted for three days, the eleventh, twelfth and thirteenth. In addition to the horses, droves of donkeys from County Clare and County Mayo were shown there and bought by the farmers and farm labourers of Meath, Louth and Monaghan. But the May fair was best known for the high quality of the horses. These were the half-breds, sired by a blood stallion out of an Irish draught mare. A foal resulting from such a cross might be anything – an *Arkle* or a *Boomerang*, a *Dundrum* or a *Limerick Lace*. They were bred by the local farmers and were in a sense a gamble because a good quality hunter might literally bring fame and fortune to his breeder.

In contrast to the high quality horses sold at Drogheda there was a small and highly serviceable type of horse kept in many parts of Ulster. These were called 'Rahery horses' and, as their name implies, they may have originated in Rathlin Island off the north coast of Antrim. In the

Statistical Survey of County Monaghan Coote wrote:

> Horses are little bred, and much less than formerly, as the size of
> farms is still more and more reduced. In this and several of the
> northern counties of Ireland they use a small though strong breed
> of horses which they call Rahery horses: they are had from the small
> island of Rathlin which lies off the coast of Antrim between that
> and Scotland to the North East of the Giant's Causeway and nearly
> opposite Ballycastle. . . . This breed of horses which are extremly
> cheap, seldom exceding three guineas in price, are most durable and
> serviceable, well calculated for a hilly country and live to a great
> age. . .
>   Asses are also very numerous here: frequently an hundred of these
> animals may be counted in the busy seasons within the circuit of a
> mile or two: they are found extremely serviceable, and are very easily
> fed: they are particularly fond of the tops of furze and green whins,
> which also contribute much to the maintainence of the Rahery
> horses.

It is not possible that the small island of Rathlin could produce a
very large number of horses, and it appears that many of them were
brought across from Scotland. There is a reference to this trade at some
fairs in County Antrim in Shaw Mason's *Parochial Survey*. In it the
writer says that 'since the weekly market for black cattle in Ballymena,
other fairs have greatly fallen off. To counterbalance this in some degree
there has been for some years past a great show of ponies from the
Highlands of Scotland at every fair day'. Similarly, in the parish of
Culdaff on the north shore of the Inishowen peninsula in County
Donegal we learn that at the same time 'small craft from the Hebrides
sometimes bring to Culdaff river herrings, barley and young horses'.

In the *Statistical Survey of County Derry* Sampson described the
local horses at some length. He said that the horse native to the county
was found in the more mountainous parts. He was a very good animal,
never more than fourteen hands, and was indefatigable. He was called
a 'clib' or a 'clibock', no doubt in reference to his long unkempt coat,
and Sampson added that he was usually sired by a one or two-year-old
colt. He went on to say that ponies from the Scottish Highlands were
highly esteemed in the Magilligan district east of Lough Foyle. There
was another type of horse which could be bought in the south-east of
the county. These he dismissed by saying that they moved slowly, were
easily kept and 'were not bad drudges'. As one might expect, the best
horses were bred by the sporting farmers in the district of Moyroe,
where the land is the best in Ireland. Like all the other good Irish horses,

they were cross-bred between the blood horse and a good type of strong mare and were excellent for all purposes.

This decline in the breeding of horses was also reported from Queen's County (Leix) during the early years of the nineteenth century. From the Barony of Cullinagh we get: 'Land is now become too high to give up to the precarious chance of brood mares which accounts for their very indifferent breed of horses'.

Much the same was reported from the barony of Upper Ossory: 'As to horses they are greatly neglected, not one brood mare now, for ten there were seven years ago: indeed Mr Vicars of Livally is the only breeder who has not slackened: he sends his mares to the best Curragh horses and generally sells his four-year-old stock at 100 guineas each'. Along the Kildare border 'several horses were bred for home use but none for sale' and the writer dismisses them as 'all of the common draught kind'. It was the same story from all the other parts of the county, and the decline was always attributed to the increased price of land. Presumably this was due to the high prices paid due to the war, though the writer doubts this and points out that where the land was truly valuable the breeding of good horses still continued.

These counties, Monaghan, Derry and Leix, were similar in some respects. They were each inhabited by numerous hardworking farmers who paid high rents. Many of these were Protestants and in addition the land was good enough to repay a hardworking farmer – and his wife – for their work. Such men would not be interested in breeding high quality horses. They did not need a heavy horse which would do damage to the land. In the best areas, as in Moyroe in Derry, or in Slewmargy in Leix, the farms were big enough and prosperous enough to afford good horses.

There were some very well-known horse fairs in Ulster. One of these, called the fair of Muff, is still held in east Cavan. It has been identified by MacNeil as a Lughnasa festival. It is held at the Rock of Muff, a few miles from Kingscourt, on 12 August and people have always spoken in superlatives when I have enquired about it.

It would seem that farmers from Monaghan and Cavan came to Muff to buy horses which had been brought there from the southern and western counties. The fair of Muff was notable for the faction fights which took place there between the Ribbonmen and the Orangemen. In one famous fight around the year 1830 some of those taking part carried guns and two men were killed.

There were some other famous Ulster horse fairs. One of these was at Moy in County Tyrone, and another was at Banbridge in County

Down. Both of these were very large fairs where the working horses needed in Belfast were bought.

Dublin city also needed large numbers of horses, and these were normally bought at neighbouring fairs. These included Carrickmines, Newcastle, Luttrellstown, Rathfarnham and Tallaght. In addition, there were some good horse fairs in County Meath, such as Dunboyne and Ballyboggan. In Offaly there was a good horse fair held in Birr in August, and a more famous one in Banagher in September.

It is probable, however, that Cork was the great county for horses and horse fairs. Two hundred years ago there were three great horse fairs in the Mallow neighbourhood. These were at Kilmacleenin on 21 June, at Kildorrery on 3 September and at Cahermee on 12 July. Of these, the best known was Cahermee and it still continues, but it is now held in the neighbouring town of Buttevant. It must be remembered that the three places also had other fairs, but these were the great horse fairs.

Another great County Cork horse fair was called Bartlemy Fair and was originally held in the field beside a holy well dedicated to St Bartholomew near Rathcormack. In Irish it was called *Aonach an Tobair*. In 1844 it was called Bartholomew's Well and was held on 4 September. Though it has long been discontinued, people still speak of it as though it had continued until recent years. They will tell you that there were two Bartlemy fairs, one on 23 August, the vigil of St Bartholomew, and the other on 3 September. This appears to be a mistake, because two major horse fairs would not be held in the same place within ten days of each other. The mistake may have occurred as a result of the calendar change in 1753 when the 4 September would be Old St Bartholomew's Day. Later, it was said that the fair was moved away from the holy well, to what are now referred to as the 'Fair Field', where the crowds assembled and the 'Trotting Field', where the horses were put through their paces.

People will also tell you that horses came to Bartlemy Fair from 'everywhere', and explain that when the railway reached Tallow the fair declined because the buyers met them at the station. It was held in a pleasant area long famous for the quality of its horses, and today the glory has not departed. In the parish notes for 1980 I read that fifty hunters and 150 thoroughbreds were still kept in the parish. Sixteen racehorses were trained there and six of them won nine races during the year.

There is still talk of the local hero, John Roche (*c.* 1840-60), a famous blacksmith and miller who always attended Bartlemy fair and set up his mobile forge. As well as attending to the horses, he was an expert tooth drawer but, even more remarkable, he was a fine sculptor and showed some of his work at the Cork Exhibition.

To people around Bartlemy the word 'Marengo' does not mean a town or a battle, but a horse. They say that this famous horse was foaled in County Wexford in 1796 and sold at Bartlemy before the year 1800, to a French Officer. Napoleon acquired it after the battle of Marengo and continued to ride it until the battle of Waterloo in 1815. My friend Father O'Donovan showed me a photocopy of an old print which he had seen in a house in his parish. It showed the Emperor riding a horse and underneath the words:

> Napoleon's famous white charger 'Marengo' was bought at Bartlemy, Middleton, Co. Cork.

No doubt people in the neighbourhood of Cahermee and Buttevant will be equally certain that Marengo was bought at Cahermee.

There were many other great horse fairs in County Cork. One which still continues is Beal Atha Buidhe (Dunmanway), which is held on the first Monday in August, and associated with this fair, races are held on the road near the town. The locals will tell you that the Beal Atha Buidhe fair has been held every year since 1615, when a patent for it was granted to a local land-owner, O'Herlihy, and the fair held in 1981 was the 366th annual fair. A cutting from the *Cork Examiner* of the following day gives details of the racing, including a number of harness races, and I have been assured that in this country made famous by the novels of Somerville and Ross various Flurry Knox types can be seen at places like Cahermee and Beal Atha Buidhe still busy about the complicated business of buying or selling a horse.

During a holiday in west Cork some years ago, I was struck by the many fine horses I saw there. I have since learned that this was known as the 'Sean Buidhe horse' and was assured by many people that the ancestor of this splendid breed was a stallion which had got ashore from one of the ships of the Spanish Armada. The same story is told about the origin of another fine breed – the Connemara Pony – and it is also told about the native horse in the Isle of Mull. There they will tell you that when the Spanish ship blew up in Tobermorey Bay the horse got ashore. When I expressed a doubt about the historical truth of such a story to a man I met in Connemara he silenced me by saying: 'Sure nobody would kill a horse'. All along the coast one can hear stories of horses and cattle which came from the sea and I believe that this story of the Armada horse is just another version of the legend.

Whatever his origin, the west Cork horse is a splendid animal and fully justifies his part of the saying heard in Bandon some years ago: 'Go east for a woman and west for a horse'. Surprisingly, Townsend, in the *Statistical Survey of County Cork*, has little to say of the horses. He says that flax, sheep and mountain ponies were sold at fairs in Bantry. Shaw Mason says about Clonakilty that the horses there were small and bred by farmers for their own use.

Here is another piece of folklore about judging the quality of a horse. It advises that a horse with one white foot is best and a horse with four white feet is bad. This is expressed in a rhyme:

Four white feet, send him far away
Three white feet, keep him for a day
Two white feet, he may never pay
One white foot, he is bred to stay.

The custom of feeding horses on the tops of green furze was common in County Cork as well as in Ulster. Once there I noticed a machine which I had never seen before and I enquired what it was. To my surprise, I was told that it was used to crush and break the green furze before feeding it to the horses.

Cork is a wonderful county for horse lore. I would be most impolite and perhaps a little unwise to doubt the story that the first steeplechase ever held took place at Buttevant. There is also of course the great showjumping event held at Millstreet where many famous horses and riders take part.

County Clare was famous for its horses and some of the fairs are still continued. The most famous of these was Kilrush, held twice yearly in May and October. In the *Parochial Survey* the writer said that the Kilrush horses had once been the finest in Ireland and added that they were still 'active and serviceable'. Dutton, however, wrote that in County Clare the quality of the horses had 'greatly declined recently' (1806). He suggested that a Suffolk Punch stallion would 'help to banish out of the county that vile breed of heavy limbed black horses that have so long usurped the place of a more generally useful kind'.

However, by the time he came to write about Dublin he was less enthusiastic. He wrote with disfavour of the big heavy horses and big heavy carts which severely damaged the roads. Then he continued:

I imagine the Cleveland bays mentioned in such high terms by Mr Cully would be a much more desirable kind of horse to introduce into this country than either the Suffolk Punch or the unwieldy dray horse, as they possess equal strength and more activity: and if a little more pains is taken in selecting the mares, a great probability arises of obtaining very fine hunters or carriage horses: but from the Suffolk Punch nothing can be obtained but a serviceable ugly drudge and I am convinced we possess many of that description already.

The horse fair of Spancel Hill, held on 24 June, also continues to flourish and good horses are shown there. Although Dutton was still complaining of the quality of the horses, he wrote that in 1807 'draught horses sold there as three-year-olds for £8–£25, and saddle horses at three years for £14–£60' and then complained that 'the fine breed of horses for which this county was formerly famous is now very rare. Lately there has been some improvement'.

Whatever may have been the reason for the decline – perhaps the buying up of the horses for the war, or, as Dutton says, the new heavy breed – he added:

> Vast numbers of mules are bred in this county but with little or no selection, consequently you seldom see one of good size. Mr Crowe of Ennis has procured a very fine ass of the Spanish blood which has greatly improved the size and shape and were any but the very worst sort of mares devoted to this purpose a very valuable breed would be introduced. Asses are very commonly used, especially by poor people, and are highly useful when the weight to be carried is moderate but yet too much for a man, an ass and a small cart or two baskets, as generally used in this county, will be found very serviceable for bringing clover or other soil to the stables and cattle sheds in summer, because the frequent journey they are obliged to make prevents that waste which is generaly made by bringing in a large quantity at once to save a lazy herd trouble.

In Connacht there were some notable horse fairs. The October fair of Ballinasloe still continues and is now a horse fair. In 1816 Dutton wrote: 'There were many horses sold at the October fair of Ballinasloe. They were greatly inferior to those twenty years ago'.

There were large horse fairs in Athlone in January and in September and horses were also sold at the fairs in March and May. The local rector, the Reverend Annesley Stream, wrote in 1815:

> Though the numbers sold in these fairs are difficult to be ascertained, the collectors of the tolls and customs say there are about 500 horses shewn for sale in the fairs of January and September besides other cattle: and in the fairs held in the months of March and May besides horses (not in such numbers as in the other fairs of the year) there

are from 3,000–4,000 sheep and about 2,000 cows and bullocks.

He went on to give some prices. Hunters made up to one hundred and fifty guineas and saddle horses made from forty to fifty guineas. Working horses sold at between twenty and thirty guineas and carriage horses sold at sixty to a hundred guineas a pair. (Prices for other livestock were: sheep £2–£3.10s.0d., bullocks £15, £25–£30, cows £15–£25). He added: 'These prices have fallen more than half within last year'. This fall occurred after the end of the Napoleonic Wars.

Other horse fairs were held in Athleague in County Roscommon and Carrignagat in County Sligo. In County Mayo the horse was the status symbol for even the smallest of small farmers. In Burrishoole and Murrisk, around Clew Bay, MacParlan wrote in 1810: 'Each village holding six acres of green (reclaimed) ground has a working garran, and, in the Barony of Gallen, almost every poor man of ever so small a holding must have his pony to work and to ride: the pony is here considered more indispensibly necessary than the cow'. Again, in the Barony of Costello, MacParlan writes of the villagers holding land in partnership and dividing 'themselves according to their numbers into four or eight parties. Each party keeps a horse, the joint property of the whole, which horses do in common the work of the village. By this method it turns out that every two villagers holding about ten or twelve acres of green ground will have one horse'.

In the Barony of Tyrawley MacParlan draws a distinction between the big farmer and the small one:

> A farmer having an hundred acres will not have more than five or six horses for the cultivation of his farm and the use of his family: but a farm of that extent occupied by villagers will support ten families, each of whom always has a horse, which they join to make up a team, and complete the spring ploughing, although they may have previously subdivided their farms, which is now most frequently done for their own convenience. In this case then the average computation would be one horse to each subdivision of ten acres.

This attitude towards the horse may be compared to that of some Africans to their horses. This from a recent letter from Lesotho: 'Only once did I see horses ploughing: horses here are for riding and admiring. . . . It's a common practice to take a pony to a sale, get offered a good price and then ride proudly home. Suppose it may even be that the higher the price offered, the less likely the sale.' Is it or was it the same in Ireland?

10
The Drover

> To Meath of the pastures,
> From the wet hills by the sea
> Through Leitrim and Longford
> Go my cattle and me.

As a small boy Padraic Collum must often have seen droves of cattle moving along the Dublin road out of Longford town, and on fair mornings he awoke to hear the lowing of cattle and the shouting of the drovers as the` cattle were driven in to the fair. As the railways spread through the country during the second half of the nineteenth century, more and more cattle were moved by rail, but on many of the roads of Ireland the drover and his cattle were commonly met, until finally the fairs died and the internal combustion engine made the roads impossible for any other form of traffic. The moving of cattle was a very profitable business for the railway companies, and one may still see very long sidings at some of the railway stations in County Meath. Cattle bought at western fairs were unloaded at Hill of Down or Enfield to be driven to the grazing farms of County Meath. Until recently a drover and his cattle had the right of way on Irish roads. This was a matter of surprise or amusement to some foreign visitors, and once I overheard a French visitor say, 'Mon Dieu! Droit aux bêtes.'

Before the railways were built, and in parts of the country where the lines were not convenient, it was necessary that livestock of every kind be moved by road. These included not only horses and cattle but sheep and even flocks of geese and turkeys. For example, horses bought at Cahermee in County Cork might be sold at Moy in County Tyrone or at Banbridge in County Down, or at some of the other horse fairs in the north of Ireland. During a radio programme in 1981 reference was made to a man with one arm who was able to take a batch of thirteen colts from Ballinasloe to Belfast.

Sheep were often difficult to drive any distance. At the outset they were usually wild and frightened, trying to get to grass, and if one of the flock managed to find an open gate or a hole in a fence all the rest were certain to follow the leader. If the drover could manage to stop the others from following, the leader would quickly rejoin the flock, but this was not always possible and it was often very difficult to get the flock back on the road and moving forward. Then when the unfortunate drover and his helper were both exhausted, some of the sheep were sure to develop sore feet from walking on the hard stoney road and were then unable to go any further. Sometimes there was a cart driven by another helper and the sheep might be put into the cart when they could not be persuaded by any means to walk any further.

Pigs were even more difficult to drive than sheep. It is quite impossible to persuade a pig to go in one direction. There is something very amusing – for the spectators – about the way a pig can change direction suddenly and slip past a man who tries to stop him. Normally the drover carried a stick made of an ash sapling, but in driving pigs such a stick would do grave damage to the animal. Instead, the drover used a piece of furze bush or sometimes a sally road.

As a class, drovers were very careful and methodical men whose job was to make sure that the stock arrived in better condition than when they set out. This was so whether the drover was himself the owner of the cattle or was driving them for the owner. In Ireland the movement of cattle was generally from the south and west to the north and east. Undoubtedly the greatest drover I ever knew was a Kerryman called John Casey who spent many years buying up yearling heifers at the fairs in County Kerry, mainly in Cahirciveen and Kilorglin. When he had gathered a herd of suitable size – about forty – he set out moving them northward across County Limerick and through the west side of county Tipperary and Offaly and through County Westmeath to end at a fair in Longford town. His route was carefully planned so that he was able to show his cattle at a number of fairs along the route, or he might sell some of them at the place where they stopped overnight. The fairs might include Abbeyfeale, Newcastle West and Rathkeale in County Limerick, Newport, Nenagh and Borrisokane in County Tipperary, as well as Birr, Banagher and Ferbane in County Offaly. The journey from Cahirciveen to Longford was more than 200 miles and might last for more than a month, and during that time they might have been shown at three or four fairs. My father, who was a very close friend of John Casey, used to say that the cattle were in better condition when they reached Longford than when they left Cahirciveen. Once I was lucky enough to see how he managed to do this, when my father, my brother and I met him and his cattle on a road north of

Ferbane in County Offaly. As we stopped to talk, the cattle, realising their drover was not following them, moved onto the roadside and started to graze on 'the long acre'. As my father and John talked they stood in the centre of the road to make sure that the cattle were not disturbed, even though there was little traffic on the road.

This movement of cattle from the high rough lands of the south-west had been going on since the end of the eighteenth century if not earlier. About the year 1800 Tighe, in the *Statistical Survey of Kilkenny* wrote: 'The Kerry cows are often driven to this county for sale: they are preferred in dairies for their quantity of milk, as well as for the low price they bear, even compared with their diminutive size. I have seen a bull and three dry cows sold for six guineas, and a bull and six dry cows for nine guineas, but these were of the smallest kind. A score has been sold for £30.'

About the same time Kerries were popular as stores in the area of County Dublin, because they fattened easily and quickly – an efficient dual-purpose breed.

About the year 1815 an effort was made to establish a ferry across the Shannon Estuary. This was necessary because many Clare farmers and butchers attended the fairs of Listowel and Killorglin in County Kerry as well as Tarbert in west Limerick, and the journey to cross the Shannon at Limerick was both long and difficult. Similarly, the ferry was to be used by buyers from the south side of the river who had bought cattle at Kilrush and Ballyket in west Clare.

Part of this movement of cattle was towards the north-east from Sligo and Leitrim and Roscommon towards fairs further north such as Enniskillen, Cavan, Cootehill, Clones and Monaghan town. There were significant developments in the area of County Derry, where some of the farmers were using turnips as winter feed. In 1802 we hear that:

Rev. Mr McCausland of Bush-hall used to plant considerable quantities of Swedish turnips in drills: he also had Norfolk turnips sown broadcast. I was sorry to see this excellent farmer beginning to decline the winter keeping of cattle, but it seems that some of the country people have made vexatious spoils of his turnips. Mr McCausland brings cattle from the County Louth, bought at Mullaghcrew etc: his usual quantity brought thence yearly was one score bullocks and one score heifers bought at a year old averaging £3.10s.0d. each: he used rear several from this stock.

In referring to the sheep in County Derry the writer did not think highly of some of the local breeds but he went on to add: 'Our best sort are bought either in the fairs of the South Western Counties, or else at Dervock to which they are driven by jobbers from these pastures'. Anyone who has ever struggled to drive sheep for twenty miles would be amazed at the skill and courage necessary to undertake a journey of more than two hundred miles from, say, Roscommon town to Dervock in north Antrim and have the sheep fit to sell at the end of the journey. Taking a drove of bullocks from County Louth to Derry or from Cavan or Fermanagh to fairs at Donaghy or Ballymena was almost routine when compared with the task of driving sheep from Roscommon to Dervock.

However, there were still more surprising feats of hardihood which appear to have been routine for some buyers and sellers of cattle. The writer of the *Parochial Survey of Dungiven* appears to have been caught between admiration for the courage, and indignation for the foolishness, of the men who did it. This is what he wrote:

> It is truly astonishing to observe with what eagerness and courage they [the Irish] engage in this last traffic which is often little better than a species of gambling. A mountaineer will travel from fair to fair, for thirty miles round with no other food than the oaten cake which he carries with him and which it requires neither fire, table knife or other instrument to use: he will lay out the whole or perhaps treble of all he is worth (to which the facility of the country banks is a great encouragement) in the purchase of thirty or one hundred head of cattle, with which when collected he sets out for England, a country with the roads, manners, and inhabitants of which he is totally unacquainted.
>
> In this journey he scarcely ever goes into a house, sleeps but little, and then generally in the open air, and lives chiefly upon his favourite oaten bread. If he fails in disposing of his cattle at the fair of Carlisle, the usual place of sale, he is probably ruined and has to begin the world, as he terms it, over again. If he succeed he returns home only to commence a new wandering and new labour and is ready in about a month perhaps to set out again for England: these also who job about from fair to fair without leaving the country are equally assiduous to take as little rest in their particular time. The wandering and unsettled habits which this species of life induces are very unfavourable to improvement: whenever by any accident the cattle trade is suspended or becomes unprofitable the persons acustomed to be employed in it being unfit for any soberer occupation remain in a great measure idle: even agriculture is burthensome to them as wanting the variety and interest which their usual business affords: thus the fruits of so much labour and enterprize are often wasted

during the long intervals of indolence and inactivity.

This practice is also mentioned in the *Statistical Survey of County Derry*. The writer says that young store bullocks, called 'nabs', from the mountains of Donegal were sometimes driven to Scotland and to England.

The writer of the *Parochial Survey* goes on to tell more about the cattle trade during the Napoleonic Wars, as it was carried out in the parish of Dungiven:

> The extent of the mountains in this parish and the excellent pasture which many of them afford, render the rearing and grazing of cattle a very important object of attention to its inhabitants: the great profits of the cattle trade for two or three years past have contributed of late to increase this attention. Many of those who purchased cows early last year, and held them over during the summer nearly doubled their money by them. These circumstances have brought a considerable influx of wealth to several of the mountain districts. Persons who but seven or eight years ago were in the situation of common day labourers can now engage two, three or four hundred pounds in this profitable business.
>
> The grazing of cattle is paid by the *summ*, which is to be understood the grazing of a cow when above three years old: the proportions of other kinds of cattle are estimated by this in the following manner, a *summ* is divided into three equal parts, called feet, which is thus applied. A year-old calf is called a foot, a two-year-old two feet, a *summ* is three feet: a horse is five feet: two colts are equal to a horse: six sheep or four ewes and four lambs the same: twenty-four geese is a *summ*: thus then if 6*s*. be the price of the *summ*, a year-old will be 2*s*., a two-year-old 4*s*., a horse 10*s*., and so on. The charge for a *summ* in the mountain from May to November varies from 6*s*. to 16*s*. according to the goodness of the pasture. In the parks which are kept up for fattening it is from 40*s*. to 50*s*. The stock of sheep in this parish is but scanty and the breed, with a few exceptions, indifferent. There is a very good breed of pigs in some townlands, but the farmers are not very skilful or attentive to rearing them.

This export of cattle from Ulster to the south-east of Scotland and England was only the continuation of a traffic which had been carried on for some centuries and it was not quite so hazardous as the writer would indicate. The cattle were mainly young stores, which could be moved efficiently, and it is likely that the journey towards Carlisle was only undertaken during the spring or early summer when there was a good demand for such cattle to fatten on the summer grass in England. The cattle could be moved from Dungiven to Larne or to Donaghadee in a few days and from either place to Portpatrick was a short sea crossing – given luck and a favourable wind. As the cattle moved towards Carlisle there were some other towns where the drover might try to sell them. Among these were Newtownstewart, New Galloway and Dumfries, all in good farming districts.

It will be remembered that Scotland had undergone an agricultural revolution following the Act of Union with England in 1707. This caused a great demand for farm labourers from the Highlands of Scotland and from Ireland, and in this way some Irishmen might have become familiar with the markets and fairs of south-west Scotland, where the store cattle of Galloway were sold. Writing about this trade, Hanley said: 'In the year ending December 1784 more than 18,000 Irish cattle and 1,200 horses passed through Portpatrick, and during the five years 1785-90 over 55,000 cattle and 10,000 horses were landed at the same Port'.

He also said that from 1707 onwards:

> The Scottish cattle trade in particular received a useful fillip which in time stimulated the cattle trade between the north of Ireland, and the south-west of Scotland. From the rough grazing of Galloway the native and Irish cattle set forth on the month's journey to the lush meadows of Norfolk and Suffolk where they fattened easily and rapidly for the Smithfield market. With the cattle that were regularly shipped from Donaghadee to Portpatrick came score of Irish droves many of whom seem to have settled in Galloway etc.

This export of cattle to Scotland continued and many Irish cattle dealers were familiar with the cattle market of Glasgow and the Tryst of Falkirk – the Ballinasloe fair of Scotland.

In the *Statistical Survey of County Derry* there is a reference to some fine, large, well shaped cows from Fermanagh or Roscommon. They were bought, to be fattened, at Raphoe, Killygordon, Strabane or Derry from the dealers.

During the early years of the nineteenth century the export of salt beef from Ireland continued. Usually the prices paid for beef cattle were good due to the war boom, but everyone knew that peace would be followed by a slump in this trade. In the *Statistical Survey of County Clare,* Dutton wrote rather dramatically of the difficulties which the grazier might experience during one of the years when the market for fat cattle was depressed. Normally the cattle were sold at the local fair, but if the owner, dissatisfied with the price offered, should decide to drive them to Limerick or Cork, there were further difficulties to be overcome. He wrote:

The principal markets for fat cattle are Cork and Limerick: a few years back an attempt was made to establish one in Clare connected with a commercial house at Liverpool but from some unfortunate circumstances it failed. . . . If contracts are made by commercial houses in England agents attend the fairs in November and December and generally give good prices: if a peace is expected or, as has been the case in 1806, the merchants are combined, the graziers are completely at their mercy, and suffer not only every kind of gross indignity. . . but suffer serious losses from the cheating of every person concerned in slaughtering these cattle. As it is scarcely known in other parts of the Kingdom it may be at least amusing to detail the business a little. The grazier finding no agent attending the fairs to buy (except some trusty friend of the merchants who reads a letter from Cork or Limerick, stating the rumours of a peace, or the expected low price) is obliged to drive his cattle to either of these markets: after driving them into either of these towns he waits upon the great man, and with all humility begs to know if he wants any fat cattle: after a good deal of pretended hurry of business, and waiting for a repetition of the question 'he believes he shall not want any thing more than what he has already engaged but to oblige Mr. . . he will endeavour to make room for them: as to the price, it is to be regulated by what any other grazier receives'. When this is settled he must drive his beasts to a slaughterhouse many of which are erected for this purpose: he pays for this a high price and must also give the heads and offal: he must sit up all night superintending the slaughtering and must silently observe every species of fraud committed by the worst kind of butchers: for, as has frequently happened if resentful language is used to those scoundrels, they begin to whet their knives and put themselves in an assassinating attitude: this is a slaughterhouse at night, and among the horrid scenes of carnage around him requires no small share of nerves. Next morning without taking any rest he must bring his meat to the cutters-up: here unless they are fee'd begins the second part of the fraud he has to suffer: first they take for their perquisite several pounds of his best beef, and if he has cows, unless they are well paid will cut away large quantities of the udder, which they call offal, and which is the property of the merchant though he pays nothing for it. The merchant also gets the tongue, and if the grazier wants a few must beg them at the rate of at least three shillings each. The third scene begins at the scales: here another perquisite must be paid, and much good meat is refused, because truly it should be a few pounds less than the stipulated weight per beast: an appeal then is made to the great man. 'Really Sir I do not wish to take your cattle: the prices I receive in England are so low. I shall lose by my contract: suppose you would try if you can do better elsewhere, but I will agree to take your beef, though below the weight if you make the terms lower'. . . . Then he enquires what mode of payment: bills at ninety days are the best terms he can get. He then applies to a chandler to buy his fat. When this is settled the tanner must be waited on, and here, as well as with the chandler, bills at a long date are the only payment he can receive, and as they are generally men of small or no capital, if their speculations should not succeed their bills are worth little.

This is but a small part of the gross indignities the grazier has to suffer: he has to transact a business totally foreign to his habits of life, and is consequently unable to cope with those, who from their infancy are used to the tricks practised in this business, and therefore able to avoid them or turn them perhaps to their own benefit. The price depends not a lot on the causes before mentioned, but on the size of the beast, those of a large size bringing more per hundredweight than those of a smaller one, which is a premium on large bone, and cows are always lower in price than oxen, though they are sent to England in the same package and if fat go as the best beef called 'Planter's Mess'.

No doubt anyone who did as Dutton says would have trouble in disposing of his cattle, and the sight of a slaughterhouse is not pleasant. The difficulties were great and probably the greatest was that concerning the payment for his beef as well as for his hides and tallow. Generally it was better to take the best price offered at a convenient fair.

The Tangler

The 'tangler' was almost as much a part of the fair as were the cattle. He was usually a man of high intelligence, or was at least very quick-witted, and a good actor. He might travel to the fair in the company of a man who wished to buy a large number of cattle, and who was prepared to pay the tangler for his expert judgement and skill in doing this. More generally the tangler was a freelance, and being an expert judge of the cattle, was able to buy well – sometimes better than a genuine buyer. When he had done this his next duty was to find a genuine buyer who was prepared to buy the animal at profit to the tangler. Many men continued for years and made a reasonable living in this way, without ever owning, or wishing to own, the price of the cattle which they could buy so expertly.

Sometimes these men were called 'blockers', and generally the word carried a slightly disreputable implication. If a genuine buyer was unable to complete a deal he might go away and allow a blocker to move in and make a bid for the cattle. The blocker moved in, examined the cattle carefully, and then made a bid, less than the price offered by the real buyer. He then proceeded to bargain loudly and dramatically, but refusing to increase his bid. As he continued 'in possession', as the expression was, no real buyer would dare to interfere and make a better bid. That would be an unforgivable crime and would almost certainly be followed by blows. Often I have heard the unfortunate seller say, 'Get out of my sight. I don't to want to dale with you.' Still, the blocker would hang on and even when he pretended to go some of the bystanders would call him back saying, 'Here ye'll divide two pound', or some other such encouragement as, 'Here he'll give her to you'. All this time the blocker would be keeping a sharp lookout for the genuine buyer, who would make a sign telling him to break off the bargain and disappear so that the genuine buyer could get in and start the genuine deal in the hope that the seller's determination to get a high price would now be less.

Sometimes the blocker was bad-mannered and would look at the animal and ask, 'How much for that ould hen roost?' or 'Where did you get the little scutty calf?' He might even go so far as to say, 'How much for that ould bag of bones?' but this was not considered proper and no decent man would do it. If he did, he was liable to get into some trouble, so a more subtle approach was often employed. The blocker would look at the cattle which he was pretending to buy and then closely examine the teeth, or the jaw, or the udder, or some other part of the animal. Then he would declare loudly, 'No. I won't buy her. She is wrong', and off he would go, leaving the seller looking anxiously at his cow and still more anxious to get rid of it quickly.

The reason for all this was because the seller sometimes did not have any clear or accurate idea of what his animal was worth, and had little idea what it might weigh. These are the reasons why the seller invariably asked more than he expected to get – so leaving himself room to bargain, and if necessary reduce his price. The rule was 'Ask plenty, you can always come down, but you can't go up'. The lowest grade of tangler was the man who specialized in selling 'wrong' ones. They were more usually found selling 'wrong' horses, but their services were sometimes required to dispose of cattle. For example, in the case of an old cow with many rings on her horns, it was necessary that these be pared down and the horns expertly smoothed with sandpaper and polished. If the toes had become noticeably long they might be cut shorter and trimmed neatly. I have also heard a story of a cow whose tail had been cut off in an accident: it was expertly fitted with a new tail before being taken to the fair.

I do not wish to give the impression that tanglers as a group were any more dishonest than any other. They were, as I have said, able and intelligent men – if they were not they would not have had any business at a fair – and they were prepared to make their knowledge and skill available to buyers. One man whom I knew, and whom I remember very kindly, was known as 'Pa Mac'. His name was Patrick Sullivan and I met him when I went to the fair of Cahirciveen with my father, where he was helping to buy the cattle and as my father said, 'Pa Mac is the best judge of a Kerry heifer that ever stood the fair of Cahirciveen'. He had one great advantage. He spoke with the local accent – unlike many tanglers, who were clearly strangers – and was known to many people at County Kerry fairs. I could never imagine that 'Pa Mac' would ever do any of these dirty little tricks I have mentioned. He was not that sort of man.

I have heard of fairs to which unusually large numbers of tanglers went. One of these was Watergrasshill, not far from Cork city. Some time during the 1920s a bus service from Cork was established and early on the morning of each fair a special bus ran from Cork. Many tanglers travelled on this bus and they became such a scourge to the sellers that ultimately nobody brought cattle there and the fair died out. In Dunmore, County Galway, I heard a disgruntled farmer say, 'You can't get your cattle into the fair with them. They are a bloody curse.' I have no doubt that the large numbers of tanglers were a disadvantage to most of the people who attended the fair of Dunmore. I used to hear that Kells was 'a tangler's town', but this did not appear to injure the fairs held there.

11

Fighting at Fairs

FOR centuries stick fighting was a common feature of such assemblies as fairs, markets, patterns and race meetings which were held in every part of Ireland. Since the middle of the eighteenth century this practice has been described many times, but it is probably much older. In his book on *Head Injuries* published in 1793 Sylvester O'Halloran (1728-1808), a very distinguished surgeon who practised in his native city, Limerick, for more than fifty years, wrote:

> Without doubt there is no part of the habitable globe that for half a century past has afforded such an ample field for observations on injuries of the head as Ireland in general: this province of Munster in particular: for our people invincably brave, notwithstanding the cruel oppressions they have suffered for a century past, and highly irritable soon catch fire: a slight offense is frequently followed by serious consequences, and sticks, stones, and every other species of offense next to hand are dealt out with great liberality. To this add the frequent abuse of spiritous liquors, particularly whiskey, which has unhappily for the morals and constitutions of the people found its way to every part of the Kingdom.
>
> From these hitherto unrestrained causes it is that many of our fairs, patrons, and hurling matches terminate in bloody conflicts. . . . From this it appears what superior advantages Irish surgeons have long possessed in this department of their profession over those of the neighbouring nations.

O'Halloran goes on to describe eighty-five cases of head injury which he had treated and in some cases gives a few details about how the injury occurred. For example, one case reads: 'Peter Meehan, aged nineteen, on the 17 March 1780 received some blows on the head and a cut of an hangar on the upper part of the right parietal which wounded the bone but did not penetrate the two tables'. It will be noticed that the injuries were sustained on St Patrick's Day, which was then, as now, a general holiday in Ireland.

Another case reads: 'In the beginning of last August I was called upon to visit one MacNamara in Broadford and another of the name of O'Rourke about a mile further along the same road. On returning from a neighbouring fair on the preceding day each received a severe fracture on the right side of the coronal bone'. MacNamara was the more severely injured and died of his injuries. O'Rourke appears to have recovered.

Stick fighting between large bodies of men was common in Ireland during the eighteenth century. One well remembered 'battle' took place in 1782 when Caesar French, a landowner who lived on the Galway-Mayo border, had a quarrel with a neighbouring landlord, George Robert Fitzgerald. French organised and led an 'army' of 300 of his tenants against Fitzgerald and defeated his tenant 'army' in a famous fight. O'Halloran makes reference to injuries received in what he called riots which occurred in different places during the eighteenth century.

There are various theories as to how the practice started. One suggests that it was a method of training the recruits for Irish regiments in the French armies at the time. This does not seem very likely, as the authorities could not fail to hear of it and would quickly stop such a treasonable practice. It is often said that the skills were taught by the dancing masters who travelled from place to place teaching dancing and deportment to the people, as well as the skills of stick fighting.

In any case, no matter what its beginning, stick fighting became a national pastime during the greater part of the nineteenth century and was likely to occur at fairs and markets. As Dr Kevin Danaher wrote, 'it was a crude and dangerous form of sport' – but one which was almost natural in the Ireland of the time when every man carried a stout heavy stick. A good stick fighter was a popular hero, much as a star footballer is regarded today. The causes of the fighting were in many cases not known, and generally the combatants bore no greater ill-will to each other when the fight was over than might be borne today by members of rival football teams. One explanation which was often heard among the stick fighters in County Mayo went:

Win or loose, we'll have a booze
Lá Fhéile Bríde Tullrahan (On St Brigid's Day in Tullrahan).

In any case there would be little difficulty in finding causes for quarrelling in rural Ireland as anyone who has ever attended a district court will know. There might be trouble about land, or about a right of way, or a failed marriage, or some personal insult real or imaginary, but often the original cause was forgotten though the fighting continued.

All through the eighteenth century the native Irish were a very depressed class, little better than serfs ruled by a landowning ascendency who would refer to them as 'the Common Enemy'. As could be expected in such circumstances, the oppressed would form secret societies in an effort to right some wrongs or to take revenge upon some specially vicious oppressor. These societies were to be found in every part of Ireland. They were called Whiteboys, Rightboys, Shanavests, Caravats, Threashers, Carders, Ribbonmen and Molly Maguires. Others were called Croppies, Chalkers, Houghers, Rockites and Terry Alts but there probably were many others. Similarly in Ulster secret societies were organised among the small farmers and farm labourers who were Protestants. These were called Hearts of Oak, Hearts of Steel, Peep o'Day Boys and, later, Orangemen.

The sticks used were of different kinds. Probably the most popular was a heavy blackthorn about 3–4 ft long and held about one-third of the way along the shaft so that the near end could be used to protect the elbow where a blow might paralyse a fighter's grip and so render him helpless. In order to prepare a good fighting stick, skill and knowledge were necessary. The thorns were cut short and the stick was put in the chimney to season. This might be continued for a year or even longer and during this time it was repeatedly oiled and polished. The best oil for this purpose was neat foot oil, made by boiling the feet of cattle and skimming off the thick yellow oil. More usually this oil was used to treat harness leather.

In Ballinamore there was a famous maker of fighting sticks whom I remember well. He was James (Rury) Reynolds, a carpenter, who lived in Chapel Lane, and in his younger days he had been a good stick fighter. Like any expert craftsman, James was proud of his skill and gave special names to some of his best sticks. One might be called 'No Opinion for Nine Days'. This made it clear that a blow from the stick would be so severe that the doctor could not give a prognosis for nine days. Another stick might be called 'Rid the Lane', i.e. Clear the Street. Still others might be called 'Dead with one Stroke' or 'Dead without the Priest', but when James was especially pleased with a stick he might be inspired to call it 'Father of the Sloes' or 'Mother of the Sloes'.

Some of the experts preferred a stick of ash: they insisted that the blackthorn was liable to crack, and an iron ferrule was fitted on the end to prevent this. The ash stick was made of a heavy ash sapling – a much heavier type than the ash plant used by the drover. According to Kevin Danaher the ash stick used for fighting was made from an ash sucker i.e. one of the shoots which grow from the stump of an ash tree which has been cut down.

In some cases the fighter might use a 'loaden butt'. This, in my opinion, was derived from the hunting crop which every 'gentleman' carried at the time and which he was inclined to use freely to beat his inferiors. It was made by hollowing out the heavier end of a stick and then filling the hollow with lead. The loaded end was then bound neatly and firmly with a covering of 'waxend', i.e. the heavy waxed linen thread used by saddlers to sew harness. This was done to make sure that the stick did not crack when used. The loaden butt was sometimes carried inside the sleeve of the coat and attached by a leather strap to the wrist, or it might be carried in the leg of the trousers, attached to a leather belt.

Occasionally other types of stick were used. Some were of oak and some were of holly. The stick had no special name. It might be referred to as a *cippín*, a *maide*, or a *bata* or, during the present century, a 'fighting stick', but it was never called a *shillelagh* or any other such word. Often hammer shaped sticks called *shillelaghs* are bought by tourists, but I cannot imagine one being used in a real stick fight.

Some of the fighters carried a bag of stones and these were sometimes used before the stick fight became general. In some descriptions of these fights one reads of women taking part, but this was rare and generally people did not approve of it. Normally it only occurred when a wife or mother saw that her man was getting the worse of the fight and tried to help him. True, there were stories of people like Big Biddy and Long Ann who were notable fighting women, using a stone tied in the toe of a woollen stocking to great effect at the fair of Tuam. These, however, were exceptional, and normally it was not considered fair to strike a woman – though a man was allowed to defend himself against her attack. Usually the women looked on and no doubt encouraged their men, and they also organised a dressing station for those who had been severely wounded.

In some cases some other weapons such as swords, knives and even guns of different kinds were used, but these were rare and only used 'when necessary'.

Faction Fighting

In some cases large numbers of men, often hundreds, took part in these fights and it is possible that the different factions were organised by the secret societies. In my native district of Ballinamore the Molly Maguires fought the Ribbonmen, when they were not combined to fight the Orangemen. In another case the Shanavests, known as the Four-Year-Olds, fought the Caravats, known as the Three-Year-Olds. According to O'Donnell, in *The Irish Faction Fighters,* this began in the year 1805, following the hanging of a certain Nicholas Hanley in Clonmel. The practice spread widely and soon faction fighting was common in every part of Ireland, as the different factions were organised.

The authorities took differing views of the fighting. In some cases they encouraged it, as in the case of Caesar French and Robert Fitzgerald. In Kerry, Thomas Ponsonby, a local landowner, helped to organise one of the factions, the Lawlor-Black Mulvihills, in a very savage faction fight on 24 June 1834. It must be realised that until the year 1830 there was no organisation in the country which could be called a police force. Following a Police Act of the Irish parliament in 1789 a police force was established. This corrupt and useless force, the baronial constables, was established and administered by the Grand Jury. The 'barneys', as they were called, were almost all elderly men and would be of no help in controlling a faction fight. In 1814 another effort was made with the establishment of the Peace Preservation Force by the Chief Secretary, Sir Robert Peel. While the baronial constables were not a serious police force, the Peace Preservation Force was highly unpopular – the word Peeler is still remembered – and was used to keep the peace in disturbed areas. The next effort was the establishment of the County Constabulary in 1822. This was still unpopular. It was a paramilitary force appointed by the local magistrates, and was not effective in preventing the faction fighting – the factions were likely to unite against the police. It was only in 1836, with the establishment of the Irish Constabulary free from the influence of the magistrates and the Grand Juries, that the police force became efficient and did its duty with impartial justice.

This was to a great extent due to a Scotsman, Thomas Drummond, the Under-Secretary. He used the new police force to put a stop to the faction fighting and when he died in 1840 it was in decline. This did not put an end to stick fighting at fairs, which was to continue until the present century, but now the local police were able to cope with the problem. There were some other causes for its decline; the passing of the Catholic Emancipation Act, the increasing opposition of the clergy, the temperance movement – which was preached by Father Mathew – and the more efficient control of private distilling.

It would be difficult to identify the different factions. In Tipperary one faction was known as the Oultachs (*na h-Ullaigh,* The Ulstermen), but who the Ulstermen were, or when they settled in Tipperary, is a very difficult question. Similarly, many of the factions were made up of family groups. It may be that the faction fighting was derived from inter-tribal rivalry but this is a matter for investigation by experts on the history of mediaeval Ireland.

At the end of the eighteenth century some faction fighting took place between Catholics and Protestants. These were more serious affairs, and both sides could dig up plenty of grievances and other causes for fighting. One famous fight occurred at Banagher in County Offaly on 6 January 1814 and has been described in detail by O'Donnell. The fight was between the men of the town and those living in the parish of Lusmagh some distance to the south. Lusmagh was in some ways a strange parish. It is on the left bank of the Shannon, yet it is part of the diocese of Clonfert and was formerly regarded as part of the province of Connacht. Until the sixteenth century it was held by an O'Madden under the De Burgo lords of south Galway. Then, during the sixteenth century, the area of west Offaly which is now the barony of Garrycastle came under the control of a family called MacCoghlan. A further complication was the establishment of the plantation town of Banagher under James I. This was a Protestant town, a pocket borough, and was strongly fortified to hold the river crossing. All this would indicate that the rivalry between Lusmagh and Banagher was very ancient and the faction fight in January 1814 was only the latest fight between the parties with the addition of religion and race as further causes for quarrelling.

In any case, a notice was posted in the town and announced that on the next Thursday, 6 January, the men of Lusmagh would attack the town. On the morning of the sixth, the Feast of the Epiphany, about 500 men of Lusmagh entered the town and the fighting began about 9.0 a.m. At about 10.0 a.m. a local magistrate, Captain Armstrong, asked for and was given a detachment of the 12th Regiment from the town garrison. The soldiers were able to come between the parties, the fighting ceased and the Lusmagh men began to move away. It was at this stage that the soldiers opened fire on them, killing three and wounding fourteen. It was said that the members of the Banagher Yeomanry took part in the fighting, though they were not wearing uniform at the time and it would seem that most of the Banagher men were Protestants.

In the province of Ulster this was known as party fighting, and there – as in Banagher – there was a religious difference between the parties. In many parts of the province the two sides were about equal in numbers and in fighting skill but the Protestants had some advantages – the law and some of the magistrates were inclined to favour them. In addition, some of them had served in the yeomanry and had guns.

One very famous fight between Catholics and Protestants took place at Garvagh, a small town in the south-east of County Derry, in the year 1813. The story is told in a fine ballad which was written shortly after the fight.

To the north and east of the town the land is good and the Protestants lived there, while the Catholics lived on the poorer land to the south and west. The trouble began at the fair of Garvagh on 23 May 1813 when the local magistrate, Alexander Purviance, reported to Dublin Castle:

> I happened to be on the street of Garvagh that day between four and five o'clock in the evening when I observed some disposition towards riot among the people and immediately sent to have the constables assembled, four in number, which I have in the town and before they had all well arrived, a riot had begun in different parts of the town, and in ten minutes were seen I dare say near 300 cudgels all up at once. For four constables and myself to do anything towards quelling such a riot you may easily conceive was impossible. Though we all used every endeavour to suppress it we were at length obliged to leave them to fight it out.
>
> Before I go further I must inform you who are the two parties that comprise this body of rioters. According to my own opinion and that of my brother magistrates it is composed of Catholics on the one side, Orangemen on the other. At this May fair which I mentioned before the Catholics were most numerous and overcame the other party by their numbers.

Purviance knew that at the next fair there was likely to be further trouble, so in his letter he asked for some soldiers to help keep the peace. He got no answer to this request, so as a last resort he asked the captain of the local corps of yeomanry to bring his yeomen to Garvagh on the fair day. The yeomen came willingly, but when the June fair was over he wrote again to Dublin Castle:

> The Orangemen seemed determined to revenge the proceedings of the last fair, and came into the town in great numbers all armed with staves. They so much exceeded the other party this day in numbers that they dare not appear to face them. Towards the evening when they were a little inflamed with whiskey they attacked a catholic house in town and broke his windows. I immediately ordered the party out and endeavoured to apprehend some of them

who had broken the windows but could not find them out: from what I saw then I determined not to apply for any Yeomanry again, unless I could have them from a distant part. I proclaimed the Riot Act repeatedly and endeavoured to disperse them by every means in my power short of ordering the military to fire but they still stayed in large groups, and when I would disperse a large assembly this moment, they got together in another part in a few minutes after, and I could perceive revenge, insolence, and a desire to riot in their looks as if they had found anyone to oppose them. I went up and down the town repeatedly endeavouring to disperse them by threats and persuasions and did not get the street cleared till past ten o'clock.

All was now set for trouble on the next fair day, 26 July. Early in the afternoon the less bellicose were on their way home, the Protestants crowding the roads to the east and the Catholics moving southward across Ballinameen Bridge. Let the ballad tell the rest of the story:

The Battle of Garvagh

I

The day before the July fair
The Ribbonmen they did prepare
For three miles round to sack and tear
The loyal town of Garvagh

II

Then to Provene we straight applied
For aid, but he soon us denied,
'Let longest stand the toughest hide
I'll send no aid to Garvagh.'

III

Then to Coleraine we straightway sent
For aid but none to us was sent
The bloody crew for to prevent
From their designs of Garvagh

IV

It's from no quarter help was found
For to support that loyal town
Then fortune did appear to frown
Upon the town of Garvagh

V

Sad news, sad news to Orangemen
Thirteen hundred Ribbonmen
Did all assemble in the glen
To burn the town of Garvagh

VI

And others did in ambush lie
In wood and thickets they were nigh,
In readiness for to supply
That bloody crew in Garvagh

VII

The day came out they did repair
In multitudes to Garvagh fair,
Some thirty miles to travel there
To burn the town of Garvagh

VIII

The Protestants and Orangemen
Like brothers did assemble then
To keep the town they did intend
Or die like men in Garvagh

IX

The Tory whistle loud and shrill
Did quick resound o'er moor and hill
Fall on brave boys destroy and kill
All Protestants in Garvagh

X

Then all prepared in great haste
White handkerchiefs around their waists
Their jackets we did soundly baste
The July fair in Garvagh

XI

We gave the word to clear the street
And numbers fled like hunted sheep
When Protestants did Papists meet,
At Davidson's in Garvagh

XII

We fired blank cartridge (to) no avail
The Orange bullets flew like hail
We soon did make them turn tail
With deadly wounds from Garvagh

XIII

Then Captain Dooley cried 'Brave boys
Maintain your guard and fear no noise
We'll massacre the Orange boys
And burn the town of Garvagh'

XIV

But scarcely had he turned round
Till he received a deadly wound
His brogues went up his head went down
At the third tree in Garvagh

XV

The Teagues they cried 'Is this the way
That we will make the massacre
The Ribbonmen will curse the day
That they attacked Garvagh'

XVI

Had you been there for to have seen
The best man first through Ballnameen
While Orange boys pursued them keen
And cleared the town of Garvagh

XVII

But mark what followed this affray,
They thought to swear our lives away
To jail we went without delay
We had no guard from Garvagh

XVIII

Against us bloodily they swore
Such swearing n'er was heard before
MacCluskey swore two hours or more
Against the boys of Garvagh

XIX

Our thanks are due to Sir George Hill
The Beresfords befriend us still
And Sir Harvey Bruce of Downhill
They cleared the boys of Garvagh

XX

The Judge he thought us to condemn
But our impartial jurymen
Our grateful thanks are due to them
They cleared the boys of Garvagh

In his book *The Irish Land Question*, George Sigerson had something to say about faction fighting and he was especially critical of the attitude of the Irish landowners to it. In 1868 he wrote:

It was long the custom for some of the Irish gentry to organise factions and placing themselves at their head lead them to sanguinary frays at the appointed fair or market. . . . The proprietorial magistrates were disposed to encourage the strife, and to inflict mere nominal penalties on those who were captured.

He went on to quote from what Sir John Hawley, a Circuit Court Judge, wrote of his experiences in dealing with men accused of faction fighting:

The greater number of the magistrates instead of assisting me as I had a right to expect in the praise-worthy and humane effort to put down faction fighting did everything they safely could to thwart me, and thereby keep alive this shameful detestable custom.

He went on to describe the first Quarter Sessions at which he presided in Nenagh where:

a farmer's son who had committed a frightful murder at a faction fight was returned for trial for manslaughter merely. But this was not all. The Jury after a short delay found a verdict of guilty and Mr Hawley was about to pronounce sentence, when one of the magistrates who crowded the bench requested him to confer with them. 'I turned round to speak to them,' he says, 'and you may guess my astonishment when I heard them all urge the necessity of inflicting on the man convicted of aggravated manslaughter only a mere nominal punishment. When I asked what they meant by 'necessity' they frankly declared they could not live in the country unless the system of faction fighting was kept up as they believed it was necessary for their own safety to have the people divided.

Although the number of big faction fights declined during the second half of the nineteenth century, this did not mean the end of stick fighting at fairs. This was liable to occur until about the year 1920. The troubles associated with the Land War and then the quarrelling between the different groups in the Irish Parliamentary Party helped to continue the fighting. During my childhood the quarrels between Parnellites and Anti-Parnellites were still very real, and might cause fighting. I saw what may have been the last party fight in County Leitrim between a group of Hibernians and some members of the newly formed Volunteers. The Hibernians were the descendants of the Molly Maguires, one of the local secret societies, and have been described as the fighting wing of the Nationalist Party.

It is difficult to collect stories about stick fighting – people have become ashamed of it and do not wish to speak about it – but I did hear a story about the selection of a candidate to contest a Westminster election around 1902. The delegates to the Convention from Ballinamore travelled in a brake, a sort of two-horse bus. Outside Carrick-on-Shannon the brake was stopped and each man was supplied with a blackthorn stick, and told what he must do in case anyone should propose a rival candidate.

Around Ballinamore there were some well-known fighting families. Probably the best known were a group of seven brothers called Mac a'Teer, who lived on the Cavan-Leitrim border. These were professional fighters who were paid for their services and were prepared to fight for any party. There was also the story of the father who decided that his two sons should fight to decide which of them would inherit the farm. Generally the fighting was between family groups, with Flynns, Dolans and Gaffneys taking part.

In asking about stick fighting, I often used to hear references to what was called 'castle money'. The implication was that the government paid some people to encourage faction fighting, but I do not think this happened during the present century. Certainly the police worked hard to keep the peace at fairs and it was probably their increasing efficiency that ended the fighting.

12
Travelling People

ANYONE who can remember the routine of an Irish fair will know that at every fair there were numbers of travelling people. Naturally they gathered in larger numbers at some fairs than at others : the October fair of Ballinasloe, the Puck fair of Killorglin, and the Monaghan Day fair at Mohill were popular with them, but there were many others, especially the horse fairs of Kilrush, Caher Mee, Tinehely, Spancel Hill, Birr and Banagher.

At the fair of Kilkenny the travellers followed a special routine. They assembled along the Callan Road a few days before the fair and then on the morning of the fair they moved to a place called 'the Closh' outside the walls of the fair green proper. There they sold their donkeys and ponies and they did not pay any tolls. In a sense they used 'the Closh' as a private fair.

It was not difficult to recognise them. Normally they were in shabby clothes, but often they might wear something colourful, such as a bright pullover, a neck cloth, or pieces of jewellery, and their hair was often well bleached by the weather. Sometimes they wore old riding breeches or jodphurs and the women continued to wear shawls long after most women had ceased to wear them. Usually they had a swaggering devil-may-care look about them, which distinguished them from the 'settled' people.

As the day of the fair approached they appeared from nowhere, as though by magic, at their traditional camping sites convenient to the town, with a collection of flat spring carts and barrel-topped caravans. Round topped canvas tents were set up, fires were lit, and clothes were washed and spread on the bushes to dry. They assembled in family groups, each with a number of animals – a batch of donkeys, a horse or two, greyhounds, terriers, a few cats and often a nanny-goat to provide milk. The family consisted of husband, wife and a number of children, as well as a grandparent or two. The sight of such an assembly was greatly admired by foreign tourists, who looked upon it as a return to 'the simple life'. They found it all quite romantic and loved to take photographs of the encampment. Little did they know about it.

Among the travelling people some family names are more common than others. In County Kerry many of the travellers are Coffeys, and O'Driscolls are found in west Cork. In south Leinster there are Cashes, Connors, Delaneys and Mahers. In Connacht the Wards and Furies are most numerous in County Galway and the Maughans in County Mayo. In the area of Sligo, Leitrim and north Roscommon are the MacDonoughs and Cawleys. The most notable of the northern families are the MacGinleys, the Heaneys and the Bonars. In the midlands there are Dorans, Purcells, Cunninghams, Hanafins, Hutchinsons and Hoares. In County Clare there are Shoeys (Joyces), Donohues and MacInerneys. These are all well recognised Irish names and are not exclusive to the travellers.

It must be recognised that the travelling people are not tramps. They were not, and are not, parasites, and they have always done useful work and contributed their fair share to the welfare of the community. They were simply people whose way of life was such that they were forced to travel for at least part of the year in order to earn a living. In some cases they left the road during the worst months of the year and lived in common lodging houses in towns. Some travelling families spent the winter in Granard in County Longford, but fifty years ago most Irish towns had common lodging houses where journeymen tradesmen, tailors, stone-masons, bakers and others stayed, as well as the travelling people.

In any study of the travellers it is necessary to learn what they say about themselves. They are likely to tell you that their ancestors have always travelled and they have always been a secret people. They might add that when St Patrick escaped from slavery in County Antrim he took refuge with the travelling people who guided him safely to the place where he got a ship for his home. It is not considered polite to refer to them as 'tinkers' and they are certainly not gypsies. When, for any reason, one of them appears in the district court he is usually described as 'an itinerant horse dealer and tinsmith', but they always speak of themselves as 'travellers' or 'the travelling people'.

During the late nineteenth century and until it was superseded by plastics, tinned sheeting was cheap and tended to replace utensils made of wood or heavy earthenware. Working in tin and other light metals, the travellers made up and sold the tinware as they travelled. This was a very useful trade and during the earlier years of this century a very profitable one. A well known tinsmith whom I remember as a child, Martin MacDonagh, told me when I last spoke to him in 1973 that in

1914 a box of tin cost £5, and when he had made it into tin cans etc. it could be sold for £20. Martin explained that it was his wife who sold the finished articles, and spoke of the fine wife she had been to him. The tin was made into cans of different sizes, basins, milk strainers, potato graters, hand lanterns in which a candle could be carried, porringers, flat pans to hold milk, billy-cans and lids for clay pipes, all looking silver bright and shining when new. Workers in metal have always been honoured in Ireland, and the many examples of their work which have survived the centuries show that they were splendid craftsmen. Joyce, writing about his youth in County Limerick about 1870, described how he had seen a tinker repair a hole in a cast iron pot. He made a crucible of clay and using anthracite or wood charcoal and a bellows he melted the cast iron in the crucible. Then using a clay mould around the pot he poured the white hot metal into the hole and repaired it neatly.

Some of them were very skilful and made such things as fish hooks, minnows and trawling spoons. I remember Martin MacDonagh explaining to me that great care was necessary to make sure that the fins of the minnow or spoon fitted exactly so that it would spin smoothly when moving through the water. Martin was also proud of his skill in fixing things such as an old pan scales or one of the wall clocks which were seen in many houses, but he would undertake most types of light metalwork.

Livestock

In addition to working as tinsmiths, many of the travellers were dealers in horses and donkeys. Until about 1950 thousands of donkeys were kept on Irish farms. They were usually bought from the travelling people who had bought them in the west of Ireland, where they had been bred. Some of the families, the Shoeys, MacInerneys and Donohues in County Clare, had organised this business and they are credited with having bred the first piebald donkey. County Meath was a very good place to sell a donkey, as they were kept by many farm labourers for bringing home firewood or moving farmyard manure. They were surprisingly cheap. A foal could be bought for 5s. and a young ass for 10s. It must be realised that many Irish farmers were much too proud to breed or deal in donkeys, so the trade was left to the travellers.

Sometimes a smart young colt could be seen trotting alongside its mother, which was pulling the caravan. The colt was well bred and it was always hoped that it would make a good price at one of the big horse fairs. As I heard the owner of one such colt say many years ago, 'That colt is money in the bank'. In addition to the mare and foal, they usually had some other horses. Some were piebald circus type horses and one often hears the story of the owner who dyed the white spots before selling such a horse to 'a bloodstock agent'. Depending on the market, they might have a number of old worn out horses which were sold to the knackers.

Some of the travellers were expert horse dealers and could make an old lame horse appear to be sound. This, of course, was only a temporary 'cure' and when the buyer discovered that he had been duped he could always find another dealer to buy the horse and have the expert again make him ready for the next fair day.

Most of the travelling people kept a goat or two, as well as a number of greyhounds or terriers. The greyhounds might be sold and tried on the race track or they might be kept to catch rabbits or hares for food, though, as Martin MacDonagh expressed it, 'You might get into trouble with the law for killing a hare'. Martin assured me that he was always careful to pull the scut out of the dead hare and make a cut in its ear, to prevent hare lip in the unborn child if he happened to meet a pregnant woman. All the travelling people agree that it is wrong to take life. Martin MacDonagh assured me that in all his eighty years he had never killed a chicken or drowned pups. Except when it is necessary to kill fish or rabbits for food, they will not do it, and they would never kill the oldest and most worn out of their animals. I have never known any of the travelling people to own cattle – they might be accused of stealing them and they had no way of feeding them. Also, they never bought or sold second-hand clothes, as they had no efficient way of keeping the clothes clean and dry. It was also recognised that they never made poitín, though some of them made the pot and worm used by the distillers. When I asked why they did not do this, it was explained that it would not be possible to make poitín at a roadside camp; everybody would know about it.

Social Life

Among the travellers marriage customs were very strict, and early marriages were encouraged in order to keep the family group together. If a young lad wished to get married he would go and discuss it with the head of his family group as well as with his parents. He was expected to give the details of the girl's pedigree so that the head of the group could know if the couple were close blood relatives. If they were too closely related he might advise that the marriage should not take place, and normally his advice was accepted by all the parties concerned. One sometimes hears stories about temporary marriages among the travellers. That is all nonsense. They were, and always have been, married by a priest; though as Martin MacDonagh said, 'There was blackguards among the travellers the same as everywhere else'. One also hears stories about the couple 'jumping the budget'. The budget was the sack in which the tinker carried his tools. The couple who were to be married jumped over it as part of the ceremony. This is imaginary – though it reads well in a novel. Usually there was one priest in the neighbourhood whom they knew well and who married them. My friend the late Canon John O'Reilly of Ballinamore often told me of the marriages which he witnessed among the travelling people.

Transport

Until about fifty years ago the travellers moved with a light spring cart on which they carried all their property, the tools of the trade and the materials to set up the tents where many of them slept. Later they acquired a type of four-wheeled caravan with a light canvas cover, fitted with a stove and with bunks for sleeping and for storage. One used to hear that this caravan had been copied from that kept by the gypsies in England but this may not be correct. The caravan used by the English gypsies is built square and of timber and is much heavier than the Irish one. My friend Sean Maher tells me that the Irish caravan is really a development of the round topped, barrel shaped tent built on the flat cart instead of on the ground. The rods which supported the canvas cover were fitted into holes in the bottom of the flat cart and the canvas spread on top of them. The caravan was completed when it was fitted with a second pair of wheels.

The caravan travelled at a walking pace, usually not more than ten miles a day and less on hilly roads. On the other hand the flat spring cart with a smart horse could travel over thirty miles a day, driven by an expert. I remember my father saying as he watched a young traveller go trotting past on his flat cart, 'The only people now who know how to trot a horse are the tinkers. Did you notice that he had the breaching loose and how he kept the horse in a steady trot? That way it will not do any damage to the harness or to the car. If he let the horse gallop he would surely break something.' At the time I did not understand much of what he said but I have often thought about it since. The flat car was used to carry such things as scrap metal, rolls of linoleum, feather ticks, mattresses, or whatever else its owner might be buying, selling or exchanging. Nowadays the caravans can be seen fitted with rubber tyres and being driven along Irish roads by tourists rather than by the travelling people, who have now equipped themselves with caravans drawn by motor cars and fitted with such things as bottled gas and television. They can often be seen running roadside markets where they sell radios, records, tapes, umbrellas and so on.

The quality which has enabled the travelling people to survive, and in some cases to flourish, was their versatility. Although, as I have said, they were officially described as 'itinerant horse dealers and tinsmiths', these were only part of their many ways of making a living. Some collected scrap metal and in this way gathered up a lot of rubbish which nobody wanted. Nowadays the shells of old motor cars look very ugly near their camps. If the scrap could not be sold at a profit they might collect old feather ticks which they exchanged for cheap fibre mattresses. In some cases they carried rolls of linoleum and wallpaper, which would appeal to the women of the house and might be exchanged for an old clock or a table lamp or for eggs or chickens. I remember some years ago near Longford town seeing a family of travellers who had a large collection of tall oil lamps made of different coloured glass. The family was busy cleaning, shining and restoring the lamps, which would fetch good prices as antiques.

In such a society different talents were identified and carefully developed. Those who were skilful buyers and sellers were encouraged to buy and sell. Those who had no such gifts could learn to gather and prepare ash plants and halters, which were sold at the fairs. Some of them could spend a profitable day selling copies of *Old Moore's Almanack*. At a fair they might earn money as drovers or by helping a more prosperous horse dealer. Then there was work to be done around the camp. Harness had to be repaired, or caravans had to be painted. Some of the women and the children were expert beggars, but the men never begged.

Music

Any special talent for music was quickly recognised and fostered carefully, and some of the travellers became well known. According to one story, Margaret Barry began her singing career as a street singer at the fair of Longford. Another family whose members have gained considerable distinction are the Furey Brothers. Their musical talent was developed by their grandfather, Charley Furey, and by their father,

Ted, who were both well-known musicians in County Galway and
County Clare. Another famous street singer was Joe O'Reilly ('Joe the
Barber') from Galway. Some people who have heard him say he was
the greatest street ballad singer in Ireland. Another famous street singer
was Joe Gaffney. Then there were three brothers called Doran. They
all had some sight defect, by they were all very able musicians.

The strangest of all these entertainers was 'Delaney the Puppet Man'
of whom I heard at the fair of Kilkenny. At the end of his visit to Ireland
in 1842, Thackeray saw a puppet show in Dublin. He was surprised
to see it and wrote, in his *Irish Sketch Book*:

> One night I paid two pence to see a puppet – such an entertainment
> as may have been popular a hundred and thirty years ago and is
> described in the *Spectator*. But the company here assembled were
> not it scarcely need be said of the Genteel sort. There were a score
> of boys however and a dozen of labouring men who were quite
> happy and contented with the piece performed and loudly
> applauded.

In some cases if one of the travellers showed special skill and talent
for it he might equip himself with a board and play the three card trick
at fairs, race meetings or such places. If he were very skilful he might
do a bit of thimble-rigging or catch a few dupes by playing trick o' the
loop.

Some of those whose names I never knew were good ballad singers,
and in addition they sold copies of the ballads. The singer usually
carried a sheaf of ballads in his hand and added to his earnings by
selling copies of them. Normally the singer could not read, so in order
to distinguish between the different ballads a suitable drawing was
printed on the sheet, for example a ship or a soldier or a horse, indicating
the subject of the song.

When I was a boy, 'bad' half-crowns were not unusual. Some of
these may have been made by the tinkers – so people said – and when
I asked Martin MacDonagh about it he answered, 'Of course I could
make money but nobody would be bothered making the kind of money
that is going now.' However, he went on to describe the method of
making such coins, which might be made of lead. The problem with
this was that the lead coins had to be silvered and there was no jingle
in them. They were best made of solder which could be got from an
old creamery can. When the can was heated over the fire the solder
would melt and drip into a pot or basin. 'If you did the job properly
you would get seven pounds of solder out of a big can.' The cake of

solder was then remelted and cleaned.

Next a plaster of Paris mould was made of one side of the coin and then of the other. The most difficult part of the process was to fit the two moulds together using a match stuck in the plaster to hold them together. The melted solder was then poured in through a tiny hole and left to cool and become solid.

I do not know how often such counterfeit coins were made by the travelling people, but they were experts at one trick which always caused great amusement when it was reported in the local newspaper. The traveller would call to the house of a well-off but notoriously mean farmer. The caller produced two freshly minted half-crowns and having explained that he had just made them, offered to sell the two for one worn half-crown. The cupidity of the farmer was aroused and he enquired how the coins were made. 'Solder and silver,' the tinker explained, 'but these are all I had the stuff to make.' He then went on to explain that for £10 he could buy enough material to make £50 worth of half-crowns. After more of such chat the farmer might be persuaded to hand over £10 in return for a promise of 200 new half-crowns.

Naturally that was the last he saw of his money, and when he realised that he had been tricked he made a complaint to the police. The travelling man was arrested and charged at the local court and in his defence told the story exactly as it happened and added that the two coins which he showed to the farmer were not counterfeit. The travelling man had never done any counterfeiting and would not do it even if he knew how it might be done. The case usually ended with a trivial sentence on the traveller, a lecture for the greedy farmer and a great laugh for all the readers of the local newspaper.

The fairs have now passed into history and the traditional way of life of the travelling people is coming to an end. Tin ware has long been replaced by plastics, there are few horses on Irish farms and fewer donkeys. The travellers continue gathering up scrap and running road-side markets, but gradually they are being persuaded to settle down so that their children get a chance to go to school and equip themselves for a new and more complex society. There is no reason to regret this. The lives of the travelling people were hard, with a short life expectancy, and they suffered all the disadvantages of an isolated minority. True, they often left their camp sites dirty and untidy and sometimes they got into trouble with the law for petty crimes like fighting and drunkenness, but the more one knows about them the more they are seen to resemble the rest of the ordinary Irish people.

13
Hiring Fairs

TODAY the idea of holding a hiring fair would seem quite archaic. Some people would no doubt think of it as a sort of slave market, but this is to misunderstand it. Like so many Irish fair customs, the hiring fair may be derived from an act of the English parliament passed during the reign of Edward III. This act, called the Statute of Labourers, declared that magistrates must fix the wages of farm labourers and the rates must then be made know to all those concerned. This was done at what were called Statute Sessions, held about 1 May or in the autumn. When the employers and the workers of the district assembled to learn what the fixed rates were, they met and made their agreements, and so the hiring fairs began. In England they were also known as Statute Fairs or Mop Fairs.

There is a very full description by Malachy Horan of what he called a Hirage fair in Tallaght, County Dublin, during the second half of the nineteenth century. He said:

> You know the old forge facing up the Tallaght street. It was there that up to fifty years ago (1880) they held the Hirage Fair. . . . It would be held a few days before 15 August. The men would come in from as far as Baltinglass. Some would be hired on the road before they reached the forge. The leaving of them would gather themselves about the forge. Each man would stick his pipe in the band of his hat, as a badge that he was free for service. When he was hired he would put it in his pocket. . . . Every man of them would be wearing his whetstone in a pouch on his left, and often enough a high crowned rush hat on his head. They were a great breed of men and civil spoken. Some could reap an acre a day. I could myself one time, aye. The street would be full, what with farmers looking for help and men anxious for work. And when all was over there would be laughing and talking and a bit of a dance or the wrestling. The ballad singer would be doing a great trade, nor were the fiddlers idle.

The custom of moving the pipe from the hat band to the pocket when a man had been hired is also reported from the hirage fair in Bandon,

County Cork in 1849.

Tallaght was an obvious place where farmers from the rich lands of County Dublin would hire men from County Wicklow to harvest their crops at a time before harvesting became mechanised. Similarly, hiring fairs were often held in places convenient to areas where farming was intensive and extra workers were needed at certain times of the year for harvesting flax or corn or for digging potatoes. The fair should also be in a place where labour was available.

One such place was Swanlinbar in West Cavan. To the west was a rough area of poor land where many farm labourers might be willing to work on the better land around Lough Erne in County Fermanagh. In this case the hiring fair was held on 29 June and when I visited it in the year 1936 it was an ordinary small summer fair. There was an unusually large number of youngish men dressed in blue serge suits, brown boots and tweed caps – the standard dress of the time. My brother was able to count more than a hundred of them, so he said, while the angelus bell rang at midday. There were plenty of girls at the fair but I don't think they were seeking employment. There were many farmers there from around Lough Erne, distinguishable by dress and accent, and many of them 'looking like Protestants' as we used to say.

As I moved along the street of the little town I saw a number of bargains being made between employers and workers, but to me it bore no resemblance to a slave market. Later there was loud talk and singing to be heard coming from the various public houses. I do not remember seeing any of the men carrying a bundle or any sign of his trade, though most of them carried a traditional ash plant. In those days the wages would have been about £2 a month or a little more. Once as a child I heard an old man tell about his life as a farm labourer before the 1914-18 war: 'I got £4 for my six months work and I only got mate twice in the half year.'

These fairs were held in most parts of Ireland, but outside Ulster the memory of them is fading. I have heard of them at Athenry, in Rathcormack and in Tullow, but could not learn any details. In New Ross it was the custom for those wishing to be hired to assemble at 'the Long Stone'. This was known as the Hiring Fair of Irishtown.

In Scotland there is a reference to what was called a 'feeing' market held as part of the Glasgow Fair. This was held at the foot of Stockwell Street and this is how it was described by a respectable citizen of Glasgow:

While this locality however forty or fifty years ago, was characterised during the greater part of the year by quietness and respectability, it cannot be denied that on Whitsun Monday in particular it was occasionally the scene of tumult and riot. On that evening all the loose, bad and elder blackguardism of the town were attracted thither to play tricks on what were designated the country 'jocks and jennies' who had assembled during the day for country hire. Frequently on such occasions have we ourselves seen the mob take possession of the street and particularly of the avenue leading to the bridge and thereafter put to rout both magistracy and police: while every man with a decent coat or a good hat was certain of being assaulted with a dead cat or some equally filthy missile.

I have not heard of any such troubles associated with Irish hiring fairs, though no doubt there was singing and drinking in the evening before the labourers set off for what was often a half year of hard, dull work.

Many hiring fairs were held on 12 May (Old May Day) and 12 November (Old Hallentide Day). These were popular fair days and fairs were often large at these times when huge numbers of cattle were for sale. Early in the nineteenth century the wages paid to labourers varied from two to four guineas for the half year and a century later they had risen to thirty shillings a month. In the Ordnance Survey letters in the Royal Irish Academy there is an interesting reference to the hiring fairs which were held in Antrim town in the year 1835. It says:

There are three annual fairs held in Antrim namely on 1 January, 12 May and 12 November. In the January fair from 80 to 100 horses of a middling description suited for small farmers and averaging not more than £10 each in value are exposed for sale.

About 150 cows and from 300 to 400 pigs are usually exposed at this fair. The other commodities exposed for sale are peddlar's goods exposed on numerous stalls arranged along the sides of the street. Old clothes, huxters' commodities such as cakes, apples, etc. Similarly exposed – a few stands with woollen stockings, shoes, tin ware, ironmongery and three or four cars of brown crockery ware from the neighbourhood of Bellaghy in the county of Derry. The other fairs in May and November are more for the purpose of hiring servants and for amusement than for business.

The number of cattle exposed in them are nearly alike – about 150 to 160 cows and from 200 to 300 pigs but no horses are exposed in them. These with the articles mentioned in the January Fair, but in much larger quantities, constitute about all the commodities for sale.

There are neither tolls nor customs demanded. These having many years ago been abolished by the Masserene family – the proprietors, from a wish to encourage farmers to come to the fair there. A curious custom is practised at the May and November fairs – namely that servants coming to them to be hired – and both Farmers and servants many of them residing eight miles off come (for) this express purpose. It matters not if the servant intends continuing with his former master he comes to the fair where his master engages him by giving him a shilling – the male servants carry a rod – the women make no sign of any kind.

The numbers who attend the May and November fairs are very great – particularly in the former and as they are chiefly for amusement, they present towards evening disgraceful scenes of drunkenness and brawling.

As the half year from May to November was the busy time on the land most labourers were hired at the May fairs and few at the November ones. These fairs were held in each of the Ulster counties and in most cases they were held in places between an area of poor rough land from where the labourers came and an area of good farming land where their labour was needed. Strabane, Newry, Enniskillen and Ballycastle illustrate this.

Many people who have read the description of the hiring fair of Strabane in Patrick MacGill's novel *Children of the Dead End* would certainly think that a hiring fair was like a slave market. There are, however, some other things which should be mentioned. Anyone who knows rural Ireland will be aware of the great social distinction between the family which owns a farm, however small or poor, and the family which has no land. To an outsider the farmer seemed no better dressed or fed, but these were matters of no importance among Irish small farmers. As well as his lack of land, the farm labourer suffered from some further social disadvantages. In moving from his home on high poor land to an area where the land was better and more intensively cultivated, he was moving from a district where Irish was the vernacular, and he might not speak very fluent English. He might also move from a Catholic area to a place where Protestantism was predominant. It is not surprising therefore that some of them should be discontented and unhappy and wish to return home to the ways of life with which they were familiar. From the point of view of the farmer, the labourer had the marks of inferiority, poverty and landlessness. This social distinction was not confined to Ulster and the low status of the Connemara farm labourer, the *spalpín,* is well known.

In an article in *Ulster Folk Life* Jonathan Bell suggests that hiring fairs became necessary when many cottagers were cleared off the land during the Napoleonic wars and it then became necessary to employ labourers from outside. Bell also says that it was generally the smaller farmers who hired the labourers, as on the larger farms there were labourers available at all seasons. He also mentions the practice of two farmers hiring one labourer between them – each had his services for three days in each week. There was also the possibility that the labourer as he worked would acquire some new skills and then he might set off to work in Scotland.

Some hiring fairs had special names. A usual name was the 'Rabble Fair' and Bell said that the hiring fair in Limavady was called 'the Gallop'. In Newry it was called the 'Loosing Fair' and I have heard it called the 'Mop Fair'.

No doubt the life of a farm labourer was hard and his diet and living conditions were often poor. It must be remembered that everybody living on a small farm 'wrought hard' and lived lives which would now be thought very rough and uncomfortable. Even if the hired labourer was treated like one of the family, life was still hard. There are two ballads which refer to the life of these men, one called *The Hiring Fairs of Ulster:*

The Farmer like a noble squire
Will come there servants for to hire
And ask them what they do require
With board and entertainment.
They'll feed you well with bread and tay
If you comply to work sincere
Your dinner will have no delay
Of butter and spuds and bacon.

The other ballad, *The Galbally Farmer,* tells a different story:

I well recollect it was Michaelmas night
To a hearty good supper he did me invite
A cup of sour milk that would physic a snipe
'Twould give you the trotting disorder.
The wet old potatoes would poison the cats
The barn where my bed was, was swarming with rats,
'Twas little I thought it would e'er be my lot
To lie in that hole until morning.

No doubt conditions varied on different farms but my own relatives spoke of this life with pleasure as they looked back on it.

The public scales, Moate, Co. Westmeath

14

Ballad Singing, Gambling and Dancing

BALLAD singing was almost as much part of the fair as was the livestock. It will be noticed that when people speak of the fairs which they attended as children they will almost always recall the ballad singers and their songs. The great time for ballad singing was the nineteenth century and most of the ballads found in different collections were written then, though some can be dated to the eighteenth century and some even to the seventeenth. The tradition continues on into the present century, and I recall hearing a ballad about Sean MacEoin sung at the fair of Longford in 1921.

A good ballad singer might travel considerable distances from fair to fair and make a living by his skill. Some of them belonged to the travelling people, but there were others who gave up a settled life and took to the road as singers. At a time when not everybody could read and people made their own music the ballad singer was a welcome guest in most places. There was always an extra drink for the singer at weddings and such places, and it was important to have a new song for these occasions.

That was most important for a ballad singer at a fair. His listeners were interested in his music, but they were even more interested in the words of his song, which told a story. They treated of all subjects: love songs and laments were popular, but they were often mawkish, and the best ballads were humorous, satirical and of course political. When the buying and selling were finished the ballad singer would appear with a sheaf of ballads in his hand. These were turned out by the local printer and copies were sold to the listeners. The singer placed his hat on the ground beside him and when the song was finished he took it around among the crowd before moving to some other part of the town. In selling the ballads the straw technique was used. In this case the singer would call out: 'Here, buy a straw from me and I'll give you a ballad for nothing,' and he would hold out a fistful of straws. I have been assured that this was not unusual at fairs in County Leitrim before the 1914-18 war.

Sometimes the ballad singers were women, though there were not many of them. Once I remember a man and a woman singing an anti-recruiting dialogue song. Here is a fragment of it:

> Come listen to my story, Molly Ban,
> I'm bound for death or glory, Molly Ban,
> For I've listed in the Army
> Where your eyes no more can harm me
> For they kill me while they charm me, Molly Ban.
>
> Ach, Brian, you've been drinking now you rogue
> And surely you are joking, Brian Oge
> For you ne'er would be the villain
> For to take the Saxon shilling
> And to do their dirty killing, Brian Oge.

And so it went on. This was a very popular ballad in its time and it is easy to see why enthusiastic supporters of the recruiting campaign at the time would think it treasonable. That was one of the difficulties experienced by ballad singers during the nineteenth century. Maura Murphy has examined the police reports during the greater part of that time and discovered many such complaints from magistrates, policemen and other such establishment figures, often with copies of the treasonable ballads enclosed. Despite the complaints, the authorities in Dublin Castle were reluctant to prosecute either the singers or the printers of the ballads. They knew well that such a prosecution might lead to further and more serious trouble. During the second half of the nineteenth century the song book appeared. This was much better value than the single sheet and the books were sold by the ballad singers as well as in some shops.

There was a famous Tipperary ballad called *The Peeler and the Goat*, a satire on the Royal Irish Constabulary which nearly drove some of the police insane with rage. It begins:

> A Bansha peeler out one night
> On duty and patrolling O
> He met a goat upon the road
> And took him for a stroller O

The policeman proceeds to question the goat, asking him to explain why:

You're absent from your dwelling place
Disorderly and idle O

Then the ballad continues:

'Excuse me sir,' the goat replied
And let me tell my story O
I am no rogue, no ribbonman,
No Croppy, Whig or Tory O
But I'm a goat that's fond of sport
And this is the rambling saison O

This satire was so effective that there were occasions when people were charged in court with insulting the police by whistling the tune, although I do not know if anyone was ever convicted.

Most of the ballads were just doggerel, and the more serious the subject the less effective they were. This next is a verse from a County Leitrim ballad of the Land War. It was written about 1890 and is called *The Emergency Men's Jennett*, describing the activities of people who took farms from which the tenants had been evicted:

These hireling paupers from poorhouses came,
Deformed by nature, both crooked and lame.
The Land Bill will give them a great overthrow,
In grief back again to workhouses they'll go.

There was a fine ballad written in County Cavan about the passing of the Reform Bill in 1832. Of course Dan O'Connell was given all the credit for it:

And on the first banner was brave Irish Dan,
The man for the people the great Liberator.
The Orange oppressor and Emancipator,
Our Daniel, they called him the great Agitator
Because he obtained the Reform.

In County Cavan in those days there was serious rivalry between Protestants and Catholics and the ballad went on to refer to Protestant as:

These beef-eating saints with their brogues and new bonnets
Make woeful complaints and what shall become of us.
Our Church it will fall and Lord Farnham look on us
Since Daniel obtained the Reform.

It is not difficult to see why 'law-abiding' and 'respectable' citizens might take exception to this ballad especially when it went on to refer to Lord Farnham as:

Lame Orange Maxwell
His blood it ran muddy.

A less controversial ballad deals with the successes of the famous greyhound bitch called Lady Harkaway, owned by Fr Tom Maguire. This is the last verse:

A rich lord from Liverpool presumptiously did say,
For £1,000 I'll run my dog against Lady Harkaway
So she hurled her defiance throughout the world wide.
Gamesters of all nations game dogs for to provide,
If they come with loaded purses, if they dare to persevere
We'll teach them all a lesson on the Curragh of Kildare.
So we'll sing her praise in future days
All around the Shamrock shore
Since Lady bravely brought the sway
To the town of Ballinamore.

Ballad singing at fairs gradually died out during the years before the Second World War. This was due partly to the increasing circulation of newspapers, but probably more so to the popularity of radio. Nowadays ballads are still popular but much of the singing is done in public houses or comes from the radio or the television. Many ballads are also available on record and tape, and today a ballad which tells a good story and tells it well can spread almost overnight literally to the ends of the earth.

Ballad singing was popular in every part of Ireland, and while the ballads have little value as literature they have some considerable value as records of our society. They are therefore well worth preserving as the material of local history.

There were some other musicians who might perform at fairs as well as singers. These included pipers and fiddle players who played for the dancers and might also make music for the crowd at the fair, but none of them were ever so popular as the ballad singer.

Gambling

I must confess that I have never felt tempted to play with such people as the three card trick man or the trick o' the loop man, though I have spent time watching others do so. My modest stake of a penny on the black at the roulette table almost always and very quickly resulted in my losing the few pence I had. Perhaps in this way I was innoculated against gambling for the rest of my life, but in addition my father used three thimbles and a dried pea to demonstrate how the thimble-rigger would win or lose by holding the pea under his thumb nail or in the palm of his hand. My father also took the trouble to demonstrate the art of the trick o' the loop man using a firm tape measure. The ends of the tape were held together to form a loop and then it was rolled up tight. The gambler tried to put a nail or some such point into the correct loop and stood to win three half-crowns to one if he succeeded, but unfortunately for him this depended on the way the trick o' the loop man unrolled the tape.

Thackeray saw a thimble-rigger at work in Killarney and, as one might expect, he did not approve of such dishonesty. He wrote:

A ragged scoundrel – the image of Hogarth's Bad Apprentice – went bustling and shouting through the crowd with his dirty tray and thimble and as soon as he had taken his post stated that this was the 'royal game of thimble' and called upon 'gentlemen' to come forward. And then a ragged fellow would be seen to approach with as innocent an air as he could assume and the bystanders might remark that the second ragged fellow almost always won. Nay he was so benevolent in many instances as to point out the various people who had a mind to bet under which thimble the pea actually was. Meanwhile the first fellow was sure to be looking away and talking to someone in the crowd: but somehow it generally happened – and how of course I cannot tell – that any man who listened to the advice of rascal number two lost his money. I believe it is so even in England.

On the following morning, Sunday, the races were over and the thousands who had crowded to the race seemed trooping to the chapels, and the streets were blue with cloaks. Walking into prayers and without his board came my young friend of the thimble rig and presently after sauntered in the fellow with the long coat who had played at cards for sovereigns. I should like to hear the confessions of himself and his friend the next time they communicate with his reverence.

The three card trick man was often to be seen at fairs. He had a little table and three playing cards, one of them a queen. The game was to select the queen from the other two as they lay face down on the table. 'Here, ladies and gentlemen', he would call, 'Find the lady.' Then as he dexterously moved the cards back and forth he continued the patter: 'Now you see her, now you don't. The quickness of the hand deceives the eye. Just watch carefully, it is all very simple.'

When he had finished moving the cards he stood back and faced the crowd, encouraging them to find the lady. The betting was three half-crowns to one and there were many gamblers ready to try. When someone succeeded in finding the queen the three card trick man paid out with a great clinking and showing of half-crowns.

If business was slow a stranger might appear and, as the three card man was turned away, he would pick up a card, see that it was not the queen, and fold a corner. When the gambler resumed his patter there was a rush to find the queen because the odds were now 2:1. Even with the odds shortened, however, few people succeeded in 'finding the lady' as the three card trick man urged them.

As I think of it now I find it difficult to believe that people could always be found who allowed themselves to be cheated. Once I saw a man at a fair who was selling money. This was not unusual because it is also mentioned by P. J. MacGill in his description of *The Parish of Ardara* in Donegal. He would take a strong brown paper bag and show that it was empty. Then he would take a fistful of half-crowns and put them one by one into the paper bag and as he did so the crowd would hear the coins jingling as he shook the bag. Then he took his big gold watch and chain and dropped them into the bag. Then he closed it, held it up, and usually found people willing to give him a pound for the bag and its contents. The person who bought it never opened it there and then. He disappeared with his treasure and did not return when he found a useless watch and a fistful of coppers in the bag.

Once a man came selling rings, watch chains, tie pins and brooches which he assured the hearers were made of 'pure Kentucky gold.' They were fresh, new, bright and shiny and one lad who bought a ring said, 'They were lovely, you would swear they were pure gold'. The same man sold 'self-filling fountain pens' in boxes on which the price was marked 30s. or £2. He explained that they were surplus stock and he would sell them at 5s. each. During the week after the fair a number of these pens would appear at our school but I never knew one of them to last more than a day.

Dancing

Dancing has long been very popular in Ireland, though the two words *damhsa* and *rince* are loan words, one from French and the other from English. It is likely that the Normans introduced the dancing of round dances and there is a reference to girls and women who went to dance in St Maula's church and in Kilkenny during the fourteenth century.

There are many references to dancing here during the seventeenth century.

In any case it is clear that during the eighteenth and nineteenth centuries dancing was a very popular pastime all over the country and was a feature of many Irish fairs. Malachy Horan mentions the dancing at Rathfarnham Fair:

> There were all kinds of sideshows in the streets. We would have trick-o'-the-loop men, wrestlers, strong men, pipers, ballad singers and the rest. But the cream of the milk was the dancing. Lads, the best dancers in Ireland, would not fail to attend. Every inn in the town would have a floor in its yard. The best of them were in the Yellow House, Connor's and Curtis's. There were all kinds of musicians but blind Kitty Shea and her daughter were as good as the best. They did well enough out of it, too, for the music was auctioned there the same as here in Killinarden. We would be selling all day and dancing all night. Them were the days.

The popularity of dancing was due mainly to the work of the dancing masters who travelled from place to place and taught the children to dance. Arthur Young, who travelled widely in Ireland between the years 1776 and 1779, mentions this in *A Tour in Ireland* and says that the dancing master usually travelled with a piper and a fiddler who provided the music. The dancing master was treated with respect and dressed well, and besides teaching his pupils to dance he taught deportment. He was a welcome visitor to the village because his presence meant a few weeks of music and dancing. In addition, he sometimes taught fencing – not with swords but with sticks, and this no doubt is how some of the best stick fighters acquired their skill.

The fees paid to the dancing master varied. Just before the Famine it was 5s. a quarter, with another 5s. to the musicians. Certainly the dancing masters taught well, and the tradition which they established lived on. The ability to dance set dances, jigs, reels or hornpipes has continued until the present day. It will also be realised that dancing was almost always part of the fun at any other outdoor festival, such as midsummer or Lughnasa. Fenton described one such dancing competition at the pattern of St Crochan on 30 July. The best dancers usually came from Caherdaniel and Sneem, where every kitchen was fitted with a dancing flag brought specially from the quarries at Valentia, where the experts practised every night.

In *It All Happened*, Fenton also describes a dancing competition at the fair of Sneem in south-west Kerry when he went there as a boy in the year 1885:

On the square of the town a number of large wooden doors were laid out side by side on which the dancing competition was held. It was the last time that Morty O'Moriarty adjudicated. He called out the names of the parishes and competitors specifying the order of the dances. On his maximum of 100 'tips' (marks) we were surprised to hear the large number who were marked high up in the nineties. The final decision was accepted without a murmur of complaint, a tribute to the honesty and efficiency of the Glenbeigh dancing master. The cheers and shouts for the victors worked echoes in the amphitheatre of the surrounding mountains. Morty worked from a dozen outposts in soth-west Kerry of which Caherdaniel was one. Those who were competent to judge said he had no equal as a teacher. He chalked the kitchen floors in oblongs and taught the most difficult traditional dances. Part of his duty on Sundays was to determine and mark off the parish champions and on fair days and pattern days to pronounce among inter-parish competitors. A very respectable wanderer, Morty was the last to train the youths to a regulated and rhythmic movement of feet and body.

MacGill, in an excellent description of the fair of Magheramore, mentions the dancing competitions which were part of it. On one famous occasion the championship of the fair was won by the son of the local landlord, 'Young Nesbitt of Woodhill', and the daughter of a tinker from Inis Caoil.

The patron fair of Muff in County Cavan was an important horse fair when farmers from County Monaghan came to buy. My friend Benny MacAdam told me how all the young lads and lasses would hurry off to the fair where there were platforms erected for dancing. Once when the weather was wet a tent was put up to protect the dancers.

I do not remember that there was much dancing at fairs in my youth – at such times I was much too busy – but I do recall one famous local performer, Willie Wrynn, known as Willie the Dancer. It may have been about the year 1924 when I heard music and cheering coming from the yard behind MacGovern's public house opposite the market yard. Inside I found that a door had been taken off its hinges and I pushed my way through the crowd and for the first time in my life saw Willie the Dancer. There were, as far as I can remember, about 200 people, mostly men, watching him and admiring his skill, and indeed he was a splendid dancer. I do not know how to describe Willie's dancing but indeed I am glad that once in my life I saw a real expert traditional Irish dancer.

As I try to recall that day I remember some of the crowd saying that Willie had won prizes in New York for his dancing when he danced on the stage there with 'bells on his dancing shoes'.

The market house, Mullingar, Co. Westmeath

15
Pedlary

IN THE *Statistical Survey of County Dublin* the fair of Lutrellstown was described as for 'horses and pedlary'. Ordinarily one thinks of the pedlar carrying his pack on his back as he travelled from place to place, but in some cases he might use a pack horse or some form of cart to carry his goods. This led to a great development of the business as roads became better and safer. Until the second quarter of the present century the efficient distance which the pedlars could travel and return in one day was about twenty miles, but the arrival of the internal combustion engine made it possible for them to travel to all parts of the country.

Over the past fifty years I have known some of these men and I have found them able and often interesting. If they were not skilful dealers they would not continue in the business. Perhaps the most interesting is Cyril Chapman, 'the bargain king', born in Christchurch Place in Dublin and reared in Glasgow and in the South of England. During the past sixty years Cyril has become familiar with such places as 'The Barrows' in Glasgow and 'The Flatiron' in Manchester as well as many famous markets in Britain, but most of his selling has been at Irish fairs and markets, from the Ould Lammas Fair of Ballycastle to the Puck Fair of Killorglin. At different times he has had stops in Castlebar and in Bundoran but he always preferred selling in the open air. Now officially retired and living in Ballymore Eustace, he travels to an occasional market 'to see what's doing'.

Mostly he sold tools and ropes to farmers, but like any dealing man he was always on the lookout for a bargain because 'if you can buy it right you can sell it right'.

His stories ranged from selling a statue of St Martin de Porres at an Orange walk in Rosnowlagh to a day in the District Court. Once at a fair a civic guard arrested the local petty thief who had stolen a few things which Cyril had laid out for sale. The case came to court, the prisoner was sentenced and when the court was finished for the day the district justice said to Cyril: 'Could that gadget really cut glass?'

Cyril got a piece of glass, showed how it was done and then went on to sell it to the justice.

He is a native speaker of the fairground slang which he tells me is rarely heard nowadays. I asked him to speak some of it and he produced this dialogue between Mike and Jack:

Mike: Hello Jack. How is it going?
Jack: Gammy enough. Done the duce all week. Not much denaro; stayed over in ——, gammy letty, clem doner and clem mujarai. Feather was tome, Bat was a lid and a half. What a doner, some nose ark. No Ben Maguire: went to graft. First to drop was the whid. Trace nicker for a bit of waxey. When I came out of his cain there was a shade piping the brief on the roller. I done a bit of wheezing and he crushed. I won't be getting any brief. The rozzer was OK.

Next stop was the lushing cain. The bunch was wide. I stalled and had a light and friskey, then wheezed about the geer. He batted a flim, then kicked and I had to bat for a croker. Some of the lush merchants in the cain were looking the geer over but no gelt.

I'm getting fed up with the knocker, but I suppose it's better than working. You can always touch for a bit of mugari on the knocker. The doner does a bit on the side with the clobber. The God Forbids got a few deener from some of the doners. That's one good thing about doing the knocker in the duce. I'm crushing now. Clem glimmers on the roller. Don't want my collar felt. By the way, had a bad dose of the flu. The croker gave me a bottle and batted me a flim. That's the graft.

Jack's speech may be translated:

Things are bad. I have been going through the country all week. Stayed in ——. Very bad lodgings, bad landlady and bad food. Bed was good. What a woman, no fire. Went to work. The first to buy was the priest. Three pounds for a square of lino. When I came out of his house there was a guard looking at the tax disc on the car. I did a lot of talking and he left. I won't be getting any summons. The policeman was OK.

First I went to the pub. The boss was in the know so I waited and had a whiskey. Then I talked about the lino. He bid me five pounds, then he baulked and bid me four pounds. Some of the customers looked at the lino but they had no money.

I am fed up with this selling but I suppose it's better than working. You can always touch for a bit of food in the country. The wife sells bits of drapery and the children can touch some of the women. That is one good thing about door-to-door selling in the country. I'm away now. There are bad lights on the van and I don't want the guards to arrest me. I had a bad dose of the flu. The doctor gave me a bottle and charged me five pounds. That is the job to be at.

Like an old time music hall comedian Cyril had a fine selection of wise cracks and smart answers for every occasion. When I asked him about this he stood up and gave a one man show of which Michael MacLiammoir would have been proud:

> This alarm clock was not made in Japan or Hong Kong by a guy called Hung One who had a brother who was hung too. A country where they sleep ten in a bed, ten under the bed and ten hanging on the hall stand waiting to go to work. Here is a scissors to cut the cost of living. This umbrella will give you the badge of respectability. You could walk into the bank and get an overdraft on the strength of it alone. When you go home with it tonight, be careful. Your dog won't know you.
>
> Sixteen yards of a rope, that would tether a goat, tie a boat or hold a woman's tongue. Here are five combs for a shilling – two dressing combs, two pocket combs and one Liverpool mousetrap [fine comb] that will kill ninety-nine out of the hundred and the one that gets away will be dead of fright before he is half way home.
>
> Here I'm selling stationery, a writing pad and two packets of envelopes with a biro thrown in. Do write and fear no man. Don't write and fear no woman. You could write to the mother-in-law and tell her you were sending her a turkey for Christmas but it got well. Talking about the mother-in-law. There's a woman, do you know, and I worship the very ground she's going into. She had two sons, one of them alive, the other in the civil service. She never puts up her hand to stop a bus, she sticks out her face. The last time she wrote she enclosed her photograph. It was taken with a high speed camera and caught her with her mouth shut.
>
> When I was serving my time in Clerys in the silk stocking department a blonde walked in. If she wasn't blonde she was fair enough. 'I want a pair of fully fashioned stockings,' she says. 'Tight at the toe, fully fashioned at the calf, tight and snug at the knee. Do you follow me?' 'Miss,' says I, 'I'm miles ahead of you.' 'I'll take six pairs, if you fit one for size,' she says. 'Miss,' I says, 'if I was caught fitting a pair of stockings on you I'd lose my job.' Well after I lost my job. . .

So it went on. When a lady examined a shopping bag and complained that it was too light he would say, 'Sure you could always put a few stones in it.' When he had handed out a few cheap biros he would then say, 'Listen, I was winking at you all to tell you to wait for the special pen. It will draw an unbroken line for ten miles. It is a pen that writes any colour you like.' A voice from the crowd might call out, 'Write green.' Cyril would grab a piece of paper and write the word 'green'. Then he would turn to the heckler and ask, 'Would you like any other colour?'

'Two months ago I sold one of these umbrellas to a farmer and he brought it back the next fair day. "It's no good," he said. "I took it with me to bring in the cows and I only hit them a couple of times when it broke."' When a lady complained that a neckline chain which she had bought turned green he replied, 'Were you expecting it to turn red, white and blue?'

When a heckler asked, 'Have you a dishwasher?' the answer was, 'Yes. I married one and you are welcome to her. The day we married I asked the priest how much I owed him. He took a look at the wife and said, "A pound will do." I handed him the pound and he took another look at her and handed me back 90p.'

Even after much more than fifty years and with his voice weak following the removal of half his larynx, Cyril was still a star performer. As he spoke he made the gesture of picking up the object he was selling. An umbrella was first hung on his left wrist and then taken in his right hand. I could almost see it as the patter went on. Then he laid down the umbrella and picked up an alarm clock and as he did so, mimed the winding of it as he held it up. Of all the dealers I have heard selling at fairs Cyril Chapman was undoubtedly the best. He was not only a shrewd and clever dealer but he was also a great actor. Even more important than these two essential qualities he enjoyed every minute of it.

The object of all dealing is to make money, and the market folk had their own words for it. A sixpence was a 'sprassey' and a shilling was a 'deener'. A 'duce of deeners' was two shillings, and a half-crown was a 'tusheroon'. Next there was a 'trace of deeners' (three shillings) and a 'croker of deeners' (four shillings). Five shillings was called an 'oxford' (scholar). A 'cow's calf' was ten shillings, and a pound was a 'licker' or a 'lid'. Five pounds was called a 'film' and ten pounds was a 'cock and a hen'.

Clearly most of these are derived from cockney rhyming slang but it would appear the words for the smaller sums are much older and are derived from the European languages.

Second-hand clothes

Many writers during the eighteenth and nineteenth centuries referred to the clothes worn by the ordinary Irish country people. Some of them said that the people dressed in rags and tatters and others said generally the people dressed neatly in warm, comfortable frieze. The reasons for this difference of opinion may have been that at his work in the fields and around his home the ordinary Irishman wore his tattered clothes and kept his good suit and his greatcoat for special occasions and Sundays, as well as fair days and holidays generally. In the north of Ireland one might hear the expression 'a Sunday go to meeting suit'.

Until the middle of the nineteenth century most people dressed in frieze or other woollen cloth which had been made at home or bought locally. In certain parts of Ulster few sheep were kept and as a result it was reported in the *Parochial Survey* from Maghera, County Derry in 1815:

> The lower classes here are worse clad than in other places from the universal practice of wearing old clothes which are brought from Scotland or bought from the military in Belfast. The King's uniform and the liveries of many of the Scottish noblemen form a considerable part of the drapery of the crowds that assemble on public days in Maghera. The comfortable slate coloured frieze which the southern counties afford to their inhabitants is unknown here. The rage for finery however prevails among the women! Many of them who labour hard all the week and live on the worst fare, appear at fairs and markets and their different houses of worship, dressed in tawdry bonnets, pellisses etc. and often times in monstrous tippets in the hottest of the dog days.

This import of second-hand clothes is mentioned during the previous century. In the year 1792 a list of goods landed at the port of Derry included 13,104 yards of old drapery and 15,373 yards of new drapery from England. The practice may be older still and there is at least one reference to the import of second-hand clothes during the seventeenth century.

Scotland appears to have been the origin of this trade. In 1824 the Irish brokers in the Briggate of Glasgow erected on a plot of ground a hollow square of buildings containing some forty shops. This second-hand depot, a landmark in the city for a century, was popularly known as 'Paddy's Market'. In time it was unable to cope with all the business transacted and in good weather booths were set up in the neighbourhood.

At the same time *The Scotsman*, the influential newspaper in Edinburgh, was complaining that old clothes dealers waylaid gentlemen in almost every thoroughfare in the New Town with invitations to dispose of their discarded clothes, adding, 'It is not a little extraordinary that a trade which in London is monopolized by the Jews should be pursued in this city exclusively by Irishmen.' This is recorded in Hanley's book, *The Irish in Scotland*.

A correspondent writing in the same newspaper suggested that Scotsmen should make a gift of their old clothes to their needy countrymen instead of allowing dealers to buy 'castoffs' and send them across the water to clothe the naked Irish. The coming of steamboats with their regular, quick and safe transport of cargoes was responsible for a rapid expansion of the trade.

Hanley also records the fact that the second-hand clothes shops in Edinburgh, kept mostly by the Irish, were wrecked by the mob.

Second-hand clothes were sold in many places. In Dublin the trade was concentrated in Plunket Street, but according to Thackeray there was such a market in Waterford:

Waterford assizes were held in the town and we ascended to the courthouse through a steep street, a sort of rag fair, but more miserable than any rag fair in St Giles's; the houses and stock of the Seven Dials look as if they belonged to capitalists when compared with the scarecrow wretchedness of the goods here hung out for sale. Who wanted to buy such things, I wondered? One would have thought that the most part of the articles had passed the possibility of barter for money, even out of the reach of the half-farthings coined of late. All the streets were lined with wretched hucksters and their merchandise of gooseberries, green apples, children's dirty capes, cheap crockeries, brushes and tinware; among which objects the people were swarming about busily. Before the Court is a wide street where a similar market was held with a vaste number of donkey carts, urged hither and thither and great shrieking, clattering and bustling. It is five hundred years ago since a poet who accompanied Richard II on his voyage hither spoke of: 'Watreforde ou moult vilaine et orde y sont la gente.'

We can leave Thackeray to continue his tour, determined to see what he wanted to see and to write what his readers expected.

Gradually the practice of selling second-hand clothes at fairs and markets spread throughout the country. As the nineteenth century went on the wearing of frieze became unfashionable, and Fenton tells of hearing cornerboys say, 'Baa' as a countryman passed dressed in his frieze coat. All my childhood I was familiar with it and the cantman who sold the second-hands could be relied on to provide entertainment for his audience. He set up his stand using the two-wheeled car on which he had brought his goods to the fair. The shafts of the car were held up by trestles and boards placed upon them to extend the floor of the flat car. Over it all he erected a scaffolding of poles and covered the scaffolding with canvas waterproofed sheeting. This served to protect the cantman and his goods against the wind and the rain as well as against the dust and dirt of the fair. The whole process of setting up what was really a tent with one open side and of dismantling it when the fair was over was highly efficient and used to remind me of the way a travelling circus party would set up the great circus tent.

When the buying and selling of the cattle was nearly over, at about eleven o'clock, the cantman stepped up on to his stage and with the presence and gestures of a true showman he addressed the crowd gathered to listen to him as he picked up and displayed a coat from the stock neatly laid out beside him. 'Here ladies and gentlemen,' he called loudly, 'Who will give me a pound for this fine coat? Look at it, it's the best tag in County Leitrim. It's all lamb's wool, mixed with ram's wool, taken from the best part of the lamb, under the tail. It was woven by a nigger and spun by a black and hopped ten times on the Rocks of Gibraltar.' As he spotted a prospective customer he would add, 'Here, fit this on you. It will do you when you are getting married.' The crowd then laughed, because the customer had long been married or else was a confirmed bachelor. 'Come on, who will give me eighteen shillings, sixteen shillings? I'll give it away at twelve shillings.' When the customers still would not buy the patter continued, 'Who will give me ten bob for this coat that will wear time out of mind,' until finally the coat was sold for perhaps five shillings.

By now the cantman had noticed a woman in the crowd with her young son. 'Ah mam, you want a pair of trousers for that lad with you. I have the very thing for him, all the way from London town. He will be able to wear them till he is getting married. Here, hould them up to him. Sure the best tailor in the country couldn't fit him better.' So it went on, sometimes jocular, sometimes bawdy, often entertaining, and always part of the fun of the fair.

Some families tended to specialise in this business and were well known for it. The O'Farrells from Cavan were well known, and the Freynes might be seen at fairs in Sligo and Mayo. The MacAllister brothers, Alec and Jack, lived in Ballinamore and were friends of my family. Jack lived opposite our house and about four times a year he would travel to Glasgow to buy more stock. Duly this would arrive at the local railway station, packed in great bales made of sacking, and by the time the bales were opened on the boxes outside Jack's door people were waiting to see what treasures or bargains he had brought home. When I see the crowd at a sale I always remember the crowd which gathered to inspect the contents of the bales from Glasgow. This was rather a private showing before the new stock was taken to be sold at all the local fairs.

Jack also bought seconds, and I remember a pair of new shoes, very shiny and with pointed toes, which my father brought home. I wore them to play football on a wet Sunday afternoon and that was the end of the shoes – but it was not the last I heard of them.

Later, in the 1920s, when the import of second-hand clothes was stopped, an enterprising man built a tin shack beside the customs post on the Fermanagh border. He stocked it with a supply of second-hands from Glasgow, and people from both sides went to buy them.

Steadily as the years went on the trade changed. It was developed by the 'Dublin women' who sold mainly coats, dresses and shoes for women. The last time I saw this was during the summer of 1966 on a wet afternoon at the fair of Kenmare in County Kerry.

Delph

Towards the end of the nineteenth century many Irish housewives were proud of the collection of crockery which they set out proudly on the kitchen dresser. As well as plates, cups and saucers there were pottery figures of heroes like Napoleon or King Billy on his white horse or of saints to be found in many houses. These were of all degrees of fineness, from pieces of Belleek, Wedgewood or Dresden china down to cheap crude imitations and plaster casts. Generally the dishes had pictures – the willow pattern was the most popular – and I remember a plate with a picture of George V which was made during the 1914-18 war.

Generally these were bought from dealers at fairs or they might be got in exchange for butter or eggs from pedlars who went from door to door. Many of the dealers who sold at fairs would sell other things as well as delph, but some of them tended to specialise in delph. In my childhood the best known of these was a man called James Whitney who kept a china shop in a County Leitrim village, Carrigallen. As I remember him he was a tall, oldish, thin man, dressed neatly in a good frock coat, and as he sold his cups and saucers he spoke in a quiet voice, unlike most fair day dealers who shouted loudly in hoarse voices.

Generally the china he sold was 'seconds' and he was able to buy a crate of these for £5 delivered at his nearest railway station from Belfast during the years before the 1914-18 war. He made a good living because, as my father said, 'He would get two good fairs out of a crate and would sell it for about £40.' He would pick up large dinner plates and sell half a dozen of them for 2s. Then he might change to selling a cup, saucer and plate for 1s. Most popular of all were large pint mugs with big handles which went for 6d. each.

If any customers needed more expensive china or glass he could provide it, but the bulk of his trade was in 'seconds'. He was a very neat worker and his stock was always set out carefully on straw. If nobody offered to buy the article when he had displayed it he always replaced it carefully before picking up another item. When the fair was over he always packed up carefully and did not leave any dirty straw or broken crockery behind him on the street.

When butter was made at home, milk was stored in large black glazed crocks. These were made in many small kilns in different parts of the country and sold at the local fairs. Such crocks came from a kiln near Florencecourt in County Fermanagh to County Leitrim fairs, and there is a tradition that they were also made near Drumahaire and in different parts of County Monaghan. Before buying one of these crocks the customer always examined it very carefully by tapping it all round with a coin to make sure it was not cracked. As I think of it I can almost hear the ringing sound.

Fir Rope

It is almost unbelievable that ropes made of specially prepared wood fibre were made and sold at Irish fairs during the present century. Generally, the rope used in rural Ireland was made of green rushes and was quite efficient, although it had a short life. In the *Statistical Survey of County Donegal* MacParlan wrote:

> Mr Richard Nisbett of Woodhill on some property of his in Boylagh found a tenant of his lately at work, twisting and making ropes with his fingers of bog fir: he showed me some of them which seemed extremely well executed, and is determined to procure for this industrious man, the necessary tools, and assistance, to forward his manufacture.

Fenton, writing of the year 1885, said:

> Sneem fair was the only mart where I saw bog deal ropes – *teada*

guimhaise – exposed for sale, and there was some history behind the cottage of the craftsman, snugly situated in a field, reclaimed from a great bog, beside the Glenlough river. The old man who made the ropes was the sixth or seventh in descent, from a *toruidhe* (tory) who had trekked westward after the debacle of Cnoc na n-Dos in 1647. Tomás O'Sullivan was known as *an toruidhe*. . . may have been descended from the man forced to eke out an existence by reclaiming a plot of bog, saving turf and more interesting than all, making bog deal ropes for farmers' haggards, and for sail tackling, often for boats that knew French and Spanish ports. Logs of bog deal without knots were seasoned, cleaned by a special tool, and finally splintered almost as fine as flax fibre. This was twisted into strands, three of which, braided, formed a strong rope eagerly purchased by farmers and boatmen, at the 1885 Sneem fair.

The third reference to such ropes is from the *Ulster Journal of Archaeology*. The wood used was straight, grained fir. It was cut in four-foot lengths with a hatchet and dried carefully in the open air. Then long thin slices were cut from it, $\frac{1}{32}$ of an inch thick and one inch broad, with a butcher's knife. This was the most skilful part of the work. Then the rope was twisted using the four-legged stool as a bobbin. A stick was bent round one of the legs and twisted, then another strip was added as the stool was rotated and the rope wound round its legs. In north Antrim a coil of this fir rope fifty feet long was sold for 3*s*.6*d*. and used for thatching.

Medicine Men

In 1896 and 1897 much of the time of the Council of the Royal College of Surgeons in Ireland was taken up discussing the details of a quarrel between two doctors, Robert Cochrane and Nathaniel Mayne, both living in Longford. Mayne had complained that Cochrane had been present at the demonstrations of a well-known healer called 'Dr Sequah' and had even sent patients to him. Cochrane appeared before the Council on 6 August 1896. He denied having sent patients to Sequah but admitted that through curiosity he had stood on Sequah's platform. He also admitted that he had circulated a pamphlet in reference to his dispute with Mayne. He expressed regrets for his behaviour and his apology was accepted by the Council. Later Mayne published a pamphlet in which he attacked the Council.

Leaving aside the dispute between the two doctors, there is no doubt that 'Dr Sequah' was a well known and very successful healer. He was a big man who travelled in style, elegantly dressed with a carriage and pair, and escorted by a brass band. He would drive into the town and set up his platform on the square and within five minutes he was surrounded by a crowd of patients all clamouring for his attention.

My father had simple views about people who needed medical attention – he never needed any – and could not understand why people whom he knew, and who appeared well, should be 'all running to Dr Sequah'. When he saw the crowd it was clear that Sequah was going to make a lot of money and he realised that all the patients were happy to be given some form of treatment, whether pills, a box of ointment, or a bottle of medicine. At the end of the fair the doctor went to a neighbouring hotel where he used to see patients in private. A few years ago I heard people speak of a 'Dr Sequah' who attended fairs in Kilkenny during the 1930s but it can hardly have been the same individual who had been so successful forty years earlier.

Most of the medicine men who attended fairs were much less exalted than Dr Sequah. One man whom I saw at a number of fairs used to address the crowd thus: 'My name is Dr Hopewell and I come from Ballinasloe. My father and mother are still living and well because every morning they each take a dose of this medicine.' As he spoke he held up a bottle containing his wonderful 'medicine' and a surprising number of people bought it.

Another was Pat MacAllister who had once been a boxer of some note, and when I saw him at the fair of Ballinamore he was still fit and active, dressed in a singlet and a smart pair of flannel trousers. Beside him he had a large tinted photograph of himself wearing boxing kit and decorated with a most elaborate looking belt. He had a good line of talk, told us all about how he used to train and, to show that he was still strong and supple, he would turn a cartwheel or stand on his hands. Then he went on to speak of the wonderful 'rub' he used which he said would cure every ache and pain. It was to be rubbed on at bedtime and all the pains and stiffness would be gone in the morning. He certainly sold many of his bottles, and I have heard many people say that it relieved their pains.

Cyril Chapman knew him well and was able to add some details. His story was that once while he was boxing in India he had become friendly with an Indian doctor who was able to cure some of the injuries he suffered in a hard fight. When he was returning home Pat asked the doctor about the medicine and was told that its power was due to 'snake oil'.

There were many sellers of corn cures, but by far the most successful was another friend of Cyril called Joseph Lawrence Reilly, a man with perfect feet. Before he began selling he set up his pitch and then took off his boots and socks and walked around smartly in his bare feet, The colder or more unpleasant the day, the longer he continued at this. Then he washed and dried his feet and applied his corn cure before putting on his boots. By then he had scores of people waiting to buy his corn cure which cured all foot ailments as well as corns.

There were many others including Dr Bernard who arrived at 'the Barrows' in Glasgow in a chauffeur driven Rolls Royce. He got out of the car and strolled among the crowd, and as he stood 6 ft 6 in. tall and wore a fur coat everybody recognised him. When a patient consulted him they returned to the car and Dr Bernard provided the necessary medicine before continuing his stroll.

Strong Men

I remember one man whom we called 'the tumbler Reilly' who used to appear at fairs sixty years ago. He set up his pitch by assembling a cartwheel, a large stone and a heavy sledge hammer. He then took off his shirt and showed off his muscled torso, as he told us about his superhuman strength. He started by asking some of the crowd to lift and examine the cart wheel and make sure it was genuine. He then asked two of them to lift the wheel and help him to balance it on his chin.

When we had all gazed in wonder at this 'the Tumbler' went on to his next act. He lay down supine on the street with a small pillow under his chest. Two helpers placed the stone gently on his chest and another struck it with the sledge hammer and continued striking it until the stone broke and the crowd cheered.

Cyril Chapman told me a story about a strong man who appeared at a fair in Derry in 1940. He was an excellent performer and was able to escape when chained and tied up. The strange thing was that none of the other people who frequented the fairs recognised him. Not long afterwards they learned that he had been arrested as a German spy.

Evangelists

I could never understand why some of the various Protestant sects ever thought it worthwhile to send preachers to fairs in the small towns of Connacht. They were not unusual during my childhood, and even then I used to wonder at their enthusiasm, because I never heard that they succeeded in getting anyone to listen to them. The fair, with streets ankle deep in dirt and cow dung, dealers selling their wares and often bawling obscenities to the delight of the crowd, ballad singers, and men going into and coming out of public houses was not a very suitable place to preach.

Nevertheless they used to appear occasionally and take a position in the midst of all the noise and confusion. Usually they began by singing a hymn and then one of the party began preaching. The sermon was usually an exhortation to read the scriptures and in some cases they had copies of the Bible which they sold for a shilling or two. I remember two of these men who were selling copies of the Douai Version of the New Testament with a recommendation to read it by Dr Troy, Archbishop of Dublin. Despite Dr Troy nobody would buy them or even accept them for nothing.

This resistance to the reading of the Bible by Catholics seems strange but it followed from the enthusiasm of some of the Protestants for Bible reading during the nineteenth century. As a result, Bible reading came to be regarded by some people as a Protestant activity, and to do so might be seen as a sign of change of faith.

I remember once seeing a preacher holding forth on a fair day in Mohill. As I stood to watch – from a safe distance, where nobody could say I was listening – I felt very sorry for him. He spoke well and clearly for nearly half an hour and one would have thought he was invisible because nobody took the slightest notice. I am happy to remember that at least nobody attacked the preacher or shouted insults at him. This would be expected in these ecumenical days, but it must be realised that this is a recent change. Fifty years ago reading the scriptures in any translation other than the Douai Version and with approved notes would be frowned on by some Catholics and thought of as a danger to the faith by some priests.

Setting off from Dunfanaghy, Co. Donegal, for the 'goose fair' in Derry

16

Some Special Fairs

Donnybrook Fair

I MUST confess that I heard more references to Donnybrook Fair when I lived outside Ireland than I heard during the time I lived within a mile or two of Donnybrook. I have met Americans who enquired about it, and when I answered that I did not know anything, they were surprised and did not believe me. Now that I think back on it, I wonder if my friends in Canada or in England believed me when I told them I knew nothing about it. Probably not. They may well have thought that I was ashamed of it, and was trying to pretend that it had never happened.

That, of course, was not so, and even though I have since learned a little about Donnybrook Fair, I did not learn of anything unusual about it. There is no doubt that fighting, drinking, dancing, love-making, pocket-pinching, thimble-rigging, cheating and horse dealing went on, but these went on at hundreds of other fairs, and at any other such assembly in Ireland and elsewhere.

It was established in the year 1204 by a charter from King John, and may have been the second such charter fair established in Ireland. According to the charter the fair began on 3 May, the Feast of the Finding of the Holy Cross, and was to continue for eight days. Apart from that little is known about it during the earlier centuries. It cannot have been a very important fair in the ordinary sense; the coastal strip of land between the mountains and the south shore of Dublin Bay is not large enough to raise the numbers of horses and cattle which would be sold at a large fair, and it is not likely that livestock from north County Dublin, Meath or Kildare would be sold at Donnybrook. There are some references to the sale of horses there in later centuries.

During the Middle Ages, when the mayor of Dublin perambulated the bounds of his jurisdiction once every three years, one of the points where the official procession stopped was Donnybrook. It would appear from the references that the Dodder marked the limit of the Mayor's area of jurisdiction and the fair was held on the flat ground on the left bank of the Dodder, part of which is now Herbert Park.

About the year 1690 the charter for the fair was sold by the Dublin City authorities to a man called Usher, a member of one of the rich Dublin merchant families. It is not likely that the fair would have been sold if it was an important commercial fair, but when people described it, it seemed largely a carnival week for the citizens of Dublin. By the second half of the eighteenth century the fair was held during the last week of August, and officially began on the Monday of that week. In practice it happened that the crowds assembled on Donnybrook Green on the previous day, known as Walking Sunday. Various explanations have been offered for this name. In my opinion, it is derived from the English word 'wake' meaning a vigil before a feast day. The same words were used for the Sunday before Rathfarnham Fair.

Whatever may have been its origin, Walking Sunday became the most notorious day of the fair week because very large crowds went out to Donnybrook, and scandalised the pious by their fighting and drinking on the Sabbath. Naturally, the righteous complained to the city authorities, who made some efforts to stop the carnival. However, some buying and selling was done at the fair and Sir Jonah Barrington, who wrote a description of it, went there to buy a horse. As he explained, 'Cattle and horses were sold at the fair but no one would buy the latter till the owners had shown off their parts.' He went on, 'The horse part of the fair was not destitute of amusement, as there was always a large ditch or drain, and a piece of wall which the sellers were always called upon to "leather their horses over" before anyone would bid for them, and the tumbles which these venturous jockeys constantly received and the indifference wherewith they mounted and began again were truly entertaining.'

The Green was a wide flat piece of ground on the side of a stream. Tents built of sods and wattles were erected for eating and drinking and, as Barrington wrote, these were 'covered with quilts, old winnowing sheets, petticoats or whatever else could be got.' In the best tents neat victuals were provided, lumps of salt beef with cabbage boiling outside on a turf fire, with potatoes and Dublin Bay herrings. For the quality who came to see the curiosities a cold round or rump of beef was provided at double price.

In the evening the dancing began, and some tents were specially equipped for this. Everyone, drunk or sober, took to the floor and they all danced until they fell down exhausted. As time went on, the number of side-shows increased, and the number and variety of musicians. These side-shows appear to have been separated from the tents intended for eating, drinking and dancing by a wide open space, and the usual collection of giants, dwarfs, tight-rope walkers, contortionists, jugglers, ventriloquists, etc. were all there, presumably come over from England, and making it more like a modern circus.

During the Napoleonic wars Donnybrook fair was a popular recruiting ground for the army. An illustration in Walker's *Hibernian Magazine* shows the crowd of holidaymakers in front of a tent called the 'Bang-up Porter and Punch House', with a hussar standing in the doorway drinking from a glass. All this was accompanied by a long recruiting speech. A few years later, when the wars were over, Dutton wrote: 'Donnybrook Fair has been long complained of as a nuisance, and a most dangerous one it is: as the recruiting service is at an end, that excuse can no longer be used. The scenes of riot and drunkenness that take place are most disgusting and can surely answer no purpose but to put money in the pockets of publicans, at the expense of the morals and health of the people. I sincerely hope to see it abolished before the next meeting, and a compensation made to the proprietor of the tolls which could easily be adjusted.'

Two signs seen over the doors of drinking tents were recorded in a recent issue of the *Dublin Historical Record*. They were in verse and one reads:

Here Paddy come to have a swig
A better one he never took
And now he'll dance an Irish jig
With Dolly Dunne of Donnybrook.

Another tent had a picture of a beehive as its sign and underneath this jingle:

In this hive we're all alive
Good whiskey makes us funny
So don't pass by, but stop and try
The sweetness of our honey.

These verses recall another sign in verse which was written over the door of a tavern on the fair green in Croom, County Limerick. I translate from memory the inscription over Sean O'Tuama's tavern:

John Tuomy welcomes all the noble Gael
And though sometimes they lack the price of ale,
Their welcome in this house will never fail.

There are few references to stick fighting at Donnybrook Fair. In

1725 Philip Skelton, then a sizar at Trinity College won a hat – the prize for the best cudgel fighter at the fair. Almost exactly one hundred years later, in 1823, Charles O'Flaherty wrote in the *Dublin Morning Post* about some visitor to the fair:

> If he sees what is not very uncommon at Donnybrok, a fellow's head thrust through a hole in a tent for the purpose of enjoying a little fresh air, he is sure to hit a crack, and says that he could not resist the desire to give it just me tip. The owner of the head, finding himself so badly treated, generally takes his friends in pursuit of the aggressor who meantime has collected a few of his friends, and thus begins the skirmish on the banks of the Dodder.

This story of someone striking a head which was stuck out of a hole in a tent wall is told about stick fighting at many fairs. The more usual version says that the aggressor was likely to strike the outline of a head seen causing a bulge in a tent wall. It was very likely that some practical joker, stimulated by a skinful of beer, would think it all very funny.

As might be expected, there were people who chose to decide that drinking and dancing were wrong, and many efforts were made to stop the fair. For example, in 1765 the drinking tents remained open late at night, so on the last day of August the High Sheriff, with constables and some soldiers, went to the fair, pulled down the tents, loaded their contents onto cars, and took them away. In 1793 there was more trouble with the city authorities, and still more in the year 1837. This time one hundred policemen were assembled on Donnybrook Green, during the evening of Saturday 26 August, and at eight o'clock the Lord Mayor, the High Sheriff, the Town Mayor, some mounted police and a troop of Hussars arrived. Within three hours not a tent remained to show that the fair had begun – all had been pulled down. The main objection to the fair was that it was a desecration of the Sabbath, and it will be remembered that in most fair charters from the year 1600 onward, it was ordered that when the fair day fell on a Sunday the fair was held on the following day, Monday.

There was more trouble in 1823, even though the owners of the various tents had tried to buy protection by contributing £40 to some Dublin charities. However, the Sabatarian lobby was stronger and the Lord Mayor ordered that tents and booths must not be set up until Monday 22 August, though he did allow the fair to continue from Monday to Saturday. The owner of the fair, a Mr Madden, petitioned the Lord Lieutenant at the time about this interference with his rights, but the Lord Lieutenant refused to override the Mayor's order. Then in the year 1835 the weather was bad so the Lord Mayor of the day extended the period of the fair by two extra days: the grateful tent owners subscribed £50 to the Mendicity Institute.

The last official fair was held on Donnybrook Green in 1854. Before the time of the next fair the opponents of it had become well organised and a committee had purchased the charter from the owner, Miss Madden, for the surprising sum of £30,000. For some years a certain Miss Dillon, who owned a public house in Donnybrook, held a fair in a field at her house, and this continued until 1860. In that year the authorities refused to renew Miss Dillon's licence, and that was the end of the fair.

Looking back at it now it would appear that Donnybrook Fair was like most pleasure fairs at the time both in Ireland and in England. Contemporary descriptions of Southwark Fair and Bartholomew Fair leave no doubt that they were used by the citizens of London very much as Donnybrook Fair was used by the people of Dublin.

When not in use for the fair Donnybrook Green was a favourite spot for the duellers of the eighteenth and nineteenth centuries, and Barrington described a duel in which he himself fought. His opponent was a certain Richard Daly, who had fought sixteen duels, three with swords, and thirteen with pistols, during the previous two years, without himself sustaining or causing any significant injury. Although Barrington had never spoken to the man in his life, the rules of the game said that he must accept the challenge, so he decided that the duel would take place on the Green at Donnybrook. Before seven o'clock on the morning of 20 March Barrington and his second, a friend called Crosby, set off walking to Donnybrook, well fortified against the cold with chocolate and cherry brandy.

When the parties met, Crosby set about organising the affair. Soon Daly's second came forward and explained that it was all a mistake and Mr Daly regretted having given Mr Barrington any trouble, and wished to shake his hand. Barrington was perfectly happy to do this but Crosby – the expert on such matters – would not hear of it. He produced a copy of the rules which declared that 'No apology can be received after the parties meet without a fire'.

They then took their positions and Barrington fired. Daly staggered back a few steps saying, 'I'm hit sir', but did not himself fire. The seconds opened his waistcoat and found a black shot the size of a crown piece on the front of his breast bone with a little blood on it. The bullet had struck a brooch, part of which was stuck in the bone. Crosby pulled it out and Daly covered the wound with his folded handkerchief. Barrington then asked why he had been challenged but Daly refused to give any explanation and his second produced another copy of the rules, reading 'If a party challenged, accepts the challenge without asking the reason of it, the challenger is never bound to divulge it afterwards'. It is hardly possible that anything more senseless ever occurred at Donnybrok Fair than that duel.

Ballinasloe October Fair

The October Fair of Ballinasloe still continues but at present it is not to be compared to the fair held in 1853 when 20,000 cattle and 100,000 sheep were offered for sale. Hardiman wrote in his history of Galway: 'The great cattle fairs of Ballinasloe (by far the most extensive in these islands) were, it is said, originally established in that place for its contiguity to Galway. These famous marts have subsisted from a very early period, although no patent for holding them appears on record before 8 June 1757 when Richard Trench of Garbaly got a patent for fairs on 15 May and 13 July.'

The site of the town marks an important crossing point on the River Suck, the only major obstacle between Athlone and Galway. It's name, Beal atha na Sluagh (The Ford Mouth of the Crowds), would indicate that it was an important meeting place, and for centuries a castle guarded the ford. In 1572 this castle was held by the Earl of Clanrickard, who had displaced the O'Kelly lords, and in 1579 it was taken over by the English and became the residence of the governor of Connacht. The fair is not mentioned in the Irish annals, nor in the State Papers, and it is most unlikely therefore that a fair comparable in importance to what it became during the eighteenth and nineteenth centuries is very old. The state of County Galway during the last quarter of the sixteenth century would also make it unlikely that such a fair could have been held at that time. The feuding of the sons of the earl and the cattle raiding by Red Hugh O'Donnell all over the Connacht plain would have made the holding of such a fair impossible. It is also to be remembered that the money to pay for such a large number of cattle was not easily available during the sixteenth century.

The great fair probably did not develop until the seventeenth century. When the country settled down under James I there was general improvement in the export trade, and it may be that Ballinasloe became a meeting place where buyers from Leinster, as well as from Galway and Limerick, met the cattle from Clare, Galway, Roscommon and

South Mayo. It is not likely that the fair could have been held between 1641 and 1652, due to the Confederate War. Petty estimated that the value of the livestock in Ireland fell during these years from £4 million to £0.5 million. However, recovery was rapid, and in 1672 he estimated that there were 3,000,000 cattle in the country. It must also be remembered that when the Earl of Clanrickard was granted patents for fairs, during the reign of James I, a patent was granted for Ballinasloe. At that time the castle of Ballinasloe may have been still held by the government.

The great increase in the export of such things as barrelled beef and hide from 1680 onward may have caused the fair to grow in size and importance. In 1718 the town and the surrounding district was acquired by a family called Trench, and it was then that the modern town was built. During this century the new English Longhorned breed of cattle was established in all the grazing lands of the west and it was these which made up the stock at the October Fairs. At this time the *Farmers' Journal* wrote enthusiastically:

It must appear that the Longhorned cattle are those to be most encouraged, especially under the influence of another most striking fact, that the total number of horned cattle above stated amounting to nearly 7,000 sold on the fair green of Ballinasloe scarcely one appeared on this or any former year except of the longhorned description – a kind too of excellent form and description according to the best English breeders who have visited the fair.

In 1844 the *Dublin Almanack* gave some statistics about the numbers of cattle brought to the fair between the years 1790 and 1843. I do not know the source of these figures, or how accurate they are, but in 1816 Dutton wrote in the *Statistical Survey of County Galway*, 'Mr Sinclair, Lord Clancarty's stewart, was the baron of the fair. He would not say how many cattle were sold at it.'

According to the figures the numbers of cattle varied from 6,200 in 1797 to 14,364 in 1842, with a mean of nearly 8,000 head. During some fairs trade was brisk, for instance in 1794 when 7,106 were sold out of 7,337. Then, when the end of the war was in sight, there was a slump in 1814. In that year 9,611 cattle were taken to the fair but 5,863 were not sold.

The *Almanack* also gives the number of sheep for the same years and these tell much the same story. The largest number of sheep was 97,384 in 1828, and of these 86,374 were sold. A bad year occurred in 1803, when out of 87,682 sheep, 33,782 were not sold.

Prices are given for the years from 1832 to 1843. First class bullocks sold for from £13 a head in 1834, up to £18.10s.0d. in 1840. Heifer prices were more uniform. They varied from £16.16s.0d. in 1841 to £13.15s. 0d. in 1834.

Sheep prices are also given. Wethers sold for £2.14s.0d. in 1833 to £2.1s.0d. in 1835.

The *Almanack* has still another reference to the fair in a section headed 'Literary, Scientific and Professional Institutions'. It appears that a society called the Connaught Club arranged that 'The Members of the club dine together at their rooms, Gills Hotel, in Ballinasloe each day during the October Fair. The President for the year is Chairman of the first day's dinner, the Vice-President, Croupier, and on each succeeding day a Chairman is appointed.' The objects of this society were 'social intercourse, universal benevolence, and local improvement'. General and local politics or other subjects likely to create discussion were strictly prohibited.

Clearly the 'quality' were not to be outdone at the brawling, eating and drinking, and had decided to organise their own show.

At present, Ballinasloe is mainly a horse fair, and on 9 October 1981 Radio Éireann transmitted a programme about it. Fitted neatly into the programme were snippets of conversations recorded on the fair green, such phrases as, 'Here, ye won't break my word', 'Let ye divide £5', 'Here, hould yer hand', and, 'Come back, he'll give them to you' – all familiar to anyone who still remembers the ritual of an Irish fair day.

Then when the dealing was finished there were more fragments of conversations recorded in a pub: 'Be gob you did alright out of the lambs'; 'Aye. I was lucky but I did them well'; 'Ah Jasus, Miley, do you mind the time we used to be clipping the sheep'; and something we can all remember – 'You'd go to your knees on the fair green. There was no tarmacadam in them days.'

One man, Barney Hamil, a horse dealer from Belfast, described how he used to take three days to drive a horse to the fair of Ballinasloe: 'You might meet with a travelling man on the way and maybe stay with him, or have a deal with him. . . . In them days you could buy a road full of horses for £200.' He also spoke of buying horses to be used as pack horses by the British army during the 1939-45 war and also about an order he had for a cargo of donkeys to be sent to the island of Sark.

On the night before the fair the town was full of people and it was not possible to get a private room. It was necessary to take great care of your money so you rolled it up inside your shirt or gave it to your wife who would put it away carefully. As an extra precaution you went to bed wearing most of your clothes and made sure to keep the light on.

The radio programme had plently of colourful details about men playing trick o' the loop, the three card trick and all the other activities associated with a great fair. All these are now gone and all that is left of the great herds of Connacht Longhorns is the Irish proverb, 'Connacht cows have long horns'.

The market house, Kilworth, Co. Cork

17
Sheep and Wool

IN MEDIAEVAL Ireland sheep were kept mainly for their wool, which was generally spun and woven at home. Until well into the seventeenth century the ordinary Irishman wore a short jacket and trousers of home-spun woollen cloth and over these he wore a great shaggy woollen cloak in which he could, if necessary, sleep out of doors. This cloak, known as a *failling*, changed little over the centuries and Stanihurst, writing around 1584, said:

> Young and old here [in Waterford] are addicted to thriving, the men commonlie to traffic, and the women to carding and spinning. As they distill the best aqua vitae, so they spin the choicest rug in Ireland. A friend of mine being of late demurrant in London, and the weather by reason of a hard hoar frost being somewhat nipping, repaired to Paris garden clad in one of the Waterford rugs. The mastiffs had no sooner espied, but deeming he had been a *beare* would fain have baited him: and were it not that the dogs were partlie muzzled and partlie chained, he doubted not he should have been well tugged in this Irish rug.

For some reason the English authorities in Dublin violently disliked the wearing of this mantle and many laws were passed in efforts to stop the practice. In the *Patent Rolls of James I* a patent dated 19 April 1613 granted the authorities the right to seize Irish mantles and clothes made of bandle linen dyed with saffron in Leinster, Munster and Meath. In consequence of this and other such acts the wearing of the mantle died out and later in the century the *cóta mór* took its place. The body of a late sixteenth-century soldier discovered some years ago in County Derry was dressed in a short coat and trousers and a mantle all made of wool and woven in a way still used in Donegal.

Early in the eighteenth century sheep were still being kept, mainly for their wool, in every part of Ireland. The wool was washed, carded, spun and woven or knitted in the homes for use there, and the surplus was sold at the local fairs. As the century went on this trade in wool increased and there were large wool fairs at Ballinasloe, Mullingar and Sligo.

During this century improving landlords were busy in Ireland. Among the things which they decided to improve was the breed of sheep, and in order to do this they imported some of the better-known English breeds. As in the case of the native Irish cattle, the improvers had very poor opinions of the quality of the native sheep. This is what Robert Frazer wrote in the *Statistical Survey for County Wexford* about the sheep there: 'Hardly anything can be worse than the common breed of sheep in the county of Wexford, long legged, narrow backed, large head, large bone, and as wild as deer.' Frazer went on to write about the good qualities of the Leicester breed and of the South Down breed and advised that 'as all farmers in this country, even the smallest, keep a few sheep for their wool, and even for their milk, they would be greatly benefited by getting into these valuable breeds'.

In County Derry, Sampson, the writer of the *Statistical Survey* (1802) was himself a sheep farmer and had this to say about the native breed: 'Our own strain is of all shapes and qualities, horned and without horns, coarse wool and fine, almost all are restless. We get a considerable number from the mountains of Inish-owen: these are small 'waghins' from seven to ten pounds a quarter. These sometimes fatten in one summer and are when fat very nice mutton.' He went on to say: 'Our best sort are bought either in the fairs of the South Western counties or else at Dervock [County Antrim] to which they are driven by jobbers from these areas.'

During the eighteenth century the growing of flax increased greatly in the northern counties, and for this and other reasons fences were erected to restrain straying animals. As a result fewer sheep were kept in these counties. This is how Sampson records it:

> Not long ago, one might see hundreds of sheep travelling from farm to farm unnoticed and unowned. Every servant boy in the country who had a few shillings saved, laid it out on a sheep or two which he let loose on the bounty of Providence and the toleration of his neighbourhood. Towards May all these flocks are driven to the mountains. The value of their wool and progeny greatly overpaid the grazing and risk. In the time of snow, these depredators like the locusts of Egypt devour everything before them. I have lost in one night's time two thousand head of curly Kale.

Now the numbers of sheep are much less because of tillage and fencing.

Sampson writes with enthusiasm of the beauty and prowess of his Connaught ram: 'I have crossed a neat selection of our own ewes with a strong Connaught ram. The success is prodigious. From one ram of the breed, I have this year sheared 12¼ pounds of fine combing wool; it was weighed as it came off. This fine animal is but two years old; he had horns: one, he lost in battle and my saw balanced his loss.'

Generally the story was the same in the Ulster counties, though sheep continued to be kept in West Donegal and on the high land west of the Glens of Antrim. In Antrim there were large sheep fairs at Donaghy, Ballycastle and Dervock or they were taken to Coleraine where they were bought to be fattened over the winter on the better land in County Derry.

As with the cattle the new breeds of sheep were more successful in the western counties. This enthusiastic report written in 1800 by James MacParlan is typical:

> In Sligo Mr Wynne has a prodigious fine flock of New Leicester ewes, purchased from Robert St George, which are this year tupped by a beautiful ram, hired of Messers Astley and St George at a very high price. Mr Richard Wynne has a few very fine ewes of the same breed: he showed me some year-old wethers which had been fed on a light rocky pasture and were thick fat, when Irish wethers three years old had scarcely flesh enough to carry their bones.

It is clear that the new breed fattened more easily than the native sheep, and when he was writing the *Statistical Survey of County Mayo* Mac Parlan was still enthusiastic about the virtues of the Leicesters. He wrote: 'One gentleman from this barony [Clanmorris] at the last fair of Ballinasloe sold 300 sheep in one lot at 54s. each.'

The Leicester breed was also established in the other western counties, but here the opinions were less enthusiastic. Dutton, writing about County Clare, has this to say about them: 'The old women regret the introduction of "the Dexters" (as they call them) which they say spoiled their wool. The mutton of these high-bred sheep is by universal consent esteemed vastly inferior to that of the native breed procured in the remote parts of the County.' Dutton went on to say that people complained that the native sheep tended to become very fat. In that case it would surely have been a simple matter to give them less food.

Although it was clear that the Leicesters grew well and fattened easily, the search continued for a more generally useful breed. From Sligo we get: 'Mr Wynne has also imported a ram, and some very nice ewes of the South Down breed purchased of Mr Ellman of Sussex.'

These South Down sheep were certainly a success and were soon taken
to County Galway, where Dutton described them a few years later:
'Recently the South Down breed has been introduced from Sligo, and
as a result the quality of the wool is much better.' This appears to have
been the main reason for their success. The wool was clearly of a much
finer quality and though the fleeces were smaller the quality of the wool
more than compensated for this.

For hundreds of years sheep continued to be moved from the west
of Ireland to the pastures of the eastern counties, such as Meath and
Kildare, as well as to some of the northern counties. This custom
continued as long as the fairs lasted and lately I learned with interest
of men who brought store sheep from County Leitrim to sell at the
autumn fairs in County Meath, where they were fattened over the
winter. In County Kilkenny there were great sheep fairs at Bawn on
27 May and 8 September where high quality ewes were for sale. It was
often a matter of great difficulty to distinguish one man's sheep from
those of another at one of the great sheep fairs. I have heard the story
of the County Galway parish priest who advised his congregation to
take better care of their sheep at the local fair. 'There is no good coming
to me saying your sheep are lost. By that time your sheep will be up in
the County Meath and they *ag luigh amach bolg le greine.*' ('Lying out
belly to the sun' – in other words, hanging up skinned in butchers'
shops.)

In Birr, County Offaly, there was a great sheep fair on 12 February,
Old St Brigid's Day, and this continued until the early years of the
century. The reason for it was because in the neighbourhood of Birr
there were many hardworking and prosperous Protestant farmers.
These men would buy hogget lambs at the autumn fairs and fatten
them for sale at the February fair. Some of the buyers came from as
far away as Cork.

Connaught sheep generally were considered of very high quality
during the nineteenth century. In the *Statistical Survey of County
Roscommon* Weld wrote:

> I was witness at Strokestown to a process of which, heretofore, I
> may have been myself the dupe, for aught I knew in purchases I have
> made of sheep, since it can only be detected by careful handling. It
> consists in a second shearing or rather trimming of the sheep, an
> operation performed with very great address, and upon which a
> considerable time is spent, whereby the points of the animal are not
> only set off to the greatest possible advantage but made to appear
> much better than they really are. A person not up to the practice

might be much deceived in the blood, for the sheep, before and after trimming, appear almost of a different race. The wool about the head, and about the tail, legs and shanks is all finely shorn down: at the same time the back is made to appear flat and broad and the haunch full: and this operation is performed with so much skill that the shears can scarcely be traced. But to guard as much as possible against detection the trimming takes place a few weeks before the great fairs, which allows time for the wool to assume a perfectly normal appearance. Those which I saw under the shears (21 August) were destined for the great fair of Ballinasloe on 11 October.

As a boy I used to wonder why my father, when he was buying sheep at a fair, would always stand on the hub of the cart wheel, and examine each sheep individually. Only when he had done this would he make an opening bid for them. Now I understand why he was so careful. Like Weld he may have been caught out – but not very often, I am sure.

Wool, Fairs and Markets

Sheep were very profitable because they produced two fleeces of wool each year, as well as one or two lambs and sometimes milk. Also they could thrive for the greater part of the year on high mountain land. During the eighteenth century some great wool markets were organised where the local wool clip was bought by manufacturers in Ireland or by exporters who shipped it to England or to the continent.

Sligo became an important fair for the sale of sheep and wool. About the year 1800 Mac Parlan wrote: 'In the wool trade Sligo is the great emporium between Connaught and the North from whence numbers come to meet the Connaught sellers, and buy up large quantities of that article.' Mac Parlan appears to have been very pleased with all the improvement he found in County Sligo and gives details of the prices paid. Wool sold for 18s. per stone (16lb) and the price of sheep varied from 25–42s. a head. Mutton fat with its high melting point was a valuable by-product and the tallow chandlers paid 9s.4d. a stone for it as raw material for making candles.

The greatest wool market in Ireland was held at the July fair of Ballinasloe and much of the wool produced in Galway, Mayo, Roscommon and Clare was sold there around the year 1800. Dutton, writing in 1806, said:

It is perfectly ridiculous to see sensible men walking about the streets of Ballinasloe, the buyers at one side, and the sellers at the other for often six weeks or more. This has been carried so far sometimes that the buyers have made parties to take a tour to Killarney or elsewhere, for a fortnight or more, thinking to tire the sellers into a bargain. Some regulations have lately been adopted which it is hoped will be for mutual benefit. Perhaps an auction, as has been practised lately in Dublin for South Down wool, would be the best method.

Dutton was right. Such nonsense destroyed the wool fair of Ballinasloe, and a few years later he wrote: 'The great wool fair of Ballinasloe that used formerly to bring together the graziers of three or four counties and buyers for Leinster and Munster has dwindled to almost nothing, and now almost all the wool is sent to Dublin, to different commission houses, where the most honourable dealings are observed.' He added that as a result of the change the price of wool had risen to 32s. per stone.

In County Wexford, despite Frazer's opinions of the native sheep, the wool produced was sent to the wool market at Waterford, where it made from 16s to 19s a stone according to its fineness. Frazer also said that some very fine wool of the mountain sheep made 30s. per stone in the Waterford market. At the same time, South Down wool sold at 2s.10d. per pound at the Dublin wool auction.

In County Leix the Leicester breed of sheep was well established, and in 1801 Coote wrote that 'their wool is of excellent quality: they generally stone with two fleeces and sell to the Cork, Dublin and Clonmel manufacturers.' The quality must have been satisfactory, because the wool sold at 18s.3d. per stone at the wool markets in Mountrath and Maryborough (Port Laoise), which were the most important in the county.

Woollen Yarn and Woollen Cloth

In many parts of the country the wool was washed and spun into yarn which was then knitted into such things as gloves, jerseys and stockings. This knitting was general in County Clare and in Connemara, and about the year 1800 there were large stocking markets in Ennistymon and in Corofin. However, the stockings knitted in County Clare were not as fine as those produced in Connemara and this was said to have been due to the Leicester wool, which was not as fine as that of the native Connemara sheep. Dutton reported that the Clare stockings were 'Much stronger and fitter for soldiers and those who prefer strength to beauty. They are bought in large quantities by dealers who attend at these towns every market day and are taken to Dublin and to the North of Ireland.' The wool of the native sheep on the Burren had been very fine, and some of it was bought by dealers and taken to Connemara where it was spun and made up into flannels and friezes or the yarn was knitted into stockings. The flannels and friezes were then bought, perhaps by the same dealers who took it to the north of Ireland. In both Clare and Galway the knitters sometimes disposed of the stockings to pedlars in exchange for small household necessaries.

This flourishing trade in knitted stockings was soon affected by the import of cotton stockings which were manufactured in Lancashire and were finer and cheaper than woollen stockings. They were also more fashionable. The import of cotton stockings appears to have begun in the north of Ireland, where wool was not common, and in the year 1795, 2,000 pairs of cotton stockings were imported through Derry.

In County Wicklow large numbers of sheep were kept on the highland. Much of their wool was spun at home and manufactured there for home use while the surplus of frieze, flannel and ratteen was sold at convenient fairs. It is of interest to discover that in County Wicklow some of the wool was made into felt hats which were sold at 3–4s. each. In the south of the county the local landlord had built a cloth hall at Rathdrum, and flannel markets were held there on the first Monday of each month. The hall was opened in 1794, and there were 5,329 pieces of flannel sold in that year. This increased to 7,304 pieces in 1796. In 1797 there was a decline in the numbers sold, due probably to the disturbances which led to the revolt in the following year, and only 3,927 pieces were sold. In 1798, 2,143 pieces had been sold by the end of May. Frieze was sold at many of the County Wicklow fairs and the frieze fairs in the village of Toger were well known.

One of the difficulties in organising and developing the woollen trade was the lack of a standard unit of length. There was a unit called the bandle (*bannlaimh*) which was officially 30 inches. This unit was used in the woollen markets in County Galway, but in Kilkenny bandle cloth was only 24 inches wide, and in County Limerick it was 21 inches wide. As a bandle was also the unit of length, a square bandle in County Galway was more than twice the area of a bandle in County Limerick. It is of interest to read that in County Monaghan 'the clothing friezes which are made at home or those for sale are had from Connaught price 2s.6d.–3s. a yard.' In County Galway the friezes were bought from the people who made them for 11d. a bandle.

Dress

The writer of the *Statistical Survey of the Queen's County* went on to say that the woollen trade there had declined due to the use of cotton. He was obviously annoyed by the thought of the lazy women in the barony of Stradbally: 'Their clothing is of the coarsest friezes and stuffs, none of which, or even their stockings, have their women anything to do with the manufacture of; and except in harvest time their only employment is the trifling cookery of their men's diet. This want of industry with the women is remarkable here and so habitual as can scarcely be expected to be abandoned by the present generation.'

All through the eighteenth century and for the greater part of the nineteenth century the ordinary Irishman and Irishwoman dressed in frieze, flannel and tweed which had been manufactured at home or bought at a local fair. In the statistical surveys of different Irish counties, one of the sections is called 'Clothing of the Lower Rank'. MacParlan, writing about North Mayo, said:

> Clothing for the men is made chiefly of the wool and flax of the barony manufactured into friezes and linens: the women also wear druggets and flannels made of the wool and flax of the country: for Sunday clothes, the women wear cottons, and stamped linen gowns, stuff petticoats with cloaks made of finer stuff than frieze: and bought in the shops: but those fineries are chiefly confined to the young and rather upper class of the peasantry: and for Sunday clothes, fairs, markets, and weddings the young beaux and artisans wear Manchester waistcoats and thickset breeches.
>
> Clothing likewise being manufactured mostly by themselves is of very trifling expense. If the frieze is bought at market it generally costs 3s.6d. a *slat* measuring four feet two inches in length and about two feet two or three inches wide: calculating then on the quantity of this necessary for a suit and on the expenses of lining and making it comes to about two guineas the full dress: the woman's about forty shillings: but the young and other persons who wear the fineries will have to pay ten or twelve shillings more. . .
>
> The men and women appear clean and decent on Sundays, generally in their own manufacture of friezes, flannels and druggets: thicksets, cottons, stuffs, and bauzes, are frequently worn by them.
>
> The common frieze sells here at 2s.–2s.4d. the bandle of thirty-two inches: ten bandles will be necessary for a suit of clothes: four yards of flannel to line it at 13d. per yard, and taylor 3s., the suit will come to £1.15s.10d., besides shoes at 5s.5d., stockings 1s.1d., hat 4s.4d., shirt 5s.5d. All this together with the great coat which they always wear, in summer for show, and for cold in Winter, value about 16s. makes £2.17s.3d.: and this calculation, to prevent repetition may serve as a standard for the cost of clothing throughout the county.

In County Sligo the writer found:

Clothing – still not very good but also in a state of improvement. It is composed of frieze of their own manufacture, a suit of which will cost about thirty-five shillings. But as the fathers of families, and settled men never can imagine a suit complete, or being decently dressed without a greatcoat of the same stuff, which they wear in all seasons and weather, this increases the expense nearly one half of the whole. Including, however, shoes at 5*s*.5*d*.: shirts made of three and a half yards of linen at 16*d*. per yard; frieze stockings at 18*d*., and hat at 3*s*., the suit, exclusive of the great coat, swells to £2.6*s*.10*d*. But most of the young and trades-people wear red and striped waistcoats of finer quality than frieze, corduroy breeches and worsted or cotton stockings.

The women are at home dressed in flannels and druggets, manufactured by themselves, a suit of which may come to five or six and twenty shillings: but on gala days, on Sundays, at weddings and dances the young women, and upper classes of the housekeepers, wear red cloaks, striped linen, and cotton gowns, cotton stockings, cambric caps and handkerchiefs, and green or red stuff petticoats: the cost of every particle worn on that day is about £2.12*s*.3*d*.

Woollen cloth made at home continued to be sold at fairs and markets until well into the present century. Seamus Fenton described the fair of Sneem, in south-west Kerry, as he remembered it as an eleven-year-old boy in 1885. This is what he wrote about the selling of woollen cloth at the fair:

Flannel and frieze were sold at the Sneem fair on improvised stands by dealers mainly from the Beara promontory and measured by the *bannamh* or bandle of twenty-five inches. Curiously the Abbé Moreux, famous French astronomer, states in his *Mysterious Science of the Pharaohs* that the measure used in constructing the Pyramids was the sacred cubit of twenty-five inches, and he adds that the measure is still used in remote parts of Europe. The custom of wearing native woollens died away with the decay of the Irish speech. They became unfashionable, and it was pitiful to see a brisk trade by traders from down the country in second-hand ready-mades. Going through the Westport fair one day I heard the small boys bleating out 'baa' to comfortably attired mountain folk in thick woollens from the Tourmakeady area.

Fenton also tells of a man whose sisters were expelled from the town school until they came dressed in 'respectable shop clothes'.

There is also a description by P. J. MacGill of a famous wool fair at

Magheramore in south-west Donegal. At the Magheramore fair in Ardara, homespun and handwoven tweeds were sold on tables and benches set up along the main street of the little town. Most of the buyers were local men, but in some cases they came from Belfast, Dublin or even London.

18
Markets

IN THE Irish language the word for a market is *margadh* and it is derived from Norse, so perhaps the Norsemen first brought the idea to Ireland. When patents for fairs were granted early in the seventeenth century, markets were usually established at the same time. In the larger towns there were usually two or three market days in each week, and during later centuries more markets were added. Markets were always held in a definite part of the town and today names such as Cornmarket, Haymarket and Buttermarket still mark these places. Tolls were collected on all the goods sold in the market, though as time went on these were abolished in most towns. In the old charter towns it was the duty of the local authority to provide a method of weighing or measuring the goods brought to the market and in other places this was the responsibility of the local landlord who owned the town.

In many places there was great rivalry between markets and this was sometimes the result of a quarrel between two landlords. One such quarrel is well described in John Healy's book, *The Death of an Irish Town*. On the Mayo border in County Sligo was the small town of Bellaghy, part of the estate owned by a certain Lord Knox, and beside it in County Mayo was the estate owned by Lord Dillon. The tenants from both estates brought their grain to the market in Bellaghy and here the trouble began when Lord Knox decided that his tenants must be first to have their grain weighed at the market scales. The agent of the Dillon estate, Charles Strickland, built a new town and beside the first completed house he erected a public scales. Knox objected and Strickland was ordered to take down the scales. He did so, and replaced it two feet away. Knox again objected and again Strickland moved the scale a couple of feet: when this happened a third time Knox realised he was beaten and gave up the struggle, and the market of Bellaghy declined as the market in Charlestown flourished.

The things sold at the markets were the ordinary produce of the farms of the district and varied from place to place.They also depended on the time of year. Generally markets were larger during the months of autumn and early winter. In some towns specially large markets were held during this time and the market held just before Christmas was often called The Big Market, or *An Margadh Mór*. It must be remembered that until the present century the people of the town were dependent on the local market for their supplies of many necessities – potatoes, vegetables, fowl, meat, butter, and eggs as well as fuel and grain. In addition, buyers for certain local industries attended to buy such thing as wool and linen yarn for weaving, and hides, skins and oak bark for tanning.

Some things which were not produced locally were brought to the market by pedlars. Salt was necessary for keeping butter, and coopers attended to sell tubs and barrels. Dried or salted fish might also be brought from a distance or heavy dark crocks which were used to keep milk. Many other examples could be cited and in come cases a market might be well known for the sale of some necessity – for example, tools used in agriculture.

Market Houses

In many cases the market was held in the central square of the town – in Ulster this is usually called the Diamond – or in some suitable open space. In most towns a market house was built by the local authority or by the local landlord who owned the market. In some cases the market area – the market yard – was enclosed by a wall with two gates, an entrance gate and an exit gate. This enclosed area was used for many purposes. It might be used by a travelling circus, or to house part of the local agricultural show, or as a place for a political meeting, as well as being a market area. It was usually equipped with a scales, a weigh-bridge, and a clock and bell which could be used to regulate the hours of trading.

In Derry city the old market house was built on the Diamond in 1692. It also served as the town hall, and on the ground floor held the mayor's office as well as a guard room, weigh house and a meal market. On the next floor the law courts were held, and the area was also used as a ballroom and no doubt had other functions. This building was removed during the nineteenth century.

I do not know if any market houses survive from the seventeenth century, but quite a number still remain from the late eighteenth century and the first half of the nineteenth century. Perhaps the most impressive example is the building in the town centre of Newtownards, County Down, which is now used as a town hall. It was built about the year

1770. Another fine example can be seen at Mullingar in County Westmeath. This has now become the headquarters of the county library service. Both these buildings add greatly to their towns. I think my favourite market house is in what is now the small village of Kilworth, a little way off the main road from Fermoy to Mitchelstown in County Cork. With the church beside it, it makes a very striking picture as one enters the village from the main road. The building has been efficiently restored and when I was there was being used as a craft centre. In Brookborough, County Fermanagh, the small market house is now being used as the local Orange hall, and in Draperstown, County Derry, the market house, built in 1839, is now the county library. In Maguire's Bridge, County Fermanagh, the market house stands in the middle of the street. It does not appear to have been changed to any extent and when I saw it the iron gates were still guarding the three entrances to the ground floor.

There is a fine example to be seen in Blessington. The entrances are now filled with glass and it is possible to see the beam of the weighing scales still in position. The platform of the weigh-bridge is still set in the ground outside and the upper floor is used as a lawyer's office. The market house of Baltinglass still stands in the central square of the town but it has been so much used and abused that it adds nothing to the townscape.

In Wexford the small building in the Corn Market is now being used as an art centre. In Kildare town the market house adds to the appearance of the square because it has been restored and is used as the Tourist Office. An elegant example is still used in Ennistymon, County Clare, and another in Callan, County Kilkenny. This one is kept very carefully and still has its outside stairs leading to the upper floor. It is used as the local office of the county council.

There are many others still to be found in towns all over the country. Some have been demolished and there is now no point in regretting this. It should be realised that they were often fine buildings and should be preserved carefully even though they are no longer needed for markets, because in many cases they add significantly to the appearance of the towns.

Thackeray, during his visit to Ireland in 1842, had something to say about Irish markets. About Dunmanway he wrote: 'Here it was market day, and as usual no lack of attendants: swarms of peasants in their blue cloaks squatting by their stalls here and there. There is a little miserable old market house where a few women were selling butter-milk: another bullocks' hearts liver and such like scraps of meat:

another had dried mackerel on a board and plenty of people huckstering of course.'

In Killarney he looked out from the hotel window and saw:

a dismal rickety building with a slated face that looks like an ex-townhall. There is a row of arches to the ground floor the angels at the base of which seem to have mouldered or to have been kicked away. Over the centre arch is a picture with a flourishing yellow inscription above importing that it is the meeting place of the total abstinence society. . . . A sort of market is held here and the place is swarming with blue cloaks and groups of men talking: here and there is a stall with coarse linens, crockery, a cheese and crowds of egg and milk women are squatted on the pavement with their ragged customers or gossips: and the yellow-haired girl with a barrel containing nothing at all.

In the *Statistical Survey of County Clare* there is a reference to the market house in Corofin. On Sundays it was used for mass, and when mass was finished it was used as a ball alley. I have also heard that early in the nineteenth century the market house in Augher, County Tyrone, was used as a Presbyterian meeting house.

Tolls at Fairs and Markets

These were normally paid to the proprietor of the fair or market, the local authority or the landlord on the goods sold there. It was fully realised that the holding of a fair or market was of benefit to everybody concerned. In practice the local landowner leased his right to collect the tolls to someone who did the actual collecting for his own profit. In the Inichiquin manuscripts there is a lease of the tolls and customs of the fairs and markets of Corofin, County Clare, from the owner, Sir Lucius O'Brien, to Patrick Kerin. The date of the lease is 4 August 1773 and the annual rent £16.16s.0d. At about the same time, in 1775, the tolls of the fairs and markets at Mallow were rented by the proprietor, Colonel Jephson, to Richard Willis for £70 a year.

These were significant sums, and the amounts paid by the people who bought or sold is listed for a number of places. At Aghaboe in County Leix 4d. a head was paid on cattle. For each sheep or pig sold 1d. was paid, and 4d. for a cartload of pigs. A pedlar who erected a standing paid 4d., and the proprietor of a tent paid 6d. Other traders, coopers and hatters also paid 6d. and tolls were paid on linen and woollen cloth. These rates were typical. About the same time (1815) a toll of 6d. was paid on every horse or cow sold at Macroom, County

Cork, and 1*d*. was paid on each sheep or pig.

Early in the nineteenth century it was reported from Maghera, County Derry:

> Until very lately at all our public fairs different bodies of men were constantly posted at the custom gaps with books in their hands administering oaths to all persons, young and old, drunk or sober, to ascertain whether the cattle they drove had been bought or sold in the fair. These twopenny bounties on perjury have been at last discontinued and a small toll is now levied on all cattle brought into fairs whether they are sold or not.

In 1817 the tolls of the fairs in Moneymore, County Derry, were leased to Sir William Rowley by the proprietors, the Drapers Company, for £27.14*s*.0*d*. a year. However, by the year 1832 it was stated that cattle were being stamped before they were taken into the fair. The report recommended that the tolls be completely abolished, and the agent be compensated. It went on to explain that the payment of tolls discouraged people from bringing their cattle to the fair, even though no distinction was then being made between tenants of the company and strangers. Formerly the tenants had been free and only strangers had paid tolls.

In 1839, the report said that even though tolls had been abolished since 1832, the size of the fair in Moneymore had not increased, due to the competition of neighbouring fairs. The report went on to say that the fairs were not badly attended, and added that the conduct of the people was orderly and quiet. At dusk they all went home.

The *Statistical Survey of County Cavan* has an interesting reference to the practice at the market in Belturbet:

> Oat meal, potatoes, and a good deal of yarn are sold here but no webbs. In the customs which are paid for commodities entering the market there is a very glaring imposition which materially injures the town and ought further to be redressed: they take their customs in kind for which they have not any lawful standard or measure, or if they have they do not use: the collector of the customs imposes a large wooden dish full of meal, the size of which is never adjusted. Consequently as the markets rise so do the tolls. The owner of a sack of meal which was lately worth near 6*s*. a stone was obliged to give this huge measure which from its size I should suppose contains considerably more than 14 pounds. I question, is there a market in Ireland where the custom in cash on such an article exceeds three pence. In the adjoining village of Ballyhays it amounts to but two pence per sack and in this little spot the market is considerably

better of course than Belturbet. These customs are now individual property, and are set annually for about £100. This terrible monopoly, which is such destruction to the town and its proprietors is now vested in two families who alternately preside over the corporation by which, and a provost, the town is governed and is now in fact their estates.

The report goes on to say that there is an excellent market house, over which there is a session house in the town.

In the neighbouring town of Cavan there were two sets of markets in 1888, one set owned by the neighbouring landowner, Lord Farnham, and the other owned and run by the town commissioners. Lord Farnham's markets were held near the market house (the old courthouse) in Main Street. They were administered by a certain John O'Reilly, J.P., who gave evidence to the royal commissioners. He said he was the weightmaster and tenant of the market house. The market yard was his own. He said he was the crane master under Lord Farnham, and paid him £70 per half year for the market house and £30 for the market yard.

In Farnham's market corn was sold on Monday and butter and flax on Tuesday, which was the general market day. In the markets run by the town commissioners, eggs, fowl and pork were sold during the winter months. These were held at the egg market in Mill Street in a space enclosed by a wall with three gates. In 1923, the town bought out Farnham. The market house in Main Street was closed in 1962 and demolished in 1969.

In my childhood I remember a big stone roughly oval in shape and about five feet high which stood on the roadside leading to the railway station of Ballinamore. On one side of the stone, the outline of a cross had been cut, facing the roadway. At this stone the collector of the tolls took his stand on fair days. In some cases the person driving the cattle might claim that they had not been sold and no tolls were due from them. If the collector doubted the word of the driver, he might ask him to place his hand on the stone and declare solemnly that the cattle had not been sold. This was regarded as having the virtue of an oath because the cross had been cut on the stone.

Gradually the collection of tolls ceased as it was realised that they were in some cases a significant disadvantage to the fair, and more and more fairs were free. The success of a fair was a great advantage to the town, much greater than the value of the tolls. I used to hear that the urban council in Longford abolished the fair tolls about 1930 because it cost more to collect them than they were worth to the council.

The end of a controversy about the fair tolls in Listowel, County Kerry, is described by Gaughan in Listowel. The proprietor, the Earl of Listowel, had sold his rights to Lloyds Bank and when in 1946 the urban council wished to buy them Lloyds asked £8,200. The council offered £4,000. Finally the Listowel Livestock Mart Company bought them for £8,000.

Money

The writers of the statistical surveys of the Irish counties were asked to enquire about what form of money was current in the different parts of the country. These enquiries revealed that even in the nineteenth century coinage was still scarce and not easily obtainable in many places. It was also found that in some places bank-notes circulated freely while in other parts of the country people would not accept them in payment for goods.

The most remarkable fact was that in all the linen markets in Ulster only gold and silver coin was accepted in payment by the sellers. This caused difficulties for the buyers, who were sometimes forced to exchange bank-notes for coinage at unfavourable rates. This was especially so in counties Derry and Monaghan.

In general, both paper money and coinage circulated freely, but there were some exceptions, and MacParlan wrote about Donegal: 'Money and paper are equally current, except in the mountain region, where I am sorry to see the degree of ignorance so great, that they totally refuse the currency of paper, being in general quite illiterate.'

In Leix, paper money circulated freely and Coote wrote: 'Paper money is the only currency and consists of Dublin bank-notes principally. The notes of Kilkenny, Clonmel and Waterford banks also circulate.' He also mentioned that some silver coins were struck at a mint run by the local colliery owners.

In County Clare, Dutton said that paper notes for small sums were in circulation in the year 1807. He wrote: 'It will be scarcely credited in Dublin that at this day they are publicly negotiated in Ennis and of the value of 1s. to a guinea. Since the liberal circulation of silver coin by the Bank of Ireland there can be no possible excuse for the emission of paper for small sums.'

From the Barony of Duhallow in County Cork there were more serious complaints. Townsend wrote:

The substitution of paper money for specie has in this part of the U.K. been productive of serious injury. . . from the prodigious number of forged notes that are every day passed.

The circulation of forged notes is become a trade and a very gainful one. Parties of swindlers attend the fairs and markets for the purpose of circulating them, and seldom fail to find a sufficient number of dupes among the simple country folk. The leniency with which these practices are treated encourages their continuance. The worst consequences a swindler had usually to apprehend is being obliged to give a good note for a bad one. Offenders are seldom brought to condign punishment for these or indeed for any other transgressions. A poor man never prosecutes with any view but compensation.

With notes being issued by all the different local banks as well as by local merchants it was only to be expected that forgeries would be put into circulation.

Weights and Measures

In every market it was essential that some honest means be available by which goods could be weighed or measured. Once I saw a quotation from the *Book of Proverbs* written over the door of a fish store, in the centre of the Donegal Gaeltacht. The notice was in Irish but as I don't remember it, I must give the English text:

Deceitful scales are an abomination to the Lord
But an accurate weight is his delight. *(Proverbs 11:1)*

The writers of the statistical surveys have much to say about the different methods used, and these were not standardised. In many markets potatoes were sold by the bushel but this was not very helpful because a bushel might mean almost any quantity – six stone in some markets, sixteen stone in others, and in some cases as much as eighteen or twenty stone. There was a further difficulty, because in summer a stone of potatoes weighed sixteen pounds and in winter eighteen pounds.

Similarly, the weighing of corn was very complicated, with measures such as long barrels and short barrels. In the grain market of Ennis a short barrel of wheat weighed twenty stone, a short barrel of oats weighed fourteen stone, and a short barrel of bran weighed four stone. A long barrel contained twice the amount in a short barrel. At the same time grain was sold by weight only in the market of Kilrush.

In Kilworth in County Cork wheat was sold in two and a half hundredweight and five hundredweight sacks and barley malt and oats were sold by measure. Here a barrel of barley contained thirty-six stone, a barrel of oats contained thirty-three stone, and a barrel of malt contained thirty stone. In Cork potatoes were sold by weight, but in Mallow the unit used to measure the amount of potatoes was the full of a butter firkin. Twenty-four of these constituted a barrel of potatoes.

In the *Statistical Survey of County Clare* the writer wrote:

> Great abuses are practised at markets and at some stores in the weighing. Frequently the weights are of stones of various sizes, pieces of iron or lead or mutilated weights. In fact the seller does not well know what they weigh as very few have scales at home, and even if he had, little notice would be taken by the infallable clerk of the scales.
>
> Magistrates and Churchwardens have the power to take up fraudulent weights and measures, but of what use is a power they have not the honesty to exert.

In County Sligo there were different measures. There, 'potatoes are sold by the peck which is substituted to and always supposed to contain half a hundred. Oaten meal is sold by the peck which must always contain a weight of ten pounds. A sack of oats contains twenty-four stone: a barrel of barley fourteen stone: but these, though bulk names, are all weighed, as is every article throughout the county except small quantities of meal, potatoes, etc.'

In County Cavan meal was sold by the hundredweight, which contained 120 lb. Oats were sold by the stone, which in this case contained 14lb, and fourteen stone made one barrel. Twelve stone of malt made a barrel, as did twenty stone of wheat. A stone of flax also contained 14 lb.

There appears to have been only one unit for weighing wool, the stone, which always contained 16 lb. A stone of feathers also contained 16 lb.

In measuring cloth, standard measures were used at the linen markets in Ulster but in other parts of the country other measures were used. One unit of length was the bandle *(bannlamh)* i.e. a cubit, which varied from place to place. In County Galway it measured 30 in., in Kilkenny 24 in. and in Limerick only 21 in. The width also varied, but in general was about 18 in. The bandle was used to measure both linen and woollen cloth. Another unit of length was the *slat* which appears to have always been 50 in.

Market Crosses

On a recently published map of mediaeval Dublin the market cross is shown at the top of Nicholas Street, at the entrance to Christchurch Place. A market cross was almost a part of any mediaeval town, and there are references to them in a number of Irish towns. Perhaps the best recorded is the cross which used to stand in High Street in Kilkenny.

In 1606 the corporation of Kilkenny made an order that the market be held between the market cross and Croker's Cross, and no one was allowed to buy elsewhere. Croker's Cross stood at the junction of High Street, Rose Inn Street and Castle Street. It also has been removed. There is also a reference to a market cross in New Ross but it has long disappeared. The only market cross of which part has survived is in Clonmel. This is known as 'the Bargain Stone' and 'the Pay on the Nail Stone', and it was used as a nail – in other words, when a deal was completed the price was paid out on it. Such nails were a feature of many towns, and a number of them can be seen in Bristol. One of which I know is made of wood and is preserved in Reginald's Tower in the city of Waterford, and there is another in Limerick.

In a number of cases ancient Irish crosses taken from adjacent monastic sites were used as market crosses in some Irish towns. The best known of these is probably the cross which can be seen as one drives through Kells, beside the entrance gate which leads to the Church of Ireland church. Another was the Cross of Dromore, County Down. This had once stood near the west door of the mediaeval cathedral, and the market was held around it. The shaft of the cross still survives and it was erected in its present position about a century ago. A tenth-century cross now stands in the Diamond in Clones, County Monaghan. Originally it stood on the monastic site there and is shown on a map of Clones painted about 1590. During the nineteenth century the markets, especially the linen markets, were held around the old cross.

The best example of what may be called a true market cross can be found in Newtownards, County Down. This was designed by one of the new planters, Sir James Montgomery, and was built in 1635. It is an octagonal building, once used as the town jail, and is decorated with coats of arms and surmounted by a cross.

Sir Thomas Philips had established the new town of Limavady in County Derry by the year 1622. By then it consisted of eighteen small houses set round a crossroads and with a stone cross at the intersection.

Some other interesting remains of markets can be found in Irish towns. Few market yards remain but I noticed what looked like one in Ballaghadereen, County Roscommon. The Shambles in Bandon is still intact and well worth preserving. Another old market can be seen leading off the Bull Ring in Wexford, and this is also of interest. I understand that the old markets in Coleraine, built in 1830, still continue and the market bell is still in position. When I read this I wondered if this was the bell which was rung at 8.0 a.m. to tell the butchers to bring their meat into the market. It was rung again at 9.0 a.m. and after that no more meat might be brought into the market. Clearly this rule was made in the interests of the customers who were thus able to see all the meat before buying. Thackeray in 1842 described the market of Coleraine in these words: 'The scene as we entered the Diamond was rather a lively one. A score of little stalls were brilliant with lights: the people were thronging in the place making their Saturday bargains: the town clock began to toll nine.'

The market cross, Newtownards, Co. Down

19
Linen and Flax

THE cultivation of linen and the manufacture of yarn have been carried out in Ireland for much more than 1,000 years. In the ancient laws of Ireland there are references to flax and it is certain that the *léine* worn by the Irish aristocracy was made of linen. Linen was also used for making vestments and altar cloths for use in church, and no doubt some of the aristocratic ladies wore fine linen clothes. Professor Donnchadh Ó Corráin of University College, Cork tells us that: 'The only other crop of importance for which ploughing was done was flax, and the law tracts and archeological finds leave us in no doubt about the domestic importance of linen production. Spinning and weaving were among the activities of the ordinary housewife and this implies that a patch of flax was normally grown by the farmer.'

Flax continued to be grown in every part of Ireland until the nineteenth century, though as the century went on the production of linen declined nearly everywhere except in the province of Ulster. In the year 1571 a licence was granted to Edmund More 'to export 3,000 packs of linen yarn and every part thereof by whole packs, half packs or otherwise.' Early in the seventeenth century a licence was granted to Sir Edmund Blunt and to Will Britten to export 1,200 packs of linen yarn each year for ten years. Each pack was to weigh four hundredweight, at six score pounds per hundredweight. A short time later, in 1607, a licence was granted to John West, one of the grooms of the privy chamber, to export 1,200 packs of linen yarn each year for twenty-one years. Each pack was to weigh four hundredweight. These grants would indicate that flax was extensively grown in Ireland during the sixteenth and early seventeenth centuries, before the plantation of Ulster and the development of the linen industry there.

Flax, linen yarn and linen cloth were sold at fairs and markets in most parts of Ireland, but when the country settled down after the Williamite wars the growing of flax increased rapidly in Ulster. The linen industry would be described in the modern jargon as having a high labour content and a high value end product. It was therefore a very suitable crop for a hardworking community of small farmers. In addition, many of the landlords in the northern counties were resident and of the improving type and they understood that the growing of flax and the production of linen were good methods of making rents. In the beginning, almost all the work of growing, harvesting, treating, spinning and weaving was done in their homes by the tenant farmers and their families. The amount of hard work necessary to produce a piece of linen cloth was very great and the success of the industry reflects great credit on the people of Ulster. The reasons given for this success may depend to some extent on one's views of history and of religion but nobody can deny its success.

Flax seed might be saved by the farmer from the crop of the previous year and seed imported from the Baltic, Holland or North America might be used. Around the year 1800 the amount of seed necessary to sow an acre of flax cost about £2.17s.0d. The ground which had been cleared of weeds the previous year by growing a crop of potatoes was ploughed and the seed sown between mid-April and mid-May. The growing crop was carefully weeded and when the blue flowers had formed the flax was pulled if it was to be used to make fine linen. If the intention was to produce seed, the flax was pulled when the flowers had faded and the head was full but in this case the fibre made a coarser linen. One bushel of seed sowed yielded eight bushels of seed as well as the flax. The heads were gathered and kept carefully dry until the next season, then they were thrashed and winnowed. All the experts agreed that Irish flax seed was as good as any foreign seed but the problem was to save it if the season was wet. A bushel of seed would yield twenty-five stone of clean scutched flax and the seed produced by an acre of flax could be sold for £16 in 1800. It was most important that the soil be well tilled and free from weeds, which do great damage to the crop.

The flax plants were pulled, tied in bundles and put in the stagnant water of the flax hole for five to twelve days to rot, depending on the temperature of the water. They were kept under the surface of the water, then taken out and spread on the grass and turned every second day to dry. When dried, the flax was tied in bundles and built into stacks. At the next stage it was heated in ovens and broken by striking it with a beetle while still warm. This was to separate the woody part from the filaments. This work was usually done by men, and the process was completed by the women, who scutched it. It was then hackled with combs and made ready for spinning, and the woody refuse was used to thatch houses. The flax filaments were then spun and the yarn steeped, washed clean, and boiled ready for the weaver.

When it was woven it was taken to the linen market and sold unbleached.

During the second half of the eighteenth century the industry gradually became organised. Very often a strong farmer would buy up the yarn at the local fair. On his land he built a number of houses, each furnished with a loom and a small piece of land, and this he let to a weaver at a rent of about £2 – 'a dry cot take'. If the weaver was also given the grass of a cow the rent was £3 – 'a wet cot take'. The farmer, now called a manufacturer, gave out the flax to be spun by the women and the yarn to be woven by the weavers. The manufacturer might also keep journeymen working in his own house and he organised the buying and selling. A journeyman weaver could earn up to 18*d*. a day, while the women earned 6*d*. a day for spinning. In Ulster there were more weavers than farm labourers, and the apprenticeship lasted three years.

The linen markets were very strictly controlled by the Linen Board. In most cases the buyers stood on benches or stone platforms in the open street as the sellers passed below them with a few folds of the linen exposed for inspection. Before this was done the web had been examined and measured by an official called the seal master who noted the length of the web. He had to give substantial security to the Linen Board before he was given his commission, and he had to be extremely accurate, because if there was any flaw in the linen, or if it was not of the same quality throughout or if any part of the web was damaged, both he and the weaver were liable to severe penalties. These were never remitted or passed over because the merchants were fully aware that the credit of the trade and its consequences could only be upheld 'by strict attention to the excellent laws which control the trade'.

For the seal master's trouble he was entitled to 2*d*. from the seller for every web he measured, and the owner of the house also received 1*d*. for every web paid for in his house. This was also deducted from the seller. In some markets there might be as many as 1,000 webs sold in one day.

The piece was bought on the security of the seal, and if any dishonesty was discovered the piece was forfeit and a heavy fine imposed. The fine was used to compensate the buyer and the rest went to the Linen Board. If the concealed part of the web was of worse quality than the rest the fine might be increased. Even for such minor faults as trying to sell the linen before the appointed time a fine of 20*s*. was imposed and this was given to the person who made the complaint. If a merchant sold bad flax seed, shown by the presence of black specks on the flax, he had to compensate the farmer.

When Arthur Young was in Lurgan in 1776, Mr Brownlow, the squire of the place, walked with him to the market to show him how the linens were sold. The cambrics – fine linens – were disposed of early in the market day:

> . . . but when the clock strikes eleven the drapers jump upon stone standings and the weavers instantly flock about them with their pieces. The bargains are not struck at a word but there is a little altercation whether the price shall be one half-penny or a penny a yard, more or less which appeared to me useless. The draper's clerk stands by him and writes his master's name on the pieces he buys, with the price, and giving it back to the seller, who goes to the draper's quarters and waits his coming. At twelve it ends: then there is an hour for measuring the pieces and paying the money, for nothing but ready money is taken and this is the way the business is carried out at all the markets. Three thousand pieces a week are sold here at 35s. each on an average of £5,250 and per annum £237,000 and this is all made in a circumference of not many miles.

In Drogheda and probably in some places further south the market routine was different. Here the linen was laid out for the inspection of the buyers on raised benches in the linen market, a large quadrangular building two storeys high. Here the buyers were mainly drapers from Dublin.

All over Ulster there were famous linen markets. These included Lurgan, Newry, Coleraine, Banbridge, Downpatrick, Randalstown and Dungannon. Outside this area there were large markets in Derry, and a good market in Monaghan town, where, in 1800, £3,000 to £4,000 was spent on the linen market held in the square near the courthouse. There were also important linen markets held in the market house in Ballybay with £1,500 a week and around the old market cross on the Diamond in Clones. This was mainly for the sale of linen yarn, as the linen cloth was sent to the market in Cootehill. This place had been developed by its landlord and was regarded as a model village. At the end of the eighteenth century its market was a busy one, and Coote wrote in 1801: 'buyers from all the linen markets of Ulster steadily frequent Cootehill market. As to the laws respecting the linen trade there is no place where they are more rigorously observed or an infringement more severely punished.' He added that most of the linen sold in Cootehill was sheeting. There was also a linen market in Killeshandra and flax and linen yarn were sold in Belturbet and in Cavan town.

Most of the flax grown in east Donegal and in Inishowen was sold in Derry as flax or as yarn. MacParlan reported in 1801 that some of the improving landlords in Donegal were keen to encourage the cultivation of flax on their estates. One of the objects of the Tyrhugh Farming Society was to establish a linen market in Ballyshannon. This was one way to discourage the growing of barley and the making of whiskey. MacParlan went on:

> Lord Conyngham and Mr Connelly have done a great deal here to encourage the linen trade. Lord Conyngham has given looms to his tenants and lends them money to carry on this trade, which already is in a very considerable degree of forwardness. . . .
> Even furnishing tenants with looms to weave their own yarns will produce a surplus saving and enrichment annually to the amount of their whole year's rent. . . . In widely extended estates such as Lord Conyngham's suppose the produce of yarn £10,000 that manufactured into linen which may be done by the tenants at times they could not work abroad would produce an increase sum of £2,700 calculating in a difference of two-sevenths between the raw and the manufactured material. . . .
> Mr Connolly also had established a linen manufactory, twenty houses at the Nadir and Corlea near Ballyshannon, with two looms in each house and a certain portion of land.

Despite all MacParlan's enthusiasm the land in Donegal was not good, and the industry did not flourish outside the fertile areas. Derry continued to be the great linen market. In the statistical survey it is stated that in 1802, 250,000 pieces of unbleached linen were sold in Derry for £562,500. There were also large linen markets in Limavady, Maghera and Moneymore encouraged by the London companies.

The busiest time in the linen markets was during February and March, and again during August, September and October. Prices varied greatly from year to year, but around the year 1800 the scutched flax was sold at from 4d. to 6d. a pound. Linen yarn cost about 4s. a pound and sacking about 1s.1d. a yard. A good web of linen 52 yards long and ¾ yard wide would sell at 2s. to 2s.4d. a yard.

The great linen areas of Ulster were very proud of their success, and some of the names were famous in the linen trade. The name Coleraine stamped on a piece of linen was a mark of very high quality. Banbridge used the name Gilford, that of a neighbouring village, and this was also a mark of high quality. Still another was Dromore, a small town in the Lagan Valley where very fine linens were sold.

The last stage in the manufacture of linen was the bleaching of the cloth, and in some cases this caused trouble. The Linen Board in Dublin registered each firm which bleached linen and gradually this business became concentrated around Belfast. Around 1800 there were fifty-eight registered bleachers. MacParlan tells the following cautionary tale about methods used to bleach linen:

> Some of these (bleachers) follow the method of boiling in pot-ash and exposure to the air. One, I have been told, in particular has launched into the new method of alternate steepings in sulphuret and oxymuriate of lime, with alternate washings and dryings, but not without a general cry of complaint against the effects, owing, no doubt, to the ignorance and mismanagement of its conductors.
>
> A very large cargo of linens bleached in this manner had been very lately returned from Jamaica to Dublin and thrown on the hands of a Northern gentleman who sold it. Law was at first resorted to, but the affaire was ultimately referred to three gentleman well versed in the trade and they awarded (the linens having proved quite rotten, though beautifully white) the Northern manufacturer to refund the price of the cargo and every expense attending the freight amounting to near £3,000. This, it will be hoped, will be a lesson to ignorant and inattentive adventurers.

It is surprising that the Linen Board allowed any bleacher to use such a method, because its rules were strictly enforced to the benefit of everyone concerned. In 1832 one writer had this to say about the linen traders of Banbridge:

> Even when almost every port was closed against the introduction of Irish linens and the trade was nearly lost to the country those of Banbridge found a ready market: and when the energies of the linen merchant on the old system were nearly paralysed by foreign competition, the merchants of this place created a new trade by commencing as manufacturers on an extensive scale and opening up an intercourse with America and other parts.

This refers to the mechanisation of the spinning and weaving of linen in Ulster. Although the landlord, the Marquis of Downshire, had built a hall for the sale of yarn and brown linens in Banbridge, Lewis found that this trade had declined and by 1832 machines were doing the spinning and weaving.

In contrast to this high degree of efficiency, Sir William Wilde described what might be called the old way of treating flax as he saw it in his native Roscommon during the early years of the nineteenth century. As he wrote, it was a time 'when flax was much grown in Connaught:

After the flax had been steeped in the boghole and bleached on the *Annagh* it was taken home, kiln dried, and in process of time broken preparatory to being hackled, scutched and spun into yarn. All which process were the result of household manufactory. The flax was generally broken by men: a large stool such as that used for the table in a peasant's cottage was everted and laid flat on the floor. The operator sat down behind it with a leg at each end, placed the sheaf of dried flax along the stool, holding it into the fork of the legs and with a long stout beetle broke up the outer husk or cuticle of the fibre, preparatory to its removal by being drawn through the hackle pins. As several people were generally engaged in the operation at a time the noise produced thereby was quite deafening, and hence the common expression in Connaught indicative of great uproar – 'it was like flax breaking'.

Wilde, in *Irish Popular Superstitions*, also mentioned one of his neighbours, a hackler, who moved around with 'his little hackle-boxes resembling creepy stools slung across his shoulders, one hanging behind, and another before.'

Early in the eighteenth century the textile trade was booming generally and the success of the linen trade in Ulster was observed with interest by some of the more acute and energetic landlords in other parts of the country. Sligo was not far from Ulster, and some of the improving landlords there set about establishing the linen industry on their estates. One of these, Charles O'Hara, built houses for eighty weavers and was able to persuade the Linen Board to supply them with looms. O'Hara also provided 'very cheap bargains of land' for the weavers. The experiment was a success and the report continues: 'These people have ever since resided and gave one of the first springs to the trade in this country. They being Protestants, Mr O'Hara got from the Board of first fruits every necessary assistance to purchase a glebe and build a church for their accommodation.'

Also in County Sligo the Fitzmaurice family established the industry in Ballymote, where Lord Shelbourne built houses for 120 linen workers and supplied them with looms. These men were also Protestants from Ulster, and clearly it was intended that they should repeat the success of the Ulster plantation. Shelbournes's successor, Thomas Fitzmaurice, continued the work and 'took his rents amounting to about £7,000 a year in linens'.

The most important markets for the sale of linen and linen yarn were in Ballymote and Sligo town. In Ballymote, linen fairs were held on 1 February, 3 September and 15 November, but Sligo was the most important market. There, a linen hall had been built and it was 'regularly and extensively conducted by Mr Holmes. Very large sums of money are every week laid out here in the purchase of linens.'

The writer of the statistical survey was quite enthusiastic about all this improvement and went on to point out that 'forty years ago there were not five pieces of linen sold yearly in the County Sligo'.

This combination of an improvement and an effort to establish a Protestant enclave among a people almost entirely Catholic was common among Irish landlords in the middle of the eighteenth century. Textile villages were established in many parts of Ireland and as part of the same improvement charter schools were founded where children were taught spinning and weaving as well as the doctrines of the established church.

In his *History of Waterford* Charles Smith wrote:

> The linen manufacture has hitherto gained little footing in this part of the kingdom. The methods of living here are very different from those in the north which these people will not comply with. If colonies of the northern inhabitants are to be invited into these parts which, it is to be presumed, is the best method of spreading the linen manufacture hither, they must have land set them at a cheaper rate than our cottagers pay for it, who can maintain a family with an acre or two of potatoes and pay a large rent for a dairy with the labour of a few hands.

This may have inspired Smith's neighbour, Lord Grandison, to settle a colony of Protestant weavers at Dromana on the River Blackwater in County Waterford in the parish of Affane. The village was built around the church there, and Lord Grandison referred to being 'at church with my weavers'.

In County Mayo too the improving landlords were busy trying to establish the linen industry. The first textile village may have been Newport, where the Pratts settled a colony of Quakers about 1720. In the north of the county the linens were sold unbleached in the market of Ballina because there was no convenient bleach green. Some of the flax was sold as yarn and may have been woven in Ulster. It is a slight surprise to read that linen was produced in the Erris district, though little if any was sold out of the district and as a result 'they dress better than the poor of the interior.'

By the year 1800 the trade was flourishing. In the barony of Burrishoole (centred on Newport) flax was extensively grown. Spinning wheels and looms were in every cabin – in some cabins there were two looms – where they spun and wove pieces of linen for the regular linen markets at Castlebar and Westport. Towards Westport, in the barony of Murrisk, it was greatly encouraged by the late Earl of Altamont, who established two bleach greens in the neighbourhood. Around Castlebar the local landowner, Lord Lucan, established three bleach greens as well as setting up a linen hall there where the linen market was held on Saturday and £500 spent.

Another such village was Manulla, founded in 1733 by one of the Brownes, and there eighty Presbyterian families from Ulster were settled to establish the linen industry. The last migration of linen workers from Ulster to Mayo occurred at the end of the century. In this case most of the new arrivals were Catholics, and MacParlan wrote: 'the migration too of the northern weavers during the late troubles into this county has very much promoted the linen manufacture', ending by saying: 'at Ballina, Costello and different parts of the county is abundance of fuel and water and consequently every aptness of situation for bleach greens, many of which are still necessary in this county so extensive and considerable is grown the linen business.'

In County Galway the cultivation of flax was widespread during the eighteenth and nineteenth centuries, and some flax was grown there early in the present century. In 1807 Dutton wrote that in County Galway women often used coarse linens and yarns to barter with pedlars for small household necessities. He went on:

> The manufacture of coarse linen is the principal one in this county. They are generally what are called bandle linen. A bandle (*bannlamh* – a cubit) may be 28 inches wide, or 30 inches or 32 inches, and sheetings may be 37½ inches or 40½ inches wide. In fact, though there is a certain breadth prescribed by Act of Parliament and a power given to inspectors who do, or should, attend every fair or market to seize those deficient in breadth, yet little or no notice is taken of it and they are generally any breadth the owner or the weaver chooses to make them. There is a considerable quantity sold every Thursday at the Linen Hall in Loughrea and a great deal of sheetings are also disposed of at the inn at Tuam, but I understand they are not of such fabric as to do any credit to the makers, as they are of a very flimsy texture and too often bleached with lime.

In County Galway a landlord called Robert French established his textile village at Monivea with its charter school, and houses for Protestant weavers from the north of Ireland, each with space for a loom.

In County Kerry also there were some landlords who encouraged the growing of flax. Some time about 1740 the local landlord settled a number of linen workers in Killarney. This effort met with some success, and when Thackeray was there in 1842 he saw some linens for sale on the market day. The linen industry was also established in Dingle, as Richard Hayworth, author of *In the Kingdom of Kerry*, found the site of an old bleach green there and learned that the local linens with the trade mark 'Bandle Tip' and 'Box and Tip' had once been famous.

In County Clare colonies of linen workers were established at Mountshannon and at Sixmilebridge. In 1735 fifty Protestant families from the north of Ireland were settled at Mountshannon by the local landowner, John Daly. About the same time Sixmilebridge was developed as a textile village by a family called Ievers. However, by 1806 Dutton wrote: 'All the linen manufactured in the county is used for home consumption and is generally coarse and of low price. A small quantity of coarse diapers for towels is made and generally sold at fairs and markets; also canvas for sacks and bags is sold in the same manner.' He went on to say that there were only three small bleach greens in the county and, as in County Galway, the women in County Clare sold bandle linen, as well as butter and eggs, to dealers from whom they bought household necessities. He also reported that flax seed from Europe was not available because of the war, but some seed grown in America could be bought in Limerick. However, most of the poorer people saved flax seed from their own crop and found it as satisfactory as the American seed.

In County Cork the most important flax-growing area was the south-west, and the centre of the linen trade was Bandon. This was mainly due to the fact that when Richard Boyle founded the town he settled a colony of Protestant weavers from Bristol there. In the town there were two market days, Wednesday on the north side of the River Bandon and Saturday on the south side. Townsend wrote in 1802 that the flax which was bought at the neighbouring fairs and markets was manufactured in Bandon into linens and tickens.

In the barony of Carbury linen-making was a cottage industry. Townsend said that women did all the spinning and weaving and usually made coarse linens – vitry and bandle cloth – mostly unbleached. He added that some fine linen was made there by the wealthier people for their own use. There was an important linen market held in Clonakilty on Fridays, and linen was also sold on the day before each of the annual fairs which were held on 25 March, 29 September and 1 November. He described the linens as home produced and unbleached, rather coarse and ¾–1 yard wide. Much yarn was also sold at the markets in Clonakilty, and the buyers, mainly merchants from Bandon, spent about £700 each week there.

There were other important linen markets and fairs held in Roscarbery, Skibbereen and Bantry. In Roscarbery many weavers lived in the town, and in addition to linens large quantities of yarn were sold at the markets and at the three annual fairs. Similarly, in Skibbereen and Bantry flax yarn and unbleached linen were offered for sale. Some of this unbleached linen, as well as the yarn and flax, were bought by strong farmers living in the neighbourhood. These men employed spinners and weavers to make a coarse linen cloth called vitry, 'and some of them bleached the linen by the profuse as well as undisguised use of caustic lime. The object of bleaching as far as colour is concerned is thus obtained but the cloth is destroyed by the corrosive quality of the lime.'

In north Cork flax was grown widely about the middle of the eighteenth century, but it appears to have died out by the end of the century. A description of the Mallow area written in 1775 tells of the decline of flax cultivation and of the manufacture of linen there. One of the reasons given for the decline was that the land around Mallow was not suitable for growing flax. The writer of the report said that formerly linen had been manufactired at Doneraile, five miles to the north of Mallow, and also at Annagh, seven miles to the north-west. He added that there were good bleach greens in both places, with twenty looms in Doneraile and twelve in Annagh.

The industry had not died out completely at the time the report was written, as the writer says that there were seven or eight weavers in the town. Three or four of these made broad linens and some few housekeepers in the town and the surrounding country sometimes made up a few pieces for sheeting and table linen. He also said that some bandle linen, as well as woollen cloth, was brought from other places to be sold at the four annual fairs at Mallow. In County Cork there were some other villages where linen-making was established. These included Dunmanway and Inishannon.

Flax growing and the making of linen were carried on in many parts of Leinster during the eighteenth century, but they declined during the nineteenth century. By 1710 it was flourishing in Meath and Louth, and both Dundalk and Drogheda had linen halls. In 1802 Robert Thompson found that in County Meath 'a yarn fair is held in each town on the market day before each fair day.' In Oldcastle finer yarns were sold at the Monday market, and in Kells yarn and some linen were sold on Saturdays. In County Offaly linen was made and sold at fairs and markets in Birr and Banagher, and in Carlow the finest linens were sold.

20

Butter and Fowl Markets

THE production of milk and the making of butter for sale has been an important source of income in many parts of Ireland since the beginning of the eighteenth century. In Leinster the best dairying districts were south Kildare, Carlow, Leix, Wexford and Kilkenny. Carlow was perhaps the best market town in Ireland, and in the *Statistical Survey of County Leix* it was said to be a great market for everything – grain, hides, tallow and wool as well as butter. The report continues:

> The great butter market there, Carlow, greatly encourages the dairies in this county for which the ground is naturally kind and favourable and perhaps in no part of Ireland does butter sell for such good prices. Many buyers here have commissions from the provision houses in Waterford to which it is all sent by the Barrow Navigation. The wholesale price this summer [1801] was £7 a hundred-weight. . . .
>
> In the parishes of Timahoe and Ballyroan are some extensive dairies which are often changed from dairying to fattening; and at Timahoe is the butter market which is a very considerable trade. The best exported butter is said to be from thence: the gentry occupy no more dairy than answers home consumption.

The report added that in the barony of Slewmargy the rents of small farms from ten to fifteen acres were paid principally in butter.

Some considerable quantities of cheese were also made in Leix early in the nineteenth century. This was mainly in the south of the county, and though the writer describes it as 'of indifferent quality' he says that a hundred tons were made each year and three-quarters of this were sold in the Dublin market at 6s.½d. a pound. Some was also sold in the market in Kilkenny.

In County Wexford the great butter markets were at Enniscorthy and Wexford, and large quantities of butter were exported from Wexford – 9,000 tubs annually around the year 1800. Even though the dairy farmers of Wexford were hardworking and efficient, Frazer was critical of the methods they used. He wrote in the *Statistical Survey of County Wexford*: 'The dairies in general are managed in a very dirty, slovenly manner and they are at very little pains in selecting dairy stock.' He may have been correct in some cases, but the fact that a County Wexford farmer made a profit of £120 from twenty-one cows would certainly show that the dairying was highly efficient.

The other great butter market in Leinster was Kilkenny, and here the quality of the butter was equal to that sold in Carlow. The output per cow was also very high and reached one and a half hundredweight on the better farms.

In Ulster, butter markets had been established by the end of the seventeenth century in such places as Lurgan and Moira in County Armagh and in Dromore and Hillsborough in County Down. Much of the butter was exported through the developing port of Belfast. In 1679 Sir George Rawdon of Lisburn feared that 'the butter trade, the chief business here, will inevitably be forestalled and Belfast merchants will have agents at Lurgan and Moira for all Armagh butter and at Hillsborough and Moira for Down.' By the year 1683 Belfast had exported 766 hundredweight of cheese and 33,881 hundredweight of butter. In Ulster the other important port for the export of butter was Newry.

The writers of the statistical surveys for the Ulster counties all speak of the poor quality of the native breeds of cattle, while agreeing that they were good milkers. Having described the cattle of east Cavan as 'very indifferent' one writer goes on: 'And it is surprising after the supply of the family's milk how much butter they regularly send to Newry market for the export trade; small parcels from each farm of course but the aggregate is very considerable.' In County Derry, after the usual complaints about the quality of the cattle, we learn that butter for the Derry market was made to the west of the city in County Donegal and taken by slide car to the city, where it was sold at 9*d.*–12*d.* a pound (18 ozs). Buttermilk was also sold in the market in Derry city.

In Coleraine milk was sold at 2*d.*–3*d.* a quart, fresh butter at 1*s.* a pound (18 ozs) while salted butter sold at 1*s.*1*d.* for 16 ozs. Cheese made of skimmed milk was sold in Coleraine at 6*d.* a pound and if full milk was used the price was 8*d.* Springing or milking cows to stock the dairy farms around Coleraine were often bought at the fairs in Enniskillen and cost 8–13 guineas each. The reason for this may be that the native cattle in County Antrim were of the Highland breed and not very good milkers.

The writer of the *Statistical Survey of County Antrim* says that, 'like

Cavan, Armagh and Down', Monaghan 'has only the small cow'. Despite this there were large butter markets in all the County Monaghan towns. At these markets the butter was bought by middlemen called commissioners on behalf of the Newry merchants – much the same system as was used in the linen markets. In Monaghan town the farmers took the butter to the market unpacked, but the commissioners also arranged for coopers to attend the markets.

There were large butter markets in some of the counties close to the Ulster border. These included Sligo, and in the year 1801 MacParlan wrote that there were:

> several dairies about Sligo and the export of butter from that town is very considerable; last year it amounted to upwards of £20,000. This vast increase in the quantity and export of butter is chiefly due to an improvement in the manner of making it up: formerly it used to be packed in crocks. Latterly the county people have been compelled to make it up in well coopered casks and this method has so improved the quality of the butter as to rival any in the Kingdom. . . . In the baronys of Liney and Carran butter and pasture furnish the principal means of paying rents.

In County Leitrim, though much of the land is poor, the Ulster system of small mixed farms was general by the end of the eighteenth century, and McParlan wrote that 'considerable quantities of butter are sold by the petty landholders who do not eat it themselves.'

In some parts of Ulster and the border counties where co-operative creameries had not been established these butter markets continued until about 1930. In my own childhood I remember the small barrels, each containing about fifty-six pounds of butter, being sold in the markets. The buyer, a middleman, carried a long, slender, hollow tube of metal which he might use to take a sample of the butter before buying it. At that time, just before the creameries finally took over the butter trade, there were continuous complaints about the quality of the butter and of the many ways it might be adulterated.

During the eighteenth and nineteenth centuries the production of butter was the most important industry in the province of Munster. Little of this butter was eaten at home, and it was almost all exported through the ports of Limerick, Waterford and Cork. Of these three, Cork had much the largest share of the trade. This predominance of the Cork butter market continued until about 1880 when it was superseded by the establishment of the creameries.

Much of the Irish butter was sent to the continent. From there it was re-exported to the colonies in the West Indies and South America where – naturally – heavily salted butter was favoured because it did not go rancid. Later in the eighteenth century, as the English market was opened to Irish produce, the amount of butter sold there increased greatly, and this continued for more than 100 years. In general it may be said that butter from County Clare, north Tipperary and most of County Limerick was exported through Limerick. The butter produced in south Tipperary and County Waterford went to the port of Waterford, and butter from Cork and Kerry went to the butter market in Cork.

This market was controlled by a group of exporters and brokers. All the butter taken to the market was inspected and graded on arrival. This was a formidable task, because during the busy season there 3,000 firkins were brought each morning and each firkin contained seventy pounds of butter. There were four inspectors employed at the market and very great efforts were made to ensure that the grading was uniform. The classes varied from grade one, the best, down to grade five.

The merchants were only allowed to deal in butter which had been graded and branded with the allotted grade. In order to ensure that this rule was observed, the butter in the stores of each of the merchants was inspected periodically by the market officials. In some cases the merchants added their own private marks. As a further precaution, there were inspectors on the quays as the butter was being loaded to make sure that it still carried the correct Cork brands. If, for example, an inspector found that the grade had been raised by one degree there was a fine of 10s. for each firkin so misgraded. It was a much more serious offence if a merchant were to remove the grade marks and then sell the butter to some unrecognised exporter. This was treated as an injury to the entire group of merchants, and a man might be expelled from the society and not be allowed to trade in the butter market.

Frauds might also occur after the butter had been exported. In 1842 a butter inspector went from Cork to Liverpool. His purpose was to investigate how a consignment of 650 casks of butter from Hamburg had reached South America bearing the label 'Casey Brothers Cork'. There was also the problem of brands and marks deliberately made to resemble those of the Cork exporters. Still another problem was the fact that by 1850 butter which had not passed through the Cork market was being exported from Cork and other Irish ports bearing the words 'Cork' or 'County Cork' branded on the casks. Then it was learned that casks bearing the brands of the Cork market were being retained in England and when emptied they were filled with a butter substitute.

It was also recognised that some of the butter sold in the Cork market was not of high quality and even as late as 1870 thirty per cent of it was graded three or lower.

Butter sent to the Cork market was consigned to brokers whose responsibility was to see that it was inspected, graded and branded. They then sold it to the exporters. There were about fifty of these brokers, and in 1853 their commission was fixed at 1s.8d. per hundredweight. Naturally they wished to have the butter sent to them, so in many cases they arranged to extend credit during the off season to the farmers who produced the butter. The debt was to be repayed by the sale of butter during the following season. This appears to have been a profitable business for the brokers, even more so than their regular commission, despite the fact that some of the producers failed to meet their debts.

Gaughan, in *Listowel*, quotes a reference to this practice from *A Tour Through Ireland* by J. Hall:

> On seeing when I got up in the morning great numbers assembled before my window I learned that they had come from a variety of parts to Listowel to borrow money. Butter merchants as they were termed, knowing the poverty of the farmers in general in this part of the country come from Cork to lend money on a certain day, which happened to be this. By lending money in this manner to enable the tenants to pay their rents, these butter merchants often secure all the butter which these poor people make in the course of the summer. Thousands of firkins are yearly received in this way at an easy rate and exported to England and elsewhere: the farmers by their agreement being obliged to carry it to Cork.

Gaughan also has a reference to the building of a road from Abbeyfeale to Newmarket so that the farmers of north Kerry might more easily bring their butter to Cork. He says that 30,000 firkins, valued at £52,000, were taken annually from Listowel to Cork. Oak casks to hold the butter were made and inspected in Cork before being given to the producers. When returned filled with butter the buyers were allowed a tare of 20 lbs as well as 2 lbs 'soakage weight' on each cask.

Butter might be adulterated by adding water. This was an old market trick and is mentioned by Archer. He wrote: 'The butter is also an object for fraud; they have a method of beating up old butter and mixing water with it to make it weigh heavy.' Sometimes in Cork the people also added an excessive amount of salt. In the early 1840s small farmers began selling fresh butter to people in the neigbouring towns. These men mixed and salted the butter and packed it in firkins for the Cork market. This practice developed, and in 1850-1 30,000 firkins of this specially packed butter reached the Cork market. Unfortunately, in preparing the butter the traders added quantities of boiling water. The authorities in Cork were slow to act against this practice, though such butter, known as 'cocks' – perhaps from an Irish word – was either reduced in price by 2s. per hundredweight or the quality reduced by one grade. It was not until 1872, and after many complaints from English buyers, that firm action was taken. Fines of £1 a firkin were imposed and in some cases the quality grade was refused.

From the year 1870 the great market was in decline. In 1869 oleomargarine, a mixture of beef fat and butter, was sold in England under the trade name 'Butterine' and at about the same time blended butter from Normandy came on to the English market. This was followed by butter from Denmark and Sweden which had been produced in large co-operative creameries using mechanical separators which gave twenty per cent more cream than the old method. By now the Danes, by feeding their cows in houses during the winter months and helped by good marketing, were increasing their share of the English market. Then, in imitation of the French, some factories designed to produce blended butter were established in Munster. These were supplied from fresh butter markets held once or twice weekly in the small Munster towns and were able to convert 'low class butter into a good secondary or first class article'. The heavily salted Cork butter went out of favour and the casks were heavy and difficult to handle. The killing blow to the Cork market was the establishment of the co-operative creameries, which spread slowly to most parts of the country. In addition, the amount of foreign butter imported into England was increasing rapidly. At the same time the amount of butter passing through the Cork market declined from 435,000 firkins in 1877-8 to 170,000 firkins in the year 1890.

Next to Cork was the city of Waterford, and through it much of the butter produced in Waterford and south Tipperary was exported. Butter also reached Waterford by way of the River Barrow. In County Tipperary there were very large butter markets in Clonmel and Tipperary town. In both these there were covered markets with facilities for inspection, weighing and branding the butter. Here, however, there was no compulsion on any of the people concerned – sellers or buyers – to use the facilities of the market. In the smaller towns the markets were held in the open air and the sellers took the firkins to the weighers who weighed them. It was then a matter of bargaining between the buyers and the sellers, without any official inspection or grading. This was done by the merchants themselves in their own store without any control and there were no brokers involved in the trade.

The butter market in Tipperary town was second in size to the Cork market and about 100,000 firkins a year were sold privately without going through the market. In such cases there was no inspection or branding, though the buyer might use a hollow slender tube to take a sample of the butter before buying it.

Fowl markets

During the eighteenth and nineteenth centuries the small farmers – or more likely their wives and daughters – reared large flocks of poultry. The eggs and fowl were easily sold at neighbouring markets and were a cheap source of protein for the family diet. The fowl kept were mainly hens but ducks, geese and turkeys were also reared in different parts of the country.

The writer of the *Statistical Survey of County Wexford* had this to say:

> In their poultry the county of Wexford is very excellent: the farmers and even cottiers rear vast numbers of turkeys and fowl of every description. In the neighbourhood of Wexford they also fatten them by cramming them with potatoes, buttermilk and barley meal. With these the market of Wexford is most abundantly supplied and certainly not inferior to any town in England in this respect, and also remarkably cheap.
>
> This is one of the advantages derived from the great number of small farmers in this county. They also send great quantities of poultry to Dublin. A couple of crammed fowls 2s.2d., a turkey very fat £2.8s.½d. A couple of turkeys alive, full grown £3.9s.½d.
>
> There is a fair at Michaelmas at Ballyhack for poultry only at which there are sold some thousands of all kinds and very cheap, that is, that in general they are on a par and in some cases, cheaper than butcher's meat. This arises from the great numbers of small occupiers of land in this county, who can from the offals of their potatoes, with a little barley meal, rear and feed poultry at small expense; for we have not found it to be the practice here, as in some parts of France, to sow maize and other grain for the sole purpose of feeding poultry.

The writer goes on to discuss the different methods of fattening poultry which were used in France and in England and advises that these methods be used by the Wexford producers.

In the Ulster counties the numerous hardworking small farmers also reared poultry for sale. In County Derry geese were kept in large numbers and the goose fair in Derry city was famous. This is what the statistical survey said: 'The geese are remarkably large and plenty in this neighbournood. They fatten in summer on the vetches and tares which abound in the bottoms: in autumn on the stubble and in winter on the potato ridge.'

Generally geese fed on grass and the value of the grazing of twenty geese was equal to one sum, in other words the grass of a cow. I have a copy of a photograph taken about 1904 outside the hotel in Dunfanaghy in County Donegal. It shows a man setting off for the Goose Fair in Derry driving a large flock of geese.

In County Derry they also reared flocks of turkeys, of which there were two distinct breeds. One was the American black breed which could be found at the start of the nineteenth century in the fertile district around Limavady. On the east side of the hills as one approached the valley of the lower Bann 'a smaller whitish grey breed is very plenty. They sell at 2s. to 4s. each.' Ducks were also kept in considerable numbers in Derry, where their eggs were generally eaten by the poor. Ducklings were produced for sale and sold at 6½d. each. In the fertile valley of the River Roe 'they have a good breed of large black poultry.' The chickens sold at 8d. a couple and the mature fowl at 13d.–16d. a couple.

West Cork also had large fowl markets in Bandon and Clonakilty. There were special turkey fairs on 29 September and 11 November in Clonakilty, where in 1806 they sold for 3s.6d.–5s. a pair. There was also a large turkey fair in Kilbrittain in west Cork.

In east Galway there were a number of large fowl markets, and poultry were the most important articles for sale at some fairs. At Aughrim in 1816, 20,000 turkeys were sold on 14 October. The writer says the birds were generally small and poorly developed – due, he said, to lack of proper care and feeding – and generally inferior to the turkeys produced in County Meath. As usual the best Galway turkeys were produced by the wives of the cottiers who took the necessary care with them. The local gentry were aware of this difference and took care to buy up the best of them. The writer implies that they were not themselves very successful at rearing them, so they bought them from the wives of the small farmers.

Similarly in Carlow, Kilkenny and Leix the industrious small farmers were the producers. There were large fowl markets in Fidtown and

Kells in County Kilkenny but the most important market there was held in Ballyragget on 10 December. In Leix the prices are given in some detail. Turkeys were sold at about 3s.3d. a pair. Geese cost 1s.10d. a pair and mature chickens 1s.8d. a pair. Ducks were cheapest: they cost 1s.4d. a pair.

Clearly the practice was the same in most parts of the country where fowl helped to balance the budget as well as the diet. Chickens cost little to rear and were able to find a considerable part of their own food. This could be supplemented with potatoes and buttermilk and whatever scraps were left over by the family. Ducks and geese were rather more troublesome, and turkeys needed a considerable degree of care. Some women were well known for their skill in the care of poultry and generally the money paid for them as well as for the eggs went to the woman of the house. She had well earned it. In addition to the poultry and the eggs there were also the feathers, and here again the skilful and careful housewife was able to add to her income. Feathers sold at £1.1s.0d. for 16 lb, and I know that one housewife sold a stone of feathers at one market.

Index